May Agnes (Early) Fleming

Carried by Storm

A Novel

May Agnes (Early) Fleming

Carried by Storm
A Novel

ISBN/EAN: 9783337029241

Printed in Europe, USA, Canada, Australia, Japan

Cover: Foto ©Thomas Meinert / pixelio.de

More available books at **www.hansebooks.com**

CARRIED BY STORM.

A Novel.

BY

MAY AGNES FLEMING,

AUTHOR OF

"SILENT AND TRUE," "A MAD MARRIAGE," "A TERRIBLE SECRET,"
"GUY EARLSCOURT'S WIFE," "A WONDERFUL WOMAN,"
"ONE NIGHT'S MYSTERY," ETC., ETC.

"When she is angry she is keen and shrewd,
And, though she is but little, she is fierce."
Midsummer Night's Dream.

NEW YORK:
Copyright, 1879, by
G. W. Carleton & Co., Publishers,
LONDON : S. LOW & CO.
MDCCCLXXX.

CONTENTS.

[v]

CARRIED BY STORM.

PART FIRST.

CHAPTER I.

WHICH IS HIGHLY SENSATIONAL.

"OOK at it well," says Miss Ventnor, " it is what you have never seen before— what you may never see again—a Haunted House !"

One slim, gloved hand, looking like a perfect hand in dark gray marble, points the dramatic speech. Miss Ventnor is given to dramatic and epigrammatic little speeches at all times, but as she is *not* given to talking nonsense at any time, I know there is " method in the madness " of this assertion now. And yet—a haunted house ! I laugh a little, as I lean out from the carriage to look.

"Do not laugh," says Miss Ventnor, austerely ; " there is nothing to laugh at. A dark and direful tragedy was enacted within the walls of that gloomy red farm-house—let me see—four—yes, nearly five years ago. Do you see that third window to the right, in the attic story ? Well, a man was murdered— stabbed to death in that room."

"Ugh ! how horrid !" I say, with a shudder. If she had told me he had drowned himself, or poisoned himself, or charcoaled himself, *a la Français*, or even hanged himself, or gone out of time into eternity by any one of those other violent but unbloody gates, her tragedy would have lost its most grisly element. But the average female mind shrinks in repulsion from the thought of a severed jugular or a pool of blood.

"And ever since the house has been haunted, of course," says Miss Ventnor, folding one gray kid calmly over the other. "It is a good house and a fine farm, and since Sleaford's time—Sleaford was the victim—the rent has been merely nominal. All in vain. Sleaford 'walks,' and in the 'dead waste and middle of the night' the struggle is re-enacted, and panic-stricken, belated wayfarers fly. It is all nonsense, of course," says Miss Ventnor, changing suddenly from a Siddons' voice to a practical, every-day one. "Slea-ford, poor wretch, lies over yonder in Potter's Field and troubles nobody. But the fact remains that peo-ple will not live in the place, and the most audacious tramp and thief will give the peach trees and melon patches of Sleaford's a wide berth, be he never so hungry. And—I do not mind admitting that even *I* would go half a dozen miles roundabout rather than pass it alone after nightfall. So take a good look at it, my dear, a *bona fide* haunted house is a sight to be respected and remembered, if only for its rarity in this degenerate age. And this evening, after dinner, I will tell you all about it."

I do not need the injunction—I *am* taking a good look at Sleaford's ! Even without Miss Ventnor's ghastly legend the place could hardly fail to impress one in a weird and dismal way. But just now the *mise en scene* is in keeping with the story. A gray, fast-drifting autumnal sky, lying low, and threatening rain ; a chill, complaining, fitful wind, rising and falling over the rich rank marshes ; a long stretch of flat farm land, sear and brown, corn-stalks rattling their melancholy dry bones, the orchard trees stripped and forlorn. In the midst the house, long, low, a dull brick-color, broken panes in the windows, broken fences around, no dog at the gate, no face at the casement, no smoke from the chimneys, no voice to welcome or warn away. Desolation has lain her lean brown hand upon it, and marked her own. Anything more forlorn, more "ramshackle," more forbidding, no fancy can picture. And from being a deserted house, no matter what the cause, from ghosts to bedbugs, to being a haunted house, there is but a step.

"There it stands," says Miss Ventnor, musingly, her elbow on her knee, her pretty chin in her hand,

> " ' Under some prodigious ban,
> Of excommunication——'

and yet I can remember when Sleaford's was the rendezvous of all that was youngest, loudest, merriest, in a radius of twenty miles—the 'jolliest old roost going,' as poor Frank Livingston used to tell me. The Sleaford girls were the handsomest, reddest-cheeked, blackest-eyed, loudest-laughing gypsies to be seen for a mile. There were two of them, as much alike as peas in a pod, as round and rosy as twin tomatoes. There were the two Sleaford boys, tall, strapping fellows, with more of the wild gypsy strain even than their sisters, the best dancers, wrestlers,

rowers, singers, fighters, everything but the best farm·
ers—they never worked. There was Giles Sleaford
himself, who went up to that attic room one moonlight night, a strong, stalwart man, and was carried
down next morning—an awful spectacle. And last of
all there was—Joanna."

Miss Ventnor's voice takes a sudden change as it
slowly—reluctantly, it seems—pronounces this name,
a touch of strong repulsion it has not had even when
telling the story of Sleaford's grisly death. She sits
suddenly erect as she utters it, and gathers up the
reins.

"Let us go," she says, with a shiver; "it is a
horrible place, haunted by evil memories if by nothing
more tangible. It is growing cold, too. Do not look
at it any more—it is uncanny. You will dream of
Sleaford's to-night."

"Wait!" I say; "look there!"

I speak in a whisper, and lay my hand on her
arm. Miss Ventnor bends forward. Over the broken
pickets of the fence the solitary figure of a man leans,
his arms folded across the top, his eyes fixed stead-
fastly on the house. A moment ago he was not there;
we have not seen him approach; the apparition could
not have been more unexpected if he had risen from
the ground.

"Ah!" Miss Ventnor says, a half-startled look
coming into her eyes, "I did not know he was here.
That is the one man of all the men on earth who
could throw light on part of the Sleaford mystery—
if he chose."

"And he does not choose?"

"He does not choose—I doubt if he ever wil.

choose. I wonder—I wonder what he has done with
her !"

"With her? with whom? One of the black-
eyed, tomato-cheeked Misses Sleaford ?"

"Misses Sleaford?" contemptuously. "No, Joanna. That is her window he is looking at—the attic
room next to the chamber of horrors. I wonder what
he has done with her," says Miss Ventnor, speaking
to herself ; "it must have been worse than having
a white elephant on his hands. That is George
Blake."

"George Blake ! H-m ! a commonplace cogno-
men enough for the hero of a melodrama. Do I
understand you to say this Mr. Blake eloped with
Mlle. Joanna ?"

"No ; Joanna eloped with *him*. He was the victim. Never mind now. I am cold, and I want my
dinner. I am going home. Get along, Frisky."

Frisky pricks up his ears, tosses his brown mane,
and gets along. The sound pierces through Mr.
Blake's brown study ; he turns sharply and sees Miss
Ventnor. She inclines her head, he lifts his hat—a
moment, and we are out of sight. In that moment I
have caught a glimpse of a sallow and rather handsome face, a slight and medium-sized figure, two dark
eyes, and a brown mustache.

"A *very* commonplace young man to be the first
lover in a melodrama," I reiterate. "Is—ah—your
Mr. Blake a gentleman, Olga ?"

" My Mr. Blake !" repeats Miss Ventnor, laughing ; "well, you wouldn't know much difference. He
is a newspaper man, a journalist, a penny-a-liner, works
on daily papers—is clever, they say, and has good

manners. A thousand times too good to have his life
spoiled by a woman."

"My dear, that is the only thing of interest about
him, the leaven that lightens the whole man. There
is always the element of the heroic in a man whose
life has been spoiled by a woman—if there is anything in him it is sure to force it out. And men bear
it so well, too! I dare say Mr. George Blake eats his
three meals per diem with as Christian a relish, and
writes twice as pungent paragraphs as before. Was
Joanna pretty? Quaint little ugly name, by-the-bye
—Joanna."

Olga Ventnor does not reply. At last she lowers
the reins and looks at me.

"Do you believe," she asks, "in people being possessed?"

"Good gracious!" I cry, aghast.

It is the second startling speech within the hour,
and really this last is quite too horrid.

"Because," says Miss Ventnor, trenchantly, "if
ever any human being was possessed of a demon Joanna was! Now, do not ask any questions, for here
we are, and thumbscrews would not extort another
syllable from me until I have had my dinner."

*   *   *   *   *   *

The threatening rain begins to fall with the falling
darkness. It is beating sharply against the panes as
we descend to the dining-room half an hour later.
But plate-glass and crimson curtains shut out wind,
and rain, and night; a fire burns in the shining grate,
the gas-lights in their ground-glass lily-cups flood the
deep red carpet, the gilt picture-frames, the polished
mahogany sideboard, the sparkling crystal, and rough

old silver of the dinner service. And Miss Ventnor,
in dark-blue silk, with a good deal of black lace about
it, and a sweet-smelling crimson rose in her hair, is
quite an ideal hostess. But all through soup and
salmon, roast and *entrees*, jellies and pastry, iced pudding and peaches, and black coffee, I think of the
Sleafords and the gloomy red farm-house, the awful
upper chamber, the tomato-faced maidens, the gypsy
sons, the mysterious Joanna, and the lonely figure
of Mr. George Blake, leaning with folded arms
on the broken rails, and gazing at the lattice of the
young woman who had eloped with him. Does Mr.
Blake prefer coming back here, and sentimentalizing
over four greenish panes of glass to gazing on the
charms of Mistress Joanna in the flesh?

After dinner, with slippers on the fender, the ruby
shine of the fire on her trailing azure silk and fine
laces, and red rose and pretty fair hair, Olga tells me
the story of the Sleafords.

Outside there is the accompaniment of fast-falling
rain, dully-sighing wind, wetness, blackness, night. I
set it down here in different words, and much more
than Miss Ventnor told me, much more than she knew
herself that memorable night. Bit by bit the strange
affair has come to light, and to the knowledge of those
interested therein, among whom no one is, or has been,
more vividly interested than myself. If I do not
carry *you* away as *I* was carried away that evening, it
is because pen, ink, and paper do not constitute a
handsome young lady in silk attire, with sweet, clear
voice, sweet, shining eyes, and a story-telling talent
that would have done honor to one of those improper
creatures in the Decameron, who told tales by moon-

light in the garden of Boccaccio to the listening
Florentines.   This, in *my* way, and with additions, is
the story Olga Ventnor told me that wet October
night—the tragic story of the Sleafords.

————————•◦•————————   •

CHAPTER II.

WHICH BEGINS AT THE BEGINNING.

HE village of Brightbrook! You do not
know it, perhaps, and yet it is not unknown
to fame or fashion in the heated months—
but it was both, twenty odd years ago,
when Olga Ventnor first set her blue, bright eyes upon
it.   A slim lassie, an only child, an heiress, a dainty,
upright, fair-haired fairy, all Swiss muslin, Valenciennes lace, Hamburg embroideries, many tucks, and
much ruffling.   Straight as a dart, white as a lily—a
delicate little aristocrat, from the crown of her golden
head to the sole of her sandaled foot ; idolized by
papa, adored by mamma, paid court to by friends,
relatives, playmates, teachers, servants, village folk—a
small princess, by royal right of beauty, birth, wealth.
That is a correct picture of Miss Olga Ventnor, *ætat*
ten.

And yet, in spite of all, of spoiling and flattery
enough to ruin an army of innocents, she was a charming child, simple and natural, with a laugh all wild
and free, pretty childish ways, full of flawless health
and rosy life.   It was for her sake—the apple of his
eye, and the pride of his life—that Colonel Ventnor

resigned Swiss mountains, Lake Como sunsets, ascents of Vesuvius, Texan plains on fleet mustangs, yachting adown the picturesque coast of Maine, camping out on the Adirondacks, mountain trout baked in cream, and all the other delights of his existence, and built this pretty villa in Brightbrook, and came down here in the month of roses, with eight "in help," and a pretty, pallid, invalid wife—foreswore all wild, wandering ways forever, so that little Olga might run wild among the clover and buttercups, and from much fresh air, and sweet milk, and strawberries picked with her own taper fingers, grow up to blooming health and maidenhood.

Colonel Ventnor—he had served with distinction in the far West—was a very rich man, and the descendant of a family of very rich men. Such a thing as a poor Ventnor perhaps had never been heard of. They were wealthy always, high-bred always, holding enviable positions under government always, never defiling their patrician fingers with trade or commerce of any kind, and, in a general way, considering their status and superiority to all earthly pursuits, with quite as many brains as was good for them. Of these mighty men, Colonel Raymond Livingston Ventnor was the last, and little Olga, in her Swiss tucks and Leghorn sun-hat, the very last daughter of the house, born, if ever embryo belle and heiress was yet, with a golden spoon in her mouth.

"We must marry her to Frank Livingston in about ten years from now," said the family conclave, "and so keep everything in the family. Pity she is not a boy—too bad to sink the Ventnor for Livingston—

but Frank can add the old name by and by, when he marries Olga."

Perhaps this imperial ukase was not read in form to the bride-elect, but it met the approval of papa and mamma, and certainly was announced to the future bridegroom, a slim, very pretty young fellow of eighteen or so, with a passion for base-ball, and another for pencil drawing. He was really a bright lad, and at this age quite a wonder to see in the way of tallness, and slimness, and straightness. And he only grinned when his fond mamma folded him with effusion in her arms, and announced, with joyful tears, that he—he—her Francis—her darling boy, and *not* Anselm Van Dyack, nor Philip Vandewelode, had been chosen for the distinguished position of prince consort to the heiress of many Ventnors.

" And you need never lower your family, nor slave yourself to death painting pictures now, my dearest, dearest boy ! Olga Ventnor's fortune must be simply immense—IMMENSE !"

"All right, mother," says Frank, still grinning ; "and when is it to be—this week or next? Or am I to wait until she grows up ? *I* am on hand always ; when you want me please to ring the bell."

"Frank, this is no theme for jesting. They will not permit it for at least ten years. Say her education is finished at eighteen, then two years of travel, then the wedding. Meantime, whenever you see little Olga be just as nice as possible—impressions made at her age often last through life."

Frank throws back his head, and laughs immoderately. "Did I ever dream in my wildest dime novel days it would come to this? Did I ever think that, like Dick Swiveller, I would have a young woman growing up for me? Don't wear that face, mother, or you will be the death of me. I'll run down to Bright-brook next week, if you like, and do a little stroke of courting, and hunt butterflies with the little dear until the end of July."

So Frank runs down, and is made welcome at the pretty white villa, all embowered in pink roses and scented honeysuckle, like a cottage in a picture, and by none more gladly than little Olga. All that mere money can buy is hers ; but even money has its limits as to power, and it cannot buy her a playmate and constant companion of her own age. The child is a little lonely, surrounded by love and splendor. Brother or sister she has never had, mamma is always ailing and lying on the sofa, papa is away a great deal, Jeannette, the *bonne*, is lazy and stupid, and says it is too hot to play, and in all Brightbrook there is no one this dainty, little curled darling may stoop to romp with. Yes, by-the-bye, there is one, just one, of whom more anon, but she is not always available. So the little princess, forgetting the repose which marks the caste of Vere de Vere, utters a scream of joy at sight of Cousin Frank, and flings herself absolutely plump into his arms.

"Oh ! I *am* so glad !" she cries out. "Oh ! Frank, how nice of you to come. I've been wanting you every day of my life since we came down here—oh, ever and ever so ! Mamma, you *know* I've been wanting Cousin Frank."

Mamma smiles. Frank lifts the little white-robed, golden-haired, rose-cheeked vision up higher than his head, kisses her, and with her perched on his shoulder,

2

and shrieking with delight, starts off for the first game
of romps. It is all as it should be. Mrs. Colonel
Ventnor settles her muslins and laces, lies back in her
blue satin chair, and resumes her book, very well
pleased.

Frank's one week lasts well on into September.
Brightbrook abounds in cool hill-side streams and
tarns, from which it takes its name, and these sparkling waters abound, in turn, with fine trout. Fishing
is dreamy, lazy, *insouciant* sort of work, suited to
sleepy, artistic fancies, and the young fellow spends a
good deal of his time armed with rod and line and
lunch-basket, and waited upon dutifully by his devoted little hand-maiden, Princess Olga. All the
world adores her, she in turn adores Frank. He is
the handsomest, the cleverest, the dearest cousin in all
the world. He paints her picture, he bears her aloft
in triumph on his shoulder, he sings her German
drinking songs, he teaches her to bait her hook and
catch fish, he takes her for long rambles in the woods,
he instructs her in the art of waltzing, he tells her
the most wonderful goblin tales ever human brains
invented.

And all this without a jot of reference to his
mother's romance of the future. *That* he laughs at—
simply because she is the prettiest little darling in the
world, and he is fond of children. Marry her in ten
years—ten years, forsooth! Why not say half a
century at once, and have done with it? He is seventeen — ten years looks a long perspective, a little
forever, to eyes seventeen years old.

October comes. With the first bleak blast and
whistling drift of maple leaves, these birds of summer

forsake their fragile nest, and flutter back to the stately family home of the Ventnors on Madison avenue. The pretty white villa, with its roses, and verandas, and conservatories, and sun-dial, is shut up, and only an old man and his daughter left to care for it until the next June honeysuckles blow.

Little Olga goes back to her books and her piano, under an all-accomplished governess ; Frank goes in for painting, and takes a trip to the everglades of Florida. Early next summer the Ventnor family return, making a mighty stir throughout Brightbrook, and in due course down comes Mr. Frank.

A year has made its mark on this young man. His fine tenor voice is changing to an ugly bass, a callow down is forming on his upper lip, and is loved and caressed as a youthful mother may her first-born babe. He is absent a great deal from the cottage, and he very seldom takes Olga with him anywhere now.

Nobody knows where he spends his time. Olga is the only one who inquires ; Olga, piqued and pouting, yet too proud even at eleven to let him see how much she cares.

"Where have you been *now?*" she will ask.

"Oh, up the village !"

It is his invariable answer, and it being a dull little village, and Mr. Francis of a lively turn, and fond of life, even rough and rollicking life, it is a little puzzling. Olga does not like it at all—he is not nearly so nice as on the preceding year, he leaves her to Jeannette and mamma, and amuses himself very well without her. The absences grow more frequent and prolonged. He stays away whole days, and his latch-key opens the hall-door gently far into the dim watches of the night.

Lying awake, looking at the summer moonlight stealing whitely in, the child will hear that cautious click,
that light footstep passing the door, and presently the
little Swiss clock on the mantel will chime out, silvery
and sharp, two or three. Three in the morning, and
up at the village ! It *is* odd. But presently the mystery is solved for Olga in quite a sudden and awful
way.

-----◆●◆-----

CHAPTER III.

HOW LITTLE OLGA GÉTS LOST.

"OUSIN Frank !"

There is no reply. Stretched on the
sun-steeped grass, his straw hat pulled
over his face, his long length casting a
prodigious shadow in the afternoon sunshine, Cousin
Frank is leagues away in the lovely land of dreams.

"Frank ! Cousin Frank ! Frank Livingston ! Oh,
dear !" sighs Olga, impatiently. "No wonder he is
asleep. It struck three this morning before—Frank !
Oh ! how stupid you are ! Do, *do* wake up !"

Thus adjured, and further urged by the pointed
toe of a most Cinderella-like shoe of blue kid, Frank
consents to slowly and lazily open his handsome blue
eyes.

"Oh !" she says, with a pout, "at last ! You are
worse than the Seven Sleepers. Here you have been
fast asleep for the past two hours, and all that tire-
some time I have been waiting here. I think it is
horrid of you, Frank Livingston, to act so !"

"'To act so! To act how, fairest of fairy cousins? What has your Frank, the most abject of thy slaves, Lady Olga, been doing now, to evoke your frown? There is no harm in taking a snooze on the grass, is there?" says Frank, with a prolonged yawn.

Miss Olga stands beside him, slim, straight, white, blonde, pouting, and very, very pretty.

"There is harm in never coming home until half-past three in the morning every night. If you didn't do that you wouldn't sleep on the grass all the next afternoon. What would mamma say?"

He rises suddenly on his elbow and looks at her. Pretty well this, for a demoiselle of eleven! She stands rolling the gravel with one blue boot-tip, her wide-brimmed leghorn shading her face, the long, almost flaxen ringlets falling to her slender waist, her delicate lips pouting, the light figure upright as a dart.

"Princess Olga," Frank says, after a pause and a stare, "what an uncommonly pretty little thing you are getting to be! I must make a sketch of you just as you stand; that sunshine on your yellow curls and white dress is capital! Do not stir, please, my sketch-book is here; I will dash you off in all your loveliness in the twinkling of a bed-post!"

Frank's sketch-book and Frank himself are never far apart. He takes it up now, as it lies at his elbow, selects a fair and unspotted page, points a broad black pencil, and begins.

"Just as you are—do not move. 'Just as I am, and waiting not, to rid myself of one—some sort of blot,'—how is it the hymn goes? And so you heard me come in last night? Now who would think such pretty little pink ears could be so sharp!"

"Last night!" pouts Olga; "this morning, you mean. Half-past three. I heard the clock strike."

"Don't believe the clock—it is a foul slanderer. Those little jeweled jimcracks that play tunes before they strike always tell lies. Did you tell mamma about it this morning, Olly?"

She flings back her head, and her blue eyes—very like Frank's own—kindle.

"Tell mamma! I am not a tell-tale, Cousin Frank."

The young fellow, sketching busily, draws a breath of relief.

"Most gracious princess, you are a little trump. I ask pardon. Turn your head just a hair-breadth this way. Ah! thanks—that will do. Well, now, Olga, I *was* out rather late; but I met some—some fellows, and we played a game or two, and so——"

"Were you up the village?"

"Yes, up the village. You see, Brightbrook is such a deadly-lively sort of place at the best, and a fellow must amuse himself a little in some way. And that reminds me—I have an engagement at five. What's the time, Olly? just look at my watch, will you?"

She obeys after a moment—a moment in which wistful longing and precocious pride struggle for mastery. Then she stoops and looks.

"A quarter of five. But you said——"

A pause.

"Well, I said——"

"You said—you promised Leo Abbott yesterday that you would drive me over there this afternoon, and we would have croquet and tea."

"Oh, did I?" carelessly. "Well, you must let me

off, Olly, and make my excuses to little Leo. Upon my honor, I cannot manage it—awfully sorry all the same. But it need not keep you, you know; your papa will drive you, or Peters will."

Peters is head coachman, the safest of charioteers. Papa is always willing to drive his darling anywhere. But Olga Ventnor turns hastily away, and the childish eyes that look at the setting sun are full of tears she is too proud to let fall.

"There!" Frank says, after five minutes more devoted to the sketch; "there you are, as large as life, but not half so handsome. Here it is for a keepsake, Olga. When you are a tall, fascinating young lady —a brilliant belle, and all that—it will help to remind you of how you looked when a chickabiddy of eleven."

He tears out the leaf, scrawls under it, "Princess Olga, with the love of the most loyal of her lieges," and hands it to her. She takes it, her lips a little compressed, pique, pain in her eyes, plainly enough in spite of her pride, if he cares to look. But Frank has a happy knack of never looking, nor wishing to look, below the surface of things, and he has something to think of besides his little cousin's whims just at present.

"I am off," he says, jumping up. "And—look here, Olly—go to sleep like a good little thing when you go to bed, and don't lie awake o' nights in this wicked way counting the clock. It will bring gray hairs and wrinkles before you reach your twelfth birthday. You will wake up some morning and find, like Marie Antoinette, all these long curls turned from gold to silver in a single night."

He pulls out one of the long tresses, fine as floss silk, to an absurd length, as he speaks.

"And besides, I am going to reform, to turn over a new leaf, numbers of new leaves, to become a good boy, and go to bed at ten. So say nothing to nobody, Olly, and, above all, above everything, shut those blue peepers the moment your head is on the pillow, and never open them, nor the dear little pink ears, until six the next morning."

He gives the pink ear an affectionate and half-anxious tweak, smiles at the grave face of the child, flings his hat on, and departs.

The little girl stands watching him until he is out of sight, then, with a deep sigh that would have infinitely amused Master Frank could he have heard, turns for consolation to the drawing. Is she really so pretty as this? How clever Cousin Frank must be to sketch so—dash off things, as he calls it—all in a moment. She has it yet, yellow, faded, stored away among the souvenirs treasured most.

"Madame votre mere says will mademoiselle not come for one leetle walk before her supper?" says the high Norman sing-song voice of Jeannette, appearing from the house; "it will give ma'amselle an appetite for her tartine and strawberries."

"Very well, Jeannette. Yes, I will go. Here, take this up to my room. I will go on this way. You can follow me."

So, with a slow and lingering step, the little heiress of many Ventnors sets off. She is a somewhat precocious little girl, old-fashioned, as it is phrased, a trifle prim in speech and manner, except now and then when the wild child-nature bursts its trammels, and she

runs, and sings, and romps as wildly as the squirrels
she chases. Just at this moment she is under a cloud.
Cousin Frank has wounded and disappointed her. He
will not tell her where he goes or what he does all
these long hours of absence.

"Up the village" is vague and unsatisfactory to a
degree ; he has broken his promise about taking her to
Abbott Wood, and she likes to play croquet with
Geoff and Leo Abbott. Frank's promises, she is beginning to discover, are very pie-crusty indeed ; he
makes them with lavish prodigality, and breaks them
without a shadow of scruple. All these things are
preying on Miss Ventnor's eleven-year-old mind for
the first few minutes, and make her step lagging and
her manner listless. Then a brilliant butterfly swings
past her, and she starts in pursuit—then a squirrel
darts out of a woodland path and challenges her to a
race—then a tempting cluster of flame-colored marsh
flowers catches her eye, and she makes a detour to get
them—then she finds herself in a thicket of raspberry
bushes, and begins to pluck and eat. Overhead there
is a hot, hot sun, sinking in a blazing western sky like
a lake of molten gold.

In these woody dells there are coolness and shadow,
sweet forest smells, the chirp of birds, the myriad
sounds of sylvan silence. A breeze is rising, too. She
goes on and on, eating, singing, chasing birds and butterflies, rabbits and field mice, all live things that
cross her path.

All at once she pauses. Where is Jeannette? She
has been rambling more than an hour, she is far from
home, the sun has set, she is tired, the place is strange,
she has never been here before. Her dress is soiled,

her boots are muddy ; woods, trees, marshes are around
her—no houses, no people.   Oh ! where is she—where
is her *bonne?*

"Jeannette ! Jeannette !"   She stops and cries
aloud : "Jeannette ! where are you ?"

Her shrill, childish voice echoes down the dim
woodland aisles.   Only that, and the gathering stillness of the lonesome evening in the wood.

"Jeannette ! Jeannette ! Jeannette !"

In wild affright the young voice peals forth its
piteous cry.   But only the fitful sighing of the twilight wind, only the mournful rustle of the leaves,
only the faint call of the little mother birds in their
nests, answer her.   Then she knows the truth—she is
lost !

Lost in the woods, far from any habitation, and
night close at hand.   Jeannette has lingered behind to
gossip ; she, Olga, has gone heedlessly on ; now it is
coming night ; she is alone, and lost in the black,
whispering, awful, lonely woods !

She stands still and looks around her.   Overhead
there is a gray and pearl-tinted sky, very bright still
in the west, but with a star or two gleaming over the
tree-tops.   In the forest it is already pitch-dark.   In
the open, where she now stands, it will be light for
half an hour yet.   To the right spreads the pine
woods, whispering, whispering mysteriously in the
solemn darkening hush ; to the left is a waste of dry
and dreary marsh land, intermediate and blankly gray
in the gloaming.   No house, no living thing to be seen
far or near !

CHAPTER IV.

A WILD GIRL OF THE WOODS.

HAT shall she do? The child is not a coward—she has been so sheltered, so loved, so encompassed by care all her short life, that fear is a sensation almost unknown. If it were noonday she would not fear now, she would wander on and on, calling for Jeannette until some one came to her aid, some one who would be sure to take care of her and bring her home. But the gathering darkness is about her, the tall black trees stand up like threatening giants, the deep recesses of the wood are as so many gaping dragon's jaws, ready to swallow her up. Perhaps there are ghosts in that grim forest—Jeannette has a wholesome horror of *revenants,* and her little mistress shares it. Oh! what shall she do? Where is papa? where is Frank, mamma, Jeannette, any one—any one she knows, to come to the rescue? She stands there in that breathless, awesome solitude, a panic-stricken, lonely little figure, in her soiled dress, and muddy, blue kid boots.

"Jeannette! JEANNETTE! JEANNETTE!"

The terrified voice pierces wildly the stillness, its desolate echo comes back to her, and frightens her more and more. Oh! *what* shall she do? Must she stay here in this awful, awful place until morning! What will become of her? Are there bears, or lions, or robbers in that spectral forest? She has on a necklace of gold beads—will they kill her for that?

"Jeannette! Jeannette!" she cries, in sobbing despair, but no Jeannette answers. She is indeed lost, hopelessly lost, and the dark, dreadful night is already here.

All this time she has been standing still, now a sudden panic seizes her. Fiery eyes glare at her out of the vast depths of the wood, strange weird moans, and voices in pain, come to her from its gloomy vastness. She turns wild with fright, and flies, flies for life from the haunted spot.

She runs headlong—how long or how far she never knows. Panting, gasping, slipping, falling, flying on! She does not cry out, she cannot, she is all spent and breathless. Something terrific is behind her, in hot pursuit, ghost, goblin, fiery dragon—who knew what? stretching forth skeleton hands to catch her—a phantom of horror and despair! And still the silvery twilight deepens, the stars shine out, and still she rushes on, a wildly-flying, small white figure in the lovely summer dusk.

At last—overtasked nature can bear no more, she falls headlong on the soft, turfy ground, her eyes closed, her hands clenched, and lies panting and still. Is she dying, she wonders; she feels dizzy and sick— is she going to die far from papa and mamma, and Frank, alone in this lonesome place? How sorry they will all be to-morrow, when they come upon her lying like this, all cold and dead. She thinks of the Babes in the Wood, and wonders if the robins will cover *her* with leaves.

"Hullo!"

It is no voice of ghost or goblin. It is unmistakably a human salute, and very close by. She lifts

herself silently, too utterly exhausted to reply, and
sees standing beside her, in the dusk of the warm
night, the figure of—a girl? *Is* it a girl? She puts
back the tangled golden locks, and gazes up in a
dazed, bewildered way, at this apparition.

"Hullo!" says the voice, again. It is not a pleasant voice; the face that looks down at her is not a
pleasant face. It *is* a girl, of twelve or so, in a scant
skirt, a boy's blouse belted with a strap of leather, a
shaggy head of unkempt reddish hair, a thin, eager,
old-young face, long bare legs, and bare feet.

"Hullo!"

For the third time she hails the prostrate Olga
with this salute, in a high-pitched, harsh tone, and for
the third time receiving no reply, varies it :

"I say, you! Ye ain't deef, are ye? Can't ye
speak? Who are you? What are you doin' here,
this time o' night?"

Still no reply. The rasping voice, the scowling
look, the wild air of the unexpected figure, have
stricken Olga mute with a new terror. No one has
ever looked at her, or spoken to her like this, in all
her life before.

"Deef are ye, or sulky—which? Git up—git up,
I say, or I'll make ye! Say, you! who are you?
What are ye about here, lying on the ground? Why
—lor! ef it ain't the Ventnor gal!"   •

She has taken a stride toward Olga, who springs
to her feet instantly. They stand confronting one
another in the dim light, the little white heiress shaking with fatigue and fear, the fierce-looking, wild
creature glancing at her with eyes like a cat.

"Say! If ye don't speak I'll scratch ye, I'll bite

ye—I'll pull your ugly long hair out by the roots!
Ain't you the Ventnor gal?   Come now—say!"

She makes a threatening step near. The poor
little princess puts up two imploring hands.

"Oh! please, please don't bite me! I don't mean
any harm. I am only lost, and fell down here!" A
great sob. "I am Olga Ventnor, and I want to go
home—oh! I want to go home!"

She breaks down in a great passion of sobs. The
impish-looking child before her bursts into a discordant, jeering laugh.

"She wants to go home! Oh, she wants to go
home! Oh! please somebody come and take this
young lady home! Look at her! Ain't she putty
with her old white dress, and muddy shoes, and shiny
beads. Say, you! give me them beads this very minute, or I'll snatch 'em off your neck."

With rapid, trembling fingers, the child unfastens
the necklace, and holds it out to her tormentor.

"What business have you, you stuck-up little pea-
cock!" continues the imp, wrenching, savagely, the
costly trinket asunder, "with hair down to your waist, ·
yellow hair too, the color of your beads, and all in nasty
ringlets! Oh, lordy! we think ourselves handsome,
don't we? And embroidery and lace on our frocks, and
pink, and blue, and white buttoned boots, with ribbon
bows! *I've* seen you. And a French servant gal to wait
on us, in a white cap and apron! And a kerridge to ride
in! And white feathers in our hats, and kid gloves,
and silk stocken's! We're a great lady, *we* are, till we
get lost in the woods, and then we can't do nothin' but
sit down and blubber like a great calf! Why, you
little devil!" she takes a step nearer, and her tone and

look grow ferocious, "do you know that I hate you, that I would like to tramp on you, that I spit at you!" which she does—"that I would like to pull out every one of them long curls by the roots! And I'll do it, too, before I let you go!"

The child is deadly white, deadly still with fear. She does not speak or move, cry out or turn to run—some terrible fascination holds her there breathless and spell-bound.

"What business have you," cries the creature, with ever-increasing ferocity, "with curls, and silk dresses, and gold beads, and servants, and kerridges, while your betters are tramping about bare-footed, and beat, and abused, and starved? You ain't no better nor me! You ain't so good, for you're a coward, and a cry-baby, and a little fool! And I'm goin' to hev them curls! And if you screech I'll kill you! I will! I hate you—I've hated you ever since I sor you first!"

She darts a step nearer. Olga recoils a step backward. Still she makes no outcry, no attempt to run. That fascination of intense terror holds her fast.

"I know you, and I know all about you," goes on the goblin. "I know your cousin, Frank Livingston; he comes to our house—he gives presents to Lora and Liz Sleaford. He's sweet on Lora, he is. *She* wears long curls, Lor bless you, too. Like tar ropes they are, over *her* shoulders. I'm Sleaford's Joanna; if I don't kill you, you'll know me next time, won't you? And I hate you because you're a young lady, with kerridges, and servants, and nothin' to do, and long yellow ringlets down your stuck-up back."

The ringlets seem to be the one unforgivable sin; she glares at them vengefully as she speaks.

SLEAFORD'S.

SLEAFORD'S.

32

"I'm goin' to pull them out. I never thought I'd hev the chance. There ain't nobody here to help or come if you yell. I don't care if they beat me to death for it, or hang me—I'll pull 'em out!"

She springs upon her victim with the leap of a wild-cat, and buries her claw-like fingers in the pale gold of the clustering hair. There is no mistaking her meaning—she fully intends it; her fierce eyes blaze with a baleful fire. And now, indeed, Olga finds her voice, and it rings out shrill, pealing, agonized.

"Papa! papa! Oh, papa!"

"Hi!" answers a sharp voice. Then a sharper whistle cuts the air. "Hi! Who's that? Call again!"

"Papa! papa! papa!"

There is a crashing among the trees, and not a second too soon. With a violent push, and—*an oath* —this diabolical Little Barefoot flings her victim from her, and leaps away into the darkness with the fleetness of a fawn.

CHAPTER V.

SLEAFORD'S.

T is not papa who comes rushing to the rescue, but it is a man who stoops and picks her up—a young man with a gypsy face, a gun over his shoulder, and two or three yelping dogs at his heels.

"What the dickens is the row?" he asks. "Hold up, little 'un. Good G—— ! she's dead!"

It looks like it. She lies across his arm, a limp
and inert little form, all white drapery, blonde curls,
and pale, still face. The moon is rising now, the big
white shield of the July night, and he takes off the
crushed Leghorn flat the better to behold his prize.

"By thunder!" he exclaims, aloud, "it's the little
Ventnor. The little great lady, the little heiress.
Now, then, here's a go, and no mistake."

He stands at a loss, utterly surprised. She has
been as a small Sultana in the eyes of all Brightbrook,
every one knows her, and to find her like this, dead, to
all seeming, murdered, it may be, appalls him.

"She wasn't dead a minute ago; she was screech-
ing for her papa like a good 'un. Perhaps she ain't dead
yet. Maybe she's fainted or that, frightened at something. Don't seem to be anybody here to frighten
her, nuther. Wonder what's gone with the French
ma'amselle? Well, I'll tote her to the house anyhow;
if she's alive at all the gals 'll fetch her round."

He swings her as he might a kitten over his shoulder. He is a long-limbed, brown-skinned young
fellow of twenty, whistles to his dogs, and starts over
the star-lit fields at a swinging pace. All the way he
whistles, all the way his keen black eyes keep a bright
lookout for any one who may be in hiding. No one
seems to be, for he reaches his destination, a solitary
red farm-house standing among some arid-looking
meadows. A field of corn at one side looks, in the
shine of the moon, like a goblin play-ground, but the
house itself seems cheery enough. Many lights twinkle
along its low front, and the lively strains of a fiddle
greet him as he opens the door.

The interior is a remarkable one enough. The

2*

room is long and low, the ceiling quite black with smoke, as are also the walls, the broad floor a trifle blacker, if possible, than either; the furniture, some yellow wooden chairs, two deal tables, a wooden sofa, and a cupboard, well stocked with coarse blue delf. It is, in fact, the farm-house kitchen, and in the wide fire-place, despite the warmth of the night, a fire is burning. Over it hangs a large pot, in which the family supper is simmering and sending forth savory odors.

The occupants of the room are four. On one of the tables is perched a youth of eighteen, black-eyed, black-haired, swarthy-skinned, playing the Virginia reel with vigor and skill.

Two girls, young women, as far as size and development make women, though evidently not more than sixteen, are dancing with might and main, their hands on their sides, their heads well up, their cheeks flushed crimson, their black eyes alight, their black hair unbound—two wild young Bacchanti.

The one spectator of the reel sits crouched in the chimney-corner, her knees drawn up, her elbows on them, her chin in her palms, a singularly witch-like attitude, barefooted, shock-headed, with gleaming, derisive dark eyes.

The door is flung wide, and enters the young man of the woods, with his burden, his gun, and his dogs. The reel comes to a sudden stop, and six big black eyes stare in wild wonder at this unexpected sight.

"Why—what is it?" one of the girls cries—"a dead child, Dan? What for the Lord's sake have you got there?"

"Ah! What?" says Dan. "Here, take her, and

see if she's living or dead. I can tell you who she is,
fast enough, or who she was, rather, for she looks as
dead as a door-nail now, blessed if she don't. Here!
fetch her to if you can, you, Lora ; it will be worth
while, let me tell you."

He lays the limp child in the arms of one of the
girls. The firelight falls full upon the waxen face as
they all crowd around. Only the crouching figure in
the ingle nook stirs not. There is a simultaneous outcry of recognition and dismay.

" It's little Missy Ventnor !"

" It's the kernal's little gal !"

" It's Frank Livingston's cousin !"

" It's the little heiress !"

Then there is a pause, an open-mouthed, round-
eyed pause, and gasp of astonishment. It requires a
moment to take this in.

" And while you're staring there like stuck pigs,"
says the sarcastic voice of Brother Dan, " the young
'un stands a good chance of becoming a stiff 'un in
reality, if she ain't now. Can't you sprinkle her with
water, you fools, or unhook her clothes, or do whatever ought to be done. You, Lora, tote her into the
next room, and bring her round, and you, Liz, dish up
that hash, for I'm as hungry as a hunter."

Issuing these commands, he draws up a chair to
the fire, as though it were December, and proceeds to
load a little black pipe to the muzzle. Thus engaged,
his eyes fall on the huddled-up figure opposite.

" Oh !" he growls, "*you're* there, Miss Fiery Head,
layin' in the chimney-corner, as usual. Git up and set
the table. D'ye hear ?"

She does not seem to ; she blinks up at him like a

toad, and does not stir. With an oath he seizes a billet of wood, and hurls it at her, but she ducks with a mocking laugh, and it goes over her head. As he stoops for another, she springs to her feet, and sets to work to do his bidding.

Meanwhile, in the next room, the two sisters are doing their unskilled best to bring Miss Ventnor " round." It is the parlor of the establishment, has a carpet on the floor, cane-seated chairs arranged primly around, a rocker to match, sundry gay and gaudy chromos on the walls, china dogs and cats on the mantel, green boughs in the fire-place, and a crimson lounge under the windows. On this lounge they lay her, they sprinkle her plentifully with water, force a little whisky into her mouth, slap her palms, undo her dress, and after some ten minutes of this manipulation there is a long-drawn sigh and shiver, the eyelids flutter, open, shut, open again, and two blue eyes look up into the gypsy faces bending above her.

"There !" says one of the sisters, with a long breath of satisfaction, " you're all right now, ain't you? Gracious ! how white and limpsy you was, to be sure. First time I ever saw anybody in a faint before in my life. Drink a little drop of this, it's whisky and water."

But Olga pushes away the nauseous beverage with disgust.

"I don't like it," she says, faintly ; " the smell makes me sick. Please take it away." She pushes back her tangled hair and looks vaguely about her. "Where am I ?" she asks, beginning to tremble. "What place is this ?"

"Oh, you're all right ; don't be scared, deary," says

the sister called Lora ; "this is Sleaford's. I'm Lora Sleaford ; this is my sister, Liz. Bless us, what a pretty little thing you are, as fair as a lily, I do de-clare ! I wish *I* was ; but I am as black as a crow. We all are, father and all, even our Joanna, in spite of her horrid red hair. Don't be frightened, little missy ; we know who you are, and you are all safe. And we know your cousin, Frank Livingston ; he is a right nice fellow, comes here most every night. Likely's not he'll be here in a little while, now, and then he can take you home. Liz ! there's the boys calling for their supper, and I hear father. You'd better go and get it for them."

"Joanna's there," says Liz, not stirring ; "let *her*."

"When you know very well she won't if she takes the notion," retorts Lora, angrily ; "there! there's father calling you. Now, you *must* go."

It seems she must, for she does. Lora turns back again to her charge. There is not much difference in these two sisters, and naturally, for they are twins, but Lora is rather the better looking, and decidedly the better natured of the pair.

"How did you come to be with our Dan, anyhow ?" she asks, curiously. "Where did he find you ? and what on earth made you faint away ?"

The question arouses memory. Olga shuts her eyes with a shudder, and turns so white that Lora thinks she is going to faint again.

"Oh ! that dreadful girl ! that dreadful girl !" she says, with a shuddering gasp.

"What dreadful girl ? What do you mean ? Did you get lost, and did somebody scare you in the woods ? What was she like ?" demands Lora, sharply.

But Olga cannot tell. She trembles, and shivers, and covers her eyes with her hands, as if to shut out some dreadful vision. "She said she would pull my hair out, and then—and then I got dizzy, and it got dark, and—and that is all," she replies, incoherently.

"Now I wonder if it wasn't our Joanna?" Miss Sleaford says, musingly. "It would be just like her —little imp ! If I thought it was—but no, Joanna was in the house ever so long before they came. Well, don't you cry, little deary. Frank Livingston will be here pretty soon, and he'll take you home. Now I'll go and get you something to eat. You're hungry, ain't you, and would like some tea ?"

" Oh, I only want papa !—nothing but papa !" sobs the child, quivering with nervous excitement. " Oh, papa, papa, papa !"

" Well, there, don't make a fuss ; your papa will come directly, I tell you. And you are all safe here, and needn't be afraid. Now I'll go and get you something—toast and tea—if there is any tea. So stop crying, or you'll make yourself sick."

Miss Sleaford departs. In the kitchen the two young men, and their father, Giles Sleaford, are seated at one of the deal tables, partaking of steaming hash with the appetites of hunters and constitutionally hungry men. The father is like the sons, a powerful, black-bearded, sullen-looking man. Evidently he has heard the story, for he looks up, with a glower, as his daughter enters. " Well ?" he says, in a growling sort of voice ; " how is she ?"

" Oh, all right," Lora responds. " Crying for her papa, of course. She won't take any of that stuff," pointing to the greasy dish of hash with some disdain ;

"I must make her some toast, if there is any raised bread."

" There ain't any raised bread," says Liz.

" Make her tea," suggests Dan ; "that's the stuff they drink. Store tea, and some short-cake."

" There ain't no tea," says Liz again.

" Get some, then," growls the master of the house ; "she's worth taking care on. Send to Brick's and get some."

" Joanna !" calls Liz, sharply ; "d'ye hear ? Go !"

She turns to the chimney-corner, where, crouched again, like a small salamander, in her former attitude, is Joanna, basking like a lizard in the heat.

" Won't !" returns Joanna, briefly ; " go yourself."

" What ?" cries Giles Sleaford, turning in sudden ferocity from the table—" what ?"

" Says she won't," says Liz, maliciously—" says go myself."

The man rises and takes down a horsewhip from a shelf near, without a word. The dark, glittering eyes of the girl follow him, but she does not stir. " Won't, won't she ?" says Mr. Sleaford. " We'll see if she won't. You little —— —— !"—two oaths and a hissing blow. " You won't go, won't you, you little foxy —— —— !"

With each imprecation, a cut of the whip falls across the shoulders of the crouching child. Two or three she bears in silence, then with a fierce scream of pain and passion, she leaps to her feet, darts across the room, and spits at him like a mad cat.

" No, I won't, I won't, I won't !--not if you cut me in pieces with your whip ! I won't go for tea for her ! I won't go for nothin' for her ! I won't go for you—not if you whip me to death! I won't go! I won't, I won't, I won't!"

The man pauses: used as he is to her paroxysms of fury she looks so like a mad thing, in her rage at this moment, that he actually holds his brutal hand.

"Oh, come, dad, you let her alone," remonstrates his younger son; "don't cut her up like that."

But recovering from his momentary check, Giles Sleaford lays hold of her to renew the attack. As he does so Joanna stoops and buries her sharp white teeth in his hand. And at that same instant a small white figure, with blanched face and dilated eyes, glides forward and stands before him.

"Don't! Oh, don't!" Olga Ventnor says. "Oh! pray, pray don't beat her like that!" She holds up her clasped hands to Giles Sleaford, who, partly from the pain of the bite, partly from surprise, recoils and lets go his hold. Instantly Joanna darts away, opens the door, and disappears.

"That's the last of _her_ till dinner-time to-morrow," says the younger Sleaford, with a laugh, "she'll roost with the blue-birds to-night. Dad mayn't think so, but he'll drive that little devil to run a knife into him yet."

There is many a true word spoken in jest, says the adage. In the dark and tragical after days that somber speech comes back to young Judson Sleaford like a prediction.

CHAPTER VI.

A DEED OF DARKNESS.

O it befalls, that in spite of threats and horsewhip, Joanna has her own way, and does not go for the tea. Giles Sleaford retires to the chimney-corner, grumbling internally, as is his sullen wont, and looking darkly askance at the small intruder. He makes uneasy signs to his daughters to take her back whence she came, as he fills his after-supper pipe. Both his sons are already smoking, and the tobacco-laden atmosphere half chokes the child.

"Come, dear," says Lora, taking her by the hand.

"But what is she to have to eat?" queries Liz. "I suppose, Jud, *you* wouldn't go for the tea?"

"No, I wouldn't," answers Jud, promptly. "I'm dead tired. I don't stir out o' this corner, 'cept to go to bunk to-night. Besides, she says she don't drink it—heerd her yourself, didn't yer?"

"Perhaps she'll take milk," suggests Dan. "Ask her, Lorry."

"Oh, yes, please, I will take milk," Olga responds, shrinking into herself; "anything. Indeed, I am not in the least hungry."

"And I'll poach her an egg," says Liz, brightening, now that this difficult question of the commissariat is settled. "I'll fetch it in in five minutes. You undress her, Lora, and put her to bed."

"But I want to go home!" Olga says, beginning to

tremble again. "I must not stay here all night.
Papa and mamma do not know where I am. You
must not undress me, please. I must go home."

"But, little missy, you can't go home to-night.
See, it is eleven o'clock now, and even if Frank
Livingston does come, which ain't likely (though what
keeps him I can't think), it will be too late for you to
go back to your home with him. It is a good three
miles if it is an inch."

"Oh! what shall I do?" poor little Olga sobs, "and
papa will be frightened to death, and mamma will
worry herself sick. Oh! I wish Cousin Frank would
come. But he will not—I know he will not. I made
him promise this afternoon."

"What?" says Lora Sleaford, blankly.

"I made him promise. He stays out so late, you
know, and I made him promise he would not any
more. And that is why he has not come," explains
Olga, with a sob.

"Well, I do declare!" cries Miss Sleaford, looking
anything but pleased. "*You* made him promise! A
bit of a dolly like you! Well—you see it's yourself
you have punished after all. If you had let him alone
he would have been here two hours ago, and you
might have been home by this."

Miss Ventnor covers her face with her mite of a
pocket-handkerchief, and sobs within its folds. She is
too much a little lady to do her weeping, or anything
else, loudly or ungracefully, but none the less they are
very real tears the cobweb cambric quenches.

"So you didn't want Mr. Frank to come here,"
goes on Lora, still sulkily; "how did you know he
came?"

"I did—didn't know. I only knew he—he stopped
out late. And he said—said—it was up the village.
And I made him prom—promise he wouldn't do so any
more. Oh, dear, dear, dear !"

" There, there, stop crying," says Lora, relenting ;
"you'll certainly make yourself sick. Here's Liz with
something to eat. It ain't what you're used to, I
dare say, but you must take something, you know, or
you won't be able to go home to-morrow either."

This argument effectually rouses the child. She
dries her tears, and remembers suddenly she *is* hungry.
Liz comes forward with a big black tray which is
found to contain a glass of milk, a poached egg, some
raspberries, a bit of butter, and a triangular wedge of
short-cake.

"Now," she says, " that's the best we can do for
you. So eat something and go to bed." She places
the tray before the child, and Lora draws her to a
window, where a whispered conference takes place.

"Well, I never !" says Miss Sleaford the second,
in high dudgeon ; " the idea ! Gracious me ! a chit
like that, too !"

It is evident Lora is retailing the embargo laid on
Master Frank's visits.

" It is lucky she doesn't know about the presents,
the jewelry and things. What an old-fashioned little
puss !"

There is more whispering, some giggling, and Olga
feels in every shrinking little nerve that it is all about
her. She drinks the milk, and eats the fruit, essays
the egg, and mingles her tears with her meat. Oh !
how alarmed papa and mamma will be, and what a
dreadful place this is to spend a whole long night.

Will they leave her alone in this room? will they
leave her in the dark——

"Now then !" exclaims Liz, briskly, " I see you've
done, so I'll just take the things, and go to bed.
Father and the boys have gone, already, and I'm as
blinky as an owl. Lora——"

"I'll stay for a bit," says Lora. She is not an ill-
natured girl, and she sees the speechless terror in the
child's eyes. "You go to bed. I can sleep it out to-
morrow morning."

Liz goes without more ado. Lora sits down beside
the little girl, and begins to unbutton her boots. "You
know you can't go home to-night," she says, sooth-
ingly, "and you are sleepy and nearly tired to death.
Now you must just let me fix you up a bed here on the
lounge, and I'll only take off your dress, because you've
no night-gown to put on. I'll stay here with you, and
to-morrow the first thing my brother Judson will go
over to your cottage, and tell your folks. Now be
good ; don't look so pale and scary ; there's nothing
to be afraid of here, and I'm going to stay with you
all night."

"All night ?" questions Olga, lifting two large
earnest eyes.

"Oh, yes, all night," says Lora, who differs from
George Washington, and *can* tell a lie. "Now, I'll
fix your bed, and sing you to sleep, and you will be at
home to-morrow morning before you know it."

She produces sheets and a quilt, and improvises a
bed, lays Olga in it, and takes a seat by her side.

"I will sing for you," she says. "You shut those
pretty blue peepers right away, and don't open them
till breakfast-time to-morrow."

She begins in a sweet, crooning voice a camp-meeting hymn. The low singing sound soothes the child's still quivering nerves. Gradually her eyelids sway heavily, close, open again, shut once more, and she is fast. Then Miss Sleaford rises with a great yawn.

"Off at last, and a tough job it was. Hush! twelve o'clock! I thought it was twenty. I wonder if that young limb, Joanna, is back? Most likely not, though. It's queer she don't take her death o' fever 'n ague, sleeping out doors."

She gives a last look at the sleeper.

"Fast as a church," she whispers.

She takes the lamp, leaves the room, shuts the door softly, and goes up-stairs under the rafters to join her sleeping sister. The old red farm-house is very still. In the kitchen black beetles hold high carnival; in the parlor the moonlight streams in on the pale hair and quiet face of the little lost heiress. Outside, the trees sway and rustle in the night breeze, and the stars burn big and bright in the mysterious silence of early morning.

One! two! three!

With a start Olga Ventnor awakes. It is the wooden Connecticut clock in the kitchen, loudly proclaiming the hour. Awakes with a chill and a thrill of terror, to find herself quite alone. Lora gone, the light fled, the pale, solemn shine of the moon filling the place, and that loud strident clock striking three. Oh, to hear Cousin Frank's footsteps *now* stealing up and on to his room! Oh, for Jeannette—Lora—any one—anything but this silent, spectral, moonlit room!

Stay! What is that?

She is *not* alone. Yonder in the corner, under the

chimney-piece, crouches a figure all huddled in a heap,
knees drawn up, and arms clasped around them. With
appalling distinctness she sees it, the shock head of
hair, the thin, fierce face, the bare feet and legs. She
has seen it before. The moonlight is full upon it, the
eyes are wide open and gleam like a cat's. The creature sits perfectly motionless, and stares before her.
Perfectly motionless, also, Olga lies, in a trance of
terror, scarcely breathing, feeling numb and frozen
with deadly fear. The thing stirs at last, shakes
itself, turns to the bed, glares at it, and rises slowly
to its feet. Olga's heart has stopped beating, she has
no voice to cry out, all her faculties are absorbed in
one—seeing. The apparition speaks in a muffled whisper to itself :

"I'll do it ! I'll do it if they kill me—if they whip
me till I'm dead. I hate her ; I always hated her. I
hate 'em all, but her most. I never thought I'd have
the chance, and now she's here and asleep, and I'll do
it, I'll do it, I'll do it !"

She tiptoes to the bed ; there is a gleam of blue
steel. Is it a knife? She is close—she stretches out
one long, thin hand, clutches a handful of fair, floating hair. The malignant face, the gleaming eyes, the
wild hair, are within three inches of Olga. Then,
with a shock, the child leaps from the bed, rushes
frantically across the room, her shrieks rending the
stillness, flings open the door, and falls headlong in
the passage.

CHAPTER VII.

SLEAFORD'S JOANNA.

UT into the moonlight five hours before the child Joanna had fled, pale with passion, pain, defiance, ablaze with wrath against all the world. It is a customary mood enough with this elfish child, twelve only in years, a score, if hatred, envy, malice, and all ill-will can age a child. To be flogged like a hound, to be sent supperless to bed, to be starved in attic or cellar, to swelter in fierce August noontides, or shiver among the rats on bitter January nights, these are old and well-known experiences in Joanna's life. To be forced to labor from day-dawn until midnight, with every bone aching ; to go barefoot through slush and snow ; to sleep and live worse than the dogs—for *they* are cared for ; to hear only brutal words, and still more brutal oaths, from her task-master's lips ; to be jeered at, to go clad in rags—this has been the life of this girl of twelve, the only life she can ever remember. Lora and Liz are well, gayly clad indeed ; they sing, they dance, they idle, they work or let it alone as they choose. Is not Joanna there, the household drudge, the homely, red-haired, rustic Cinderella, with never godmother or other mother, in fairyland or out of it, to come to the rescue with a pumpkin coach and a pair of glass slippers ? She knows that lovely legend of happy childhood, this most unhappy little outcast, and sighs bitterly sometimes as she looks at the big golden globes she cuts up for the cows and pigs.

There are fairy godmothers in the world, no doubt, and handsome young princesses, but they never, oh, never come near Sleaford's Farm. And who ever conceived a Cinderella with fiery-red hair, freckles, and long mottled shins ? A cinder-sifter she has been born, a cinder-sifter she must die.

She has these thoughts sometimes, formless and vague mostly, but bitter always. It would have been better if Giles Sleaford had left her in the gutter to starve ten years ago, instead of fishing her out of it, as he says he has done. He makes a great deal of that far-off city gutter in his grumbling way, for she is not his daughter, this bare-limbed unfortunate ; she is nobody's daughter, so far as she can find.

He has taken her out of the slime where she was born, he tells her, and slaves early and late to give her a home, and this is her thanks, dash her ! Her mother afore her was a good-for-nothin'—dash, dash her— what can be expected from the unlicked cub of such a dam—dash her ! double-dash everything and everybody, his own eyes and limbs included. Giles Sleaford was an Englishman once, he is a cosmopolitan now ; has tramped over the world in a vagabond sort of way, is a man under a cloud, banned and shunned by his neighbors. He has neither bought nor rented this farm, and yet he is in undisturbed possession. He does not work ; he fishes, shoots, prowls, drinks, fights ; is a worthless brute generally. Yet he has plenty of money, his daughters dress in expensive finery, and there is a rough sort of plenty always at their house. He is of horses horsey, and bets and loses heavily. He is a bit of a prize-fighter, a little of a gambler, a dark and dangerous fellow always. Some mystery shrouds

him ; he throws out vague hints now and then of the
power he holds over a certain very rich man and magnate of the place. He is brutal to all, to his own sons
and daughters, but most of all to the hapless creature
known as Sleaford's Joanna. That he has not killed
her outright in one of his fits of fury is not due to him,
one of the Sleaford boys or girls generally interfering
in bare nick of time. Their drudge is useful, they do
not want her beaten to death, or the prying eyes of
the land brought to bear on their rustic household. So
Joanna is still alive to scour the woods, and terrify
small, fair-haired heiresses into fits.

The moon is shining brilliantly as she leaves the
house. She looks up at it, her hands locked together
in a tense clench, her teeth set, her eyes aflame with
the fires of rage and hatred, her shoulders red and
welted with the stinging blows of the whip. It is a
mute appeal to Heaven against the brutality and cruelty of earth—that Heaven of which she knows nothing, except that it is a word to swear by.

She wanders slowly on, not crying—she hardly
ever cries. The silence, the coolness, the beauty of
the night calms her ; she does not mind spending it
among the dewy clover, or under a tree ; she sleeps
there oftener in summer than anywhere else. She
takes a path well known to her bare feet—it leads to
her favorite *sulking* place, as the Sleaford girls call it,
and is perhaps the ugliest spot within a radius of
twenty miles. It is called Black's Dam. An old dis-
used mill falling to pieces stands there, the water in
the stagnant pond is muddy and foul. It is a desolate
spot in broad day, it is utterly dismal and dark by
night. Some fellow-feeling draws her to it—it, too, is

3

lonely, is ugly, is shunned. Black's Dam is her one friend. The ruined mill is haunted, of course ; corpse candles burn there, shrieks are heard there, it is peopled by a whole colony of bogies. But Joanna is not afraid of ghosts. Ghosts never horsewhip, never swear, never throws sticks of hickory at people's heads—do nothing, in fact, but go about in white sheets after nightfall, and squeal to scare people. The only corpse-lights she has ever seen are lightning-bugs, the only supernatural screams the whoo-whoo of a belated owl. The sheeted specters never appear to her ; when she is exceptionally lonely sometimes she would rather be glad of the company of one or two. But ghosts are not sociable, they never seem to have much to say for themselves, so perhaps it is as well. On rainy nights she sleeps in the old mill ; after unusually bad beatings she has staid there for days, feeding on berries, and been found and forced back again at last, a gaunt skeleton. More than once she has sat and stared at the green, slimy water until the desire to spring in and end it all grows almost more than she can resist. "Only old Giles Sleaford will be glad of it," she thinks ; "I'll keep alive just to spite him." And, sad to say, it is this motive that actually holds the creature back from self-destruction many a time.

The tempter is very strong within her to-night, but Giles Sleaford is not the object of her vindictive, suppressed wrath. It is Olga Ventnor. She has grown so used to his oaths and blows that she looks for nothing else ; but a hundred demons seem aroused within her by the sight of the beautiful, golden-haired, richly-robed child. *This* is the sort to whom fairy god-mothers come, for whom magic wands are struck, who go to balls, and dance with the handsome prince, and marry him, and live happy forever after. This is what she might have been, but never can be. All the beauty, and the riches, and the fairy gifts are for this little curled darling of the gods ; for her—the lash, the feeding of the pigs, the rags, the rye bread, the ugly, ugly red hair !

She has reached the dam, and sits down on a flat stone on the brink. It is unspeakably lonely—the moon shines in a cloudless midnight sky ; the water lies black, solemn, still ; the old mill stands sinister, mysterious, casting long shadows. Hardly a breath stirs ; some frogs croak dismally in the green depths—that is all.

She sits in her favorite attitude, her knees drawn up, her chin in her palms, and stares vacantly before her. One thought, one only, possesses her—her hatred of this delicate little beauty and heiress, with her pearl-fair face and long light hair. She would kill her if she could ; she has all the will in the world at this moment to be a little murderess. Shocking—unreal ? Well, no ; think how she has been brought up—think of the records of juvenile depravity you read and shudder at in the newspaper every day. The demon of envy holds her—a passionate outcry against the injustice of her fate, that has given the golden apples of life to this one, the scourings of the pig-trough to her. "Unjust ! unjust !" something within her cries, "why has she all—I nothing ?" It is the spirit that has hurled kings from thrones, wrought revolutions, filled the world with communism—that will beat the air impotently to the end of time. No savage could be more untaught than this child. There was a Power

up there who had created her, but who looked down
on all this and made no sign. There was a Heaven for
well-dressed, respectable ladies and gentlemen, and
little heiresses. There was a Hell for such as she,
wicked and poor, where they would go when they
died, and burn in torment forever. This much she believes—it comprises her whole theory of religion.

She sits for a long time brooding, brooding. She
meant to have done something to that girl that would
mark her for life—spoil her beauty in some way—but
she has been prevented. No doubt by this time
Frank Livingston has come and fetched her home,
and her chance is gone forever. Frank Livingston,
too, is a lily of the field, a handsome dandy, but he
awakens none of this slumbering gall and bitterness
within her. *He* is simply something to be silently ad-
mired, revered, and wondered at, a being of brightness and beauty, of splendid raiment, lacquered boots,
diamond studs, and a general odor of roses and Ess.
Bouquet. He is the prince to be worshiped at a distance, and not to be lightly touched or spoken to.
She wonders sometimes to behold him pulling Lora
about in very unprincely fashion, and to see that
buxom damsel slap his face, and frowsle his silky
chestnut hair. For him, he takes no more notice of
this uncanny-looking child, with the eldritch red locks,
than of one of the half-dozen ill-conditioned dogs
that yelp about the premises. That he is the object
of her silent idolatry would have tickled Master Frank
beyond everything.

She rises at last, shivering in the bleak night wind.
She is as nearly nude as it is possible to be in a state
of civilization, and the chill damp pierces through her

tatters. Why she does not go into the mill until the morning she never knows; she turns, instead, and walks slowly back to the farm.

The house is all dark and silent. The dogs fly at her, but a word quiets them; they, too, know Joanna's witch-like ways. Jud Sleaford swears she spends half her nights riding the air on a broom-stick—she comes and goes, like the night-wind, where she listeth.

She goes to the parlor window, and flattens her nose against the pane. Her eyes are keen as any ferret's. Yes, there she is—she has not gone home— asleep—*alone!*—in her power! The girl's eyes light; they glitter in the dark. There she is, asleep, alone, in her power!

She goes round to a side window, opens it, and enters. Dogs, guns, and men are plentiful at Slea- ford's—bolts are scarce; there is no fear of burglars. She enters, drops lightly to the ground, goes straight to a shelf in the kitchen, takes down something bright and steely, and steals into the parlor without a sound. Instead of going straight to the bed she crouches in her corner, to brood, perhaps, over the deed of dark- ness she is about to do, or it may be to count the cost. She will be blamed in the morning, no doubt—is she not blamed for everything that goes wrong? she will be beaten nearly to death—quite to death, perhaps, by Giles Sleaford. Well, she does not care. They will hang him for it. If she were quite sure about the hanging, she feels she would be whipped to death without a groan.

The clock striking three arouses her. It is time to be up and doing—in an hour or two the boys will be down. Indecision forms no part of her character;

she gets up at once, and approaches the bed with her formidable weapon. It is the family shears, bright, large, keen as a razor, and her object is—*not* to cut off Olga Ventnor's head, but—her hair !

Olga is awake, is staring at her, frozen with fright. She has not counted on that, and with a snarl of baffled malice, she plunges her hand in the golden tresses, and uplifts the scissors. But in the twinkling of an eye the child springs from the bed, rushes from the room, shrieking like a mad thing. There is a heavy fall, the sound of startled voices up-stairs, and opening doors. In that moment the scissors are flung aside. Joanna is out of the window, and away like the wind to Black's Dam.

———◆●◆———

CHAPTER VIII.

THE ABBOTTS OF ABBOTT WOOD.

HREE miles away from Sleaford's Farm, and nearly four from Ventnor Villa, there stands the stateliest mansion in all the country round, the pride, the marvel, the show place of Brightbrook. It is down on the coast ; the waves of the Atlantic wash up to the low sea wall that divides it. from a shelving and sandy beach. A beautiful beach, of late years known to fame, and spoiled for all lovers of the quietly picturesque by being transformed into a popular watering-place. But in these days, fashion and capitalists have not marked it for their own, and Brightbrook Beach is an en-

chanted spot, on whose fine white sands you may lie
the long summer day through, lazy, and happy, and
cool, and watch the sea-gulls swirl overhead, and the
little, limpid, oily waves wash and whisper up to your
very feet.

The thermometer may stand among the hundreds
elsewhere, down here it is cool as some merman's grot.
There are always breezes, and fishing boats, and far-
off yachts, and forever and forever the beautiful,
changeful, illimitable sea. Or you may lean over Mr.
Abbott's low stone wall in wild weather, the wind
blowing great guns, both hands clutching your hat,
and watch with awe-stricken eyes the spirit of the
storm abroad on the waters. The great beetling
green waves leap up like Titans, dashing their frothy
spray in your face ; the roar is as the crash of Niagara.
Fascinated, you may stand for hours watching this
war of the gods, and go home, at last, inclined to
opine that Brightbrook Beach in a storm is even more
bewitching than Brightbrook Beach in summer sweetness and sunshine, and to envy John Abbott, Esquire,
his handsome home, his beautiful wife, his pretty little
daughter, his colossal bank account, and, most of all,
that grand old ocean lying there for his perpetual
pleasure, a thing of beauty and a joy forever.

If Mr. Abbott's taste in a site is good, his style of
architecture lies open to question. It is a house as
much like an old Baronial Hall as a genuine American
country-house can ever make up its mind to be.
What Mr. Abbott's idea in building a castle is, is
known to Mr. Abbott only. A grand Elizabethan
manor, with turrets, and peaked gables, and quaint,

vine-clad stone porches, and painted windows, with stone mullions.

It is new, and it looks three hundred years old at least, and reflects some of its seeming grandeur and antiquity upon its master, perhaps. And Mr. Abbott needs it. He is painfully new. He would like a moat and a drawbridge, and battlements, and a donjon keep, and a man-at-arms on the outer bastion, and he could have afforded them all. For, though extremely new, he is oppressively rich. He is so rich that his wealth forces itself upon you aggressively. You are disposed to resent it as a direct personal affront ; no one man can logically have a right to so many millions in bank shares, and bonds, and stocks, to whole blocks in New York and Philadelphia, to the larger half of all Brightbrook, to such gorgeous furniture, inlaid with precious woods and metals, to pictures worth treble their weight in gold, to sculpture such as no one short of a prince, or grand duke, or Yankee billionaire can possess, to horses shod with the shoes of swiftness, to wines like molten gold and rubies, to diamonds— Koh-i-noors, says Brightbrook, every gem of them. It is true Mrs. Abbott seldom wears these rich and rare ornaments, never, indeed, in Brightbrook, but she has them all the same, and then, in some ways, Mrs. Abbott is a very—well, *peculiar* lady.

For that matter, Mr. Abbott is a—peculiar—gentleman also. His servants say so, with bated breath, and furtive glances behind them ; all Brightbrook says it, as he rides by, monarch of all he surveys, pompous and stout. Colonel Ventnor says it with a shrug, and holds rather aloof from him, although his claret and cigars are, like Cæsar's wife, above re-

proach, and he is the only man of quite his own
standing in the place. The two ladies are much
better friends, despite the valetudinarian state of the
one, and the—peculiarity of the other.

When Brightbrook points out to the stranger and
pilgrim within its gates the wonderful castellated
mansion known as Abbott Wood, and expatiates on
its manifold beauties, it never fails to add a word of
the still greater beauty of Mr. Abbott's wife. She
was a widow, Brightbrook will tell you confidentially,
when Mr. Abbott married her, a Mrs. Lamar, widow
of a young Southern officer, and mother of a six-year-
old boy, very poor, very proud, with the bluest of all
blue Virginian blood in her veins, and a pedigree——

"Oh! if you come to pedigree," says Brightbrook,
with suppressed triumph, "*there's* a line of ancestry,
if you like! Dates back to the days of Charles the
Second, and Pocahontas, and nobody knows how long
before. But she was poor, quite destitute, they do
say, after the war, and—and Mr. Abbott came along,
immensely rich, as you may see, and—she married him."

"But you do not mean to say," cries the tourist, a
little scandalized, "that that was *why* she married
him. Because she was quite destitute, and he was
immensely rich?"

"And a very good reason," responds Brightbrook,
stoutly, "only—they do say, he and she don't quite hit
it off as—well, *you* understand! She's a great lady,
and very proud—oh! most uncommonly proud, we
must say, and he——"

A shrug is apt to finish the sentence.

"And he is not," supplements the stranger. "No,
I should think not, when he marries any man's widow

3*

on these terms, and consents to be snubbed forever
after. You say she snubs him? flings her genealogical
tree in his face ; invokes the spirit of Pocahontas and
the dead and gone Lamar, and all that sort of thing ?"

"Oh, dear no !" cries out Brightbrook, shocked,
"nothing of the kind. Much too proud a lady for
anything of that sort. Only—only she has a crushing
sort of way with her—holds herself like this !"
Brightbrook draws itself haughtily up, folds its
arms, and flings back its head, "and looks at you out
of a pair of scornful eyes. Never says a word, you
know, but sweeps out of the room, like an empress
going to the block. That sort of thing puts a man
down, you know. And then Mr. Abbott, he
curses."

"Ah ! curses, does he ?" says the tourist, laughing.
"Well, that shows he is human, at any rate. I
think I might curse myself under such provocation.
The sweeping, empress sort of style must be deucedly
uncomfortable in a wife."

"And when he curses, Mrs. Abbott looks more
haughty and scornful than ever. She's a very pious
lady, Mrs. Abbott."

"Yes, I should think so ; pride and piety make a
happy combination—a pleasant curricle for any man
to drive. So this magnificent dame condescends to
go to the village church on Sundays, and kneel among
you rustics, in perfumed silks and laces, and call herself a miserable sinner? Or," seeing Brightbrook
vigorously shaking its head, "perhaps she stoops still
lower, and patronizes the camp-meetings for which
your fine woods are so famous? No again ! Then
where *does* she go ?"

"Bless you!" cries Brightbrook, exultingly, "she
has a chapel of her own! *And* a chaplain. *And* an
altar. And vestments. And candles—wax. And in-
cense. And a little boy in a purple silk dress, and a
white lace overdress. And the Rev. Mr. Lamb comes
down every Saturday night, and stays until Monday
morning. They say she goes to confession to him. I
shouldn't think Mr. Abbott would like that. Bless
you, she's high—ever so high—what's that other word
now——"

"Ritualistic—Anglican?"

"Thanks, yes. And the chapel, St. Walburga's, is
a wonder; you really must go over and see it. The
carved wood from Belgium, and the painted windows,
with most beautiful saints, and the gold candlesticks,
and the floor of inlaid wood, and carved stails along
the sides, and no pews! The pulpit, they say, is a
work of art, and cost a little fortune abroad. Artists
and that come down from the city and rave about it.
Oh! you really must go to St. Walburga's on Sunday."

"I really think I must," says the stranger and pilgrim, and very likely he goes. He finds the park
thrown open; it actually is a park of many acres, with
green bosky glades where deer disport, sunlit terraces,
where peacocks strut, statues gleaming palely amid
green gloom, flashing fountains, casting high, cool jets,
velvet lawns, all dotted with brilliant beads of flowers,
rose gardens, where every rose that grows blooms in
fragrant sweetness, and, best of all, with thick woodland of maple and hemlock, beech and elm, willow
and chestnut sloping down to the very sea. Rustic
seats are everywhere, cool avenues tempt the unwary,
with arching boughs meeting overhead, and shutting out

the hot summer Sunday afternoon sun, artificial lakes spanned by miniature bridges, and tiny gondolas, fish-ponds, where swans float, and gold and silver beauties sparkle. There is a gate-lodge that is a very bower of sweetbriar and climbing pink roses. All this loveli-ness is thrown open to Brightbrook every Sunday, and nothing pleases the master of Abbott Wood better than to see his grounds filled with wondering, admir-ing, well-dressed people. He comes out among these faithful retainers, nearly all his tenants, and patronizes them blandly and oppressively.

Strains of music float from the painted windows of St. Walburga's, and you are expected to assist at "vespers," as a delicate attention to my lady. If you are a city stranger, you will most probably be singled out by the watchful eye of Mr. Abbott, and taken through the house. You will see armor and stags' heads in the hall—a hall wide enough to drive the pro-verbial " coach-and-four " through, a great carved chim-ney-piece with a coat-of-arms. It is the heraldic de-vice of Mrs. Abbott's family, and it is everywhere, emblazoned in the panes, in the wood-work, on the covers of the books. The rooms are all lofty, frescoed or satin-draped, filled with objects of "bigotry and virtue,"—the furniture—but the pen of an upholsterer, or a Jenkins, would be required to describe *that.* There are rooms in blue satin, rooms in ruby velvet, rooms in amber reps, rooms in white and gold, a libra-ry all rose-red and dark oak, a picture-gallery with portraits of the present house of Abbott, master and mistress, Mr. Geoffrey, and Miss Leonora. There are flowers, and birds, and beauty, and brilliance every-where.

You go into the chapel, and its dim religious light
soothes your dazzled eyes and excited senses. The organ is playing—my lady herself is organist—some soft
Mozartian melody. Up in the pulpit, that costly an-
tique work of art and oak, kneels the Reverend Ignatius Lamb, in surplice and stole, his eyes closed, his
hands clasped, in an ecstasy! He is suspected of a
leaning Rome-ward, but it certainly does not extend
to his nose, which is snub. A pretty, curly-haired boy
in the purple silk and snowy laces of acolyte, stands
slowly swinging his censer, *vice* Master Geoffrey Lamar,
retired. Geoffrey Lamar is there, though, a strong-
looking young fellow of sixteen or so, with close-
cropped dark hair, a sallow complexion, and a rather
haughty-looking face. He has not inherited his
mother's beauty—he is by no means a handsome boy.
By his side, very simply dressed, in dotted muslin,
sits his half-sister, Miss Leonora Abbott, a tiny fairy
of eight, with a dark, piquant face, dark loose hair,
the little young lady of the house, sole child of John
Abbott, millionaire. Sole child, but not one whit
more to him than his wife's son, the scion of the dead
and blue-blooded Lamar. It is well known that Abbott Wood and half his fortune are to be his, that he
looks to this lad to perpetuate the family greatness—
to merge his own obscurity in the blaze of the Lamar
brilliance, and become the ancestor of a long line
of highly-fed, highly-bred, highly-wed descendants.
Every man has his hobby, this is John Abbott's. He
is self-made, he takes a boisterous, Bounderby sort of
pride in proclaiming it. He is an uneducated man,
that speaks for itself, it is unnecessary to proclaim it.
He is a vulgar man, a loud-talking, deep-drinking,

aggressive, pompous, purse-proud man. His wife's
guests were wont to shrug their shoulders, suppress
significant smiles, or protrude delicate under lips as
they listened.   And seeing this, Mrs. Abbott has given
up society, that super-refined pride of hers has been
excoriated a hundred times a day by the rich clod she
calls husband.   She has renounced society, buried her
self in the solitude of Abbott Wood, with only her
books, her music, her casel, her children, for company.
She sees as little of Mr. Abbott as possible ; she is
always perfectly polite to him, she defers to his wishes,
and is a supremely miserable woman.   Even her piety
fails to comfort her, and she is very much in earnest,
poor lady, with her pretty, picturesque, lady-like religion.   She works altar-cloths and copes, with gorgeous
silks, and bullion, and gold fringe ; she reads her high-
church novels ; she plays Mozart in the twilight, and
sings in Gregorian chant in the chapel, but all in vain—
that settled unrest and misery leaves her not.   " Dona
nobis pacem " sounds from her lips like the very cry
of a soul in pain, but peace is not given.   She despises
her husband, his loud vulgarity and blatant purse-pride,
while her own heart is eaten to the core with that other
pride which the world tolerates and honors, pride of
birth and long lineage, and which, perhaps, in the eyes
of Him before whom kings are dust, is quite as odious
as the other.   Perhaps that peace she seeks so despair-
ingly might be found, if she hearkened a little to the
text from which the Reverend Ignatius is fond of
preaching, " Learn of Me, for I am meek and humble
of heart, and ye shall find rest for your souls."

    For Mr. Abbott—well, he is sharper-sighted than
his wife gives him credit for, in spite of chill defer-

ence and proud politeness, he knows that she scorns
and disdains—that she has scorned and disdained him
from the first. And he resents it, silently, passionately. He loves his wife. She would open those dark,
lustrous eyes of hers in wondering contempt, if she
knew how well. But she does not know it—the scorn
in her eyes would drive him to murder her almost, and
he knows that scorn would be there. Coarse braggart
and rich upstart he may be, but he would lay down
that strong life of his for her sake. And that she is
colder than marble, less responsive than ice, is at the
bottom of more than half these fierce outbursts of
anger that so disgust and repel her. Abbott Wood is
a roomy mansion, and more than one skeleton abides
therein.

It has been said that something of mystery hangs
over, and makes interesting, the master of the house.
Colonel Ventnor, riding with him one day, has seen a
little corner of that dark curtain which shrouds his
past, lifted. It was at the time Ventnor Villa was
being built. Mr. Abbott, glad of such a neighbor,
had interested himself a good deal in the proceedings,
and saved the colonel a number of trips down from
the city. Colonel Ventnor, a refined man in all his
instincts, did not much like the rough-and-ready lord
of Abbott Wood, but he was obliged by his good-
nature, and accepted it. It had happened some four
years before this memorable evening on which little
Olga loses herself in the woods.

It is a dark and overcast autumn evening, threatening rain. Leaving the villa and the workmen,
they ride slowly along the high-road, Mr. Abbott de-
tailing, with the gusto customary with him when talk-

ing of himself, some of his adventures as a San Francisco broker and speculator in '49. Suddenly his horse
shies as a man springs forward from under a tree, and
stands directly before him.

"Blast you !" roars Mr. Abbott, "what the ——
are you about ? You nearly threw me, you beggar !
What d'ye mean by jumping before a gentleman's
horse like this ?"

"Beg pardon, sir," says the man, with a grin and
a most insolent manner, "didn't go for to do it, Mr.
Abbott. Don't use your horsewhip, sir," for Mr. Abbott has raised it ; "you might be sorry to strike an
old friend."

He removes his ragged hat as he speaks, and the
fading light falls full upon him. John Abbott reels
in his saddle, the whip drops from his hand, his florid
face turns livid.

"It is Sleaford !" he gasps, "by G—— !"

Colonel Ventnor looks at him. He is a gentleman
in the best sense of the much-abused word—he swears
not at all. Then he looks at the tramp. He is a
swarth-skinned, black-looking vagabond, as perfect a
type of the loafer and blackguard, he thinks, as he
has ever seen.

"I will ride on, Mr. Abbott," he says, quietly ;
"much obliged for your good-nature about those men.
Good-night."

"Stay ! hold on !" cries Mr. Abbott. The color
comes back with a purple rush to his face, his eyes
look wild and dilated. "I—I do—I have known this
fellow in California. He's a poor devil that used to
work for me. I haven't anything to say to him in
private. You needn't hurry on *his* account, you know."

"Oh, certainly not," responds Colonel Ventnor. "Still, as there is a storm brewing, I think it will be well to get to the hotel at once, and so avoid a drenching. I will see you again before I return to town."

He lifts his hat and rides away, but not before he has heard the hoarse laugh of the tramp, as he lays his hand with the same impudent familiarity on Mr. Abbott's bridle.

Next day, when he returns to the villa, he finds that gentleman waiting for him, and issuing sonorous orders to the masons. He is almost offensive in his officious friendliness and voluble explanations.

"A poor beggar, sir, that I knew out in 'Frisco. Knew all sorts out there—hundreds of the great unwashed, miners, gamblers, blacklegs, all sorts. Had to, you know, in my business. Sometimes made some of them useful—a man has to handle dirty tools in most trades, you know. This fellow was one of them. Sleaford his name is—Giles Sleaford, a harmless beggar, but lazy as the deuce. Think I must do something for him for old acquaintance sake. Got a large family, too—lots of boys and girls—quite a 'numerous father,' as they say. Where's the good of being as rich as Rothschild if a man's not to do good with it? D—— it all! let us help one another, I say, and when we see an unfortunate chap down, let us set him on his legs again. I think I'll let Sleaford have the Red Farm; there's nobody there, and it's a capital bit of land. He wasn't half a bad sort; there were a devilish deal worse fellows than Black Giles out in San Francisco."

Colonel Ventnor assents politely, and keeps his own

opinion of Mr. Abbott's dark friend to himself. Mr.
Abbott has been looking him in the eye, in a very
marked manner, during this little speech. It is a
glance that says plainly enough, " This is my version
of the affair—I expect you to believe it, or take the
consequences." But Colonel Ventnor's quiet high-
breeding is too much for poor Mr. Abbott always. It
puts him in a silent rage, much as his wife's calm, uplifted repose of manner does.

" Curse them all !" he thinks ; "these aristocrats
are all alike. Look down on a man as the dirt under
their feet, if he ain't brought up to parley voo fransey
and jabber German and that. And they can do it
with a look too, without a word of bluster or noise. I
defy any man alive to stand up before the missis when
she's in one of her white, speechless rages, and look
her in the eye. I wish I knew how they do it."

He sighs, takes off his hat, scratches his head perplexedly with his big, brown, brawny hand, and slaps
it on again a little more defiantly cocked than before.
" And now here's Black Giles," he thinks, gloomily,
" as if I hadn't enough on my mind without *him*. I
wonder how much he knows—I wonder—— "

He mounts his horse and rides off, pondering
gloomily, in the direction of the Red Farm. It was a
different-looking place in those days to what it became
later. Mr. Abbott was a very thorough landlord, no
tenant might wreck and ruin any farm of his. This
Red Farm, so called from the color of the house, and
the great maples burning scarlet about it, was one of
the choicest bits of land in the State, and in high cultivation. And here the Sleaford family came, two
boys, three girls, the youngest a mere child then, but

a weird-looking, cowed starveling—and *squatted.* It could not be called anything else; Giles Sleaford laughed from the first at the notion of his farming, or even making the pretext. The boys were like wild Indians—they fished, shot, snared birds and rabbits, stole melons, robbed orchards, were a nuisance generally, and let the farm look after itself. The girls were of the same ne'er-do-well stamp, boisterous young hoidens, handsome "prize animal" sort of damsels, with flashing black eyes, and impudent retorts for all who accost them. The neighbors wonder—*why* does Mr. Abbott, that most particular gentleman, let this wild lot ruin the Red Farm, and bear it like the meekest of men? Why does Giles Sleaford always have well-filled pockets, good horses and clothes, whether he works or idles? They ask the question more than once, and he laughs loud and long.

"*Why* does he?" he cries. "Lord love you, that's little of what he would do for me. He loves me like a brother. He's an uncommon fine gentleman, ain't he? and got a lovely place, and a handsome wife—so I hear. I haven't been there to leave my card yet. Why does he? Bless your souls, he would turn out of his big house and give it to me, if I coaxed him hard enough."

Brightbrook does not know what to make of it. It whispers a good deal, and looks furtively at the rich man riding by. What secret has he in his life, that Giles Sleaford is paid to keep? He looks like a man who might have a dark record behind him. And what would Mrs. Abbott say if she knew? But Mrs. Abbott does not know, gossip does not reach her; she lives in a rarefied atmosphere of her own, with her

dainty work, her ornaments, her children, and the plebeian name of Sleaford penetrates it not.

And so years go on. The Red Farm goes to ruin.
Colonel Ventnor and family come with the primroses,
and depart with the swallows. Abbott Wood grows
more beautiful with every passing year, and the skele-
tons in its closets grin silently there still, when it falls
out that this summer evening Olga Ventnor goes
astray in the woods, and before ten at night all
Brightbrook is up and in quest.

*   *   *   *   *   *

"She may be at Abbott Wood," Frank Livingston
suggests—Frank Livingston, calm and unflurried in
the midst of general dismay. It is a theory of this
young man's that things are sure to come right in the
end, and that nothing is worth bothering about ; so,
though a trifle anxious, he is calm. "She spoke to
me," he adds, with a twinge of remorse, "this afternoon about taking her there. Promised to go over
and play croquet with Leo and Geoff."

Colonel Ventnor waits for no more. He dashes
spurs into his red roan steed, and gallops like a madman to Abbott Wood. On the steps of the great
portico entrance he sees the master of the mansion,
smoking a cigar, and looking flushed and angry. A
domestic white squall has just blown over—not with
the " missis ;" there are never squalls, white or black,
in that quarter—with one of the kitchen-maids, who
had done, or undone, something to offend him. He
has flown into a tremendous passion with the frightened woman, cursing up hill and down dale with a
heartiness and fluency that would have done credit to
that past-master of the art of blasphemy, Sleaford him-

self. The fact is, his wife had put him out at dinner, as she has a way of doing, and his slumbering wrath has had to find vent somewhere. Now the fuming volcano is calming itself down in the peaceful night air, with the help of a soothing cigar. He stares to see the colonel ride up, all white and breathless.

"Little Olga?   No, she wasn't there—hadn't been —was perfectly sure of it. Lost!—the colonel did not say so! How was it?"

In a few rapid sentences Colonel Ventnor tells him. Mr. Abbott listens with open mouth.

"By jingo! poor little lass! He will join the hunt immediately. That French woman ought to have her neck wrung. He would be after the colonel in a twinkling."

And he is—mounted on his powerful black horse. And all night long the woods are searched, and morning comes, and finds the missing one still missing. The sun rises, and its first beams fall upon John Abbott, tired and jaded, coming upon Sleaford's. It is a place he avoids; he looks at it now with a scowl, and for a moment forgets what he is in search of. No one has thought of looking here; neither does he. He is about to turn away, when the house door opens, and Giles Sleaford, unwashed and unshorn, comes forth.

"Hullo!" he says, roughly; "you! What may *you* want this time o' day?"

"We are looking for the colonel's little girl. You haven't seen her, I suppose?" says Mr. Abbott, quite civilly.

"Haven't I?" growls Black Giles; "that's all you know about it. I have seen her. She's here, and I wish she was anywhere else, keeping honest people from their sleep. She's in there fast enough if you want her. Why doesn't her own dad come after her? I should think *you* had enough to do to mind your own young 'uns, and your wife, from all I hear."

He laughs a hoarse, impudent laugh, that brings the choleric blood into John Abbott's face, and a demon into either eye. But, wonderful to relate, he restrains himself.

Other members of the hunt ride up now, and it is discovered that little Miss Olga is very ill, and nearly out of her senses—why, nobody knows. She woke up in the night, Lora supposes, and finding herself alone, took fright, and ran screaming out into the passage, and there fell, striking her head against the bottom stair, and hurting herself badly. Whether from the hurt or the fright, she is at present in a very bad way, and there is not a moment to be lost in removing her. Frank is of the party. He takes his insensible little cousin in his arms and kisses her, with tears of genuine remorse in his boyish eyes. If he had gone with her as she wished, this would never have happened. Now she may never ask him for anything in this world again. As he carries her out, a small figure, looking like a walking scarecrow, with wild hair, pale face, torn skirts, bare legs and feet, comes slowly and sullenly forward, and watches him and his burden with lowering, scowling glance.

"Here you, Joanna!" calls out one of the Sleaford girls, sharply. "Come into the house, and help redd up. Come in, this minute!" with a stamp of her foot, "if you don't want a little more of what you got last night."

The girl makes no reply. She slowly obeys, but her eyes linger to the last on Frank Livingston and his cousin. All the long light curls fall over his shoulder, the poor little fever-flushed face is hidden on his breast.

"One of yours, Sleaford?" says Mr. Abbott, graciously, looking after Joanna. "I didn't know you had one so young."

There is nothing in this speech apparently to provoke laughter, nor is it a time for mirth, but such is its effect on Mr. Sleaford. He opens his huge mouth, and emits such a roar that the whole group turn and look at him indignantly. The joke is so exquisite that he heeds not, but laughs until the tears start from his bleary eyes.

"Glad you find me so funny," says Mr. Abbott, huffily. "You ain't always in such good humor this time of morning, are you?" And then, as Mr. Sleaford's only response is to take out his pipe, and indulge in another fit of hilarity, he turns and rides indignantly away in the rear of his party.

Mr. Giles Sleaford, left alone in his retreat, smokes between his expiring gasps of laughter, and soliloquizes :

"'Is she one of yours, Sleaford?' And 'I didn't know you had one so young!' O Lord! I haven't laughed so much in a month of Sundays. Old Jack Abbott don't often make jokes, maybe, but when he does they're rum 'uns. 'Didn't know I had one so young!' It's the best thing I've heerd this many a day—I'm dashed if it ain't."

CHAPTER IX.

THE MISSES SLEAFORD AT HOME.

" HE story they tell is one that won't wash," says Frank Livingston. "I appeal to you, Geoff. The notion of meeting a wild girl in the woods, and being half scalped when Dan Sleaford finds her ! Then, when they have her safely housed and asleep, of that same wild creature coming down the chimney——"

" Down the chimney ?" exclaims Geoffrey Lamar, amazed.

" Oh ! well, something very like it, and going at her again with uplifted dagger. It's a fishy sort of yarn as they tell it. But," adds Frank, reflectively, " it is a peculiarity of Dan Sleaford's stories that they all *have* a piscatorial flavor."

The two young gentlemen are pacing arm in arm under the horse chestnuts surrounding Ventnor Villa. They form a contrast as they slowly saunter there— young Livingston two years the elder, tall, slender, very handsome, quick, volatile, restless ; young Lamar shorter, stouter, with a face that even at fifteen has a look of thought and power—a mouth with that square cut at the corners that betokens sweetness as well as strength, steady gray eyes, close-cut dark hair, and the careless, high-bred air of one born to the purple.

" It does sound rather oddly," he remarks ; " but what motive have they for telling an untruth ? And *something* has frightened her, that is patent enough. Poor little Olga !"

"They're a queer lot, these Sleafords," says Frank, reflectively—"a most uncommonly queer lot. And there's a mystery of some sort hanging over the head of the house. You don't mean to say, old fellow, that, living in Brightbrook so long, you don't know any of them—eh?"

"Well, in point of fact, you see, I do *not* live in Brightbrook much. I spend Christmas and New Year weeks down here, and either the July or August of every long—but that is all. One month I give to yachting, and then, of course, all the rest of the year is spent at college. You are here a good deal more than I am, and Abbott Wood is so out of the way. As it happens, I have never even heard of these people until to-day."

Frank stares at him, then straight ahead, and whistles.

"Well, that is—— I say—you don't mind my asking, do you? have you never heard your governor speak of them?"

"Never."

"Because Black Giles seems to know *him* most remarkably well. Says he used to be a pal of his, long ago, out in San Francisco."

"What?"

"Yes, I know it's a queer statement. And up the village they say——"

He pauses. A deep line graves itself between Geoffrey Lamar's eyebrows. His step-father is a sensitive subject with him.

"Well," he says, rather coldly, "they say—what?"

"I wouldn't mention this sort of thing if you were Mr. Abbott's son," goes on Frank, magnanimously,

4

"but it is different you know. Giles Sleaford, when
half seas over, has a way of talking—nasty, swearing
sort of way that makes a fellow long to pitch him out
of the window—of your governor. Red Jack Abbott
—so the disrespectful old bloke calls him—used to be
out there in San Francisco the Damon to his Pythias.
But never mind," says Frank, pulling himself up, "you
don't like the subject ; beg pardon for introducing it,
but I am such a fellow to say whatever comes upper-
most. All these returned Californians have a shady
sidewalk in their past pathway, if we only knew it, I
dare say."

Geoffrey Lamar does not seem to derive the cheerful
consolation Frank intends from this philosophical
remark. A frown contracts his forehead, and there
is a pause.

" *You* know those people very well," he says, after
that full stop.

" Oh ! uncommon. I'm *l'ami de la maison*—I have
the run of the whole house, like the family cat. It's
uncommonly jolly. I'll fetch you some evening, if you
like. We have musical and danceable reunions. Jud
plays the fiddle, Dan the flute, Lora the banjo, and
they all can sing. Lora gives me lessons on the
banjo !" Here Frank tries to look grave, but suddenly
explodes into a great laugh. " And we play euchre
and seven-up, and I lose all my loose cash regularly.
It's the best fun going. George Blake comes, and lots
more. I would have asked you long ago, only you *are*
such a solemn old duffer, and of too aristocratic a
stomach to digest such vulgar doings. But if you'll
come I'll present you. They'll kow-tow before you,
for are you not, oh, potent young seigneur, the lord of

the land, and you shall have a good time. Not just at
once, of course ; must wait until the princess, poor
little ducky, is on her little pins again before I go anywhere."

It will be observed that Mr. Frank's style of conversation is exceedingly *degagé*—quite free and easy,
and of the slang a trifle slangy. The prince of wild
Joanna's imagination has a most unprincely way of
expressing himself.

"Say you'll come. Get rid of that owl-like face,
and stop trying to look like your own grandfather.
What a fellow you are, Lamar ! I would mope myself
into the horrors if I lived as you do. Say you'll come
to the very next Sleaford swarry. We have clam-
bakes after the concert and the valse à deux-temps ;
codfish chowder, barbecued rabbit, and sich—everything highly genteel and *en regle*. And you can wash
it down with whisky ad libitum, or you can join the
ladies in cider-cup and bottled lager, if you prefer such
effeminate tipple. You will come ?"

"Yes, I will come," Geoffrey answers, laughing.
" These are attractions not to be declined. I say !
stop a moment, Livingston—whom have we here ?"

A brilliant, black-eyed, buxom brunette, dressed in
the loudest possible style, pink, and purple, and yellow all swearing at each other in her costume, advances toward them, a green parasol shading her
already over-ripe charms from the too ardent glances
of the sun.

" What !" cries Frank, falling back and striking an
attitude. " Do these eyes deceive me ? That form—
that smile—that green umbrella ! 'Tis she ! Lora !
light of my eyes, beloved of my soul, whither away

in such haste with the thermometer up in the nineties.
What! still silent! Speak, loveliest of thy sex—
speak, ere I perish! Whither goest thou in such
haste?"

Miss Lora Sleaford furls her green parasol, not at
all discomposed by this impassioned address, and ad-
ministers a gentle rebuke with the nozzle across
Frank's shapely nose.

"Don't be a donkey," is her retort. "I suppose,
considering I lost a night's sleep with that little girl,
and had a sight of trouble with her every way, I have
a right to walk up and ask how she gets along. Why
weren't you there last night?"

"Pressing business engagements, over which I had
no control, my dearest Lora; but I see those beauteous
orbs are riveted on the manly countenance of my
friend. He is perishing for an introduction—was
begging me with tears in his eyes, just before you came
up, to obtain him the *entree* to Sleaford's, and the acquaintance of Sleaford's two lovely daughters. Come
here, Geoff, a moment, will you. Miss Lora Sleaford,
allow me to present to you my young friend, Geoffrey
Valandigham Lamar."

Miss Sleaford bows gracefully, really gracefully,
smiles radiantly—black eyes, red cheeks, coral lips,
dazzling white teeth, all a-sparkle together. She evidently takes Frank's chaff as a thing of course, and is
perfectly well used to that style of address. Geoffrey
laughs, but reddens a little, with some of that becoming boyish bashfulness that Frank Livingston has
never known.

"Blush not, my Geoffrey!" says that young man of
the world, with an encouraging slap on the back,

"Miss Lora's charms floor us all at first, but we get used to 'em after a time. So will you. Don't bo ashamed of yourself—speak to her prettily—she's not half so dignified, bless you, nor unapproachable, as she looks. So you're going to the house, are you, Lora? That is a very pretty attention on your part. The little one is asleep now. Doctor says she'll pull through. But what a queer go it all is, this cock-and-bull story Dan tells, about a wild girl, and the rest of it!"

"It is true enough. I guess it was our Joanna," replies Lora, complacently adjusting a pair of flat gilt bracelets.

"You don't say so! Joanna! What a little devil's doll she is, to be sure. Shall we see you home, my friend and I, after your call, my Lora? Nothing would give us greater rapture, you know."

But Miss Sleaford declines, with a toss of her white feathers. She is not going home, she is en route for Brightbrook—Dan and the trap are waiting outside the gate. And so, with a parting bow and smile, intended to do deadly execution on young Lamar, Lora trips away to the hall door.

Mrs. Ventnor, looking pale and anxious, receives her, and thanks her in very fervent words, and a handsome present of jewelry, for her kindness to her child. She has summed up Miss Sleaford at a glance, and sees she is the type to whom breastpin and bracelets are always acceptable. There is another lady in the room, a lady who looks like a queen in a picture, Lora thinks, so grand, so stately, so beautiful is she. She awes even Miss Sleaford, who is not easily awed. It is Mrs. Abbott, she knows ; she has seen her more

than once ; the mother of that dull, plain-looking young
fellow outside. And yet, though one is beautiful and
the other almost devoid of beauty, there is a resemblance between the two faces, in the firm mouth and
proudly-curved chin, in the level, rather chill glance
of the full dark eye, in the haughty poise of the head
and shoulders. For you need not look twice at young
Geoffrey Lamar to know that although he has not
fallen heir to his mother's beauty, he has to her pride.

This grand dame goes up to Lora, and holds out
one long, slim white hand.

"We are all your debtors," she says, in a slow,
sweet, trained voice. "In saving our dear little Olga
you have served us all. If you will accept this, as a
little token of my great regard——"

She slips from her finger a circlet of rubies, and
the quick blood comes into Lora Sleaford's face.

"Thank you, ma'am," she says, almost bashfully.
With some trouble she gets the rich hoop on one of
her fat fingers, and makes her courtesy and departs,
enchanted with her visit and its results.

But little Olga is really very ill, and lies tossing
through the warm July days, fever-flushed, wild-eyed,
thirsty, wandering.

Over and over again the wild girl of the woods is
bending above her, her hands in her hair, her deadly
weapon poised, and Olga's shrieks ring through the
room, and they have to hold her in her bed by force.
All the long lovely locks are cut off close, cruelly
close to the poor little burning head, and there are days
when neither doctor nor nurse can tell how that fierce
struggle is to end.

Lora Sleaford comes often to inquire, and Joanna,

crouching like a toad in her corner, hears the story of
the severed golden hair. A moment after she has
slipped from her place, and gone out into the night.
She throws herself down on the dark, dewy grass, and
buries her face in her folded arms. She has got the
desire of her heart, and she is not glad ; a vague sort
of remorse and unrest fills her. She did not want to
kill this little heiress, only to frighten her ; to cut off
her hair, not to give her a brain fever. If she dies,
will they hang her—Joanna ? She knows Lora knows,
and has told others. Well, let them hang her if they
like ; she did not mean to do it, and hanging cannot
hurt much worse than horsewhipping. She does not
care ; she is past care, past hope, past help. It does
not matter—nothing matters. Better to be dead at
once, and done with it. But she hopes this little girl
will not die. And presently—perhaps it is because
she is all aching and half sick to-night, great tears
well up, and fill and fall from her eyes, that burn generally with so baleful a light.

She has been beaten by Giles Sleaford, she has had
her ears boxed by Dan, she has been scolded by Liz,
she has worked like a slave since early morning, she is
sore, and hungry, and hopeless, and sick.

"I wish I was dead," she sobs, her face hidden in
the sweet wet grass. "I wish I had never been born !"

*   *   *   *   *   *

But little Olga does not die. She is a delicate
child, and it requires the best of medical skill and
ceaseless care to bring her through. There comes
what is called the crisis—there is a night when no one
at Ventnor Villa nor Abbott Wood thinks of sleep—a
night when Frank Livingston paces the wet grass,

under the summer stars, until day-dawn, filled with
fear and remorse for his share in the tragedy—a night
when Colonel Ventnor walks the halls and passages,
pale as no one has ever seen him pale before—a night
when Mrs. Abbott sits through the long mute hours
clasping the hand of the sick child's mother in her
own, and with bated breath watching for that dread
change.   It comes, it passes, and burning heat changes
to profound slumber, and tossing delirium to gentle
perspiration, and little Olga is saved !

The news flies—it visits many homes, and sometime that day reaches Sleaford's, where Lora relates it
to the family assembled at supper.

"So you see, little monkey," she winds up, address-
ing Joanna, "you ain't a murderer after all, and won't
be hanged *this* time.   But you had better look out,
and not try that sort of thing again.   You mayn't get
off so easy another time."

"It's only a question of a year or two—eh, Jo?"
says Jud Sleaford, tweaking the girl's ear.   "You're
bound to come to it some day.   Of all the little limbs
of Old Nick *I* ever met, you top the lot.".

"I am what you all have made me," the child
flashes out, with sudden fire, jerking herself free.   "I
only wonder I haven't killed somebody long ago—
some of *you*, I mean.   I will yet, if you don't let me
alone."

A growl from Giles silences her, but in her poor,
darkened, heathenish little soul that night there is a
wordless thanksgiving for the news she has heard.

"I don't know what got into me," she thinks, with
a feeling akin to compunction ; "she never did nothin'
to me when all's said and done.   I'm sorry I scared

her ; I'm sorry, yes, I am, that she's had to lose all her pretty hair."

The other members of the Sleaford family circle are relieved also, but for a different reason.

"I'm sure I'm glad of it," Liz says, in a querulous tone ; "the place has been like a grave-yard ever since that night ; not a soul's been near the house, except once, George Blake. Can't we have a dance, Dan, some night next week ?"

"And tell Frank Livingston, Dan, to fetch young Lamar," suggests Lora. "I am dying for a dance. I saw two or three of the girls down at the Corners yesterday, and they were asking when we meant to have another spree."

"Dad means to go to the city next Tuesday," suggests Jud, "and as he ain't particularly useful or ornamental on an occasion like that, I vote we have the high jinks while he's gone."

This resolution is unanimously carried by the house, and next Tuesday is fixed for the Sleaford *fête*. The young ladies at once set to work to prepare their costumes and decorate the house. Dan issues the invitations verbally, and all are accepted, including that extended to Master Geoffrey Lamar. Frank goes without saying. With a load off his conscience now that Olga is recovering, Frank is in wild high spirits and ready for anything. He is generating a great deal of steam in these days of Olga's convalescence, and requires a safety-valve of some sort. He spends considerable of his precious time in the sick-room, and it is found does Olga more good by his lively presence than all the doctor's stimulants. Geoffrey Lamar and little Leo Abbott, too, are there a great deal—their conver-

4*

sation and company excite the child a little, but the
good results counterbalance the evil. Still, four or five
days of this sort of thing—this state of unnatural
goodness—has a depressing effect on Frank, and the
Sleaford "swarry" is hailed with rejoicing.

"We always present some little delicate offering
to the young ladies on these occasions," he remarks to
Geoffrey, "not bouquets or floral litter of that sort;
but something sensible and solid. On various festive
seasons of this nature, I myself have contributed a
ham, a plum cake, a turkey, some port wine, and other
graceful trifles of that sort. The present being a
special festival, it is my intention to appear in company with two imperial quarts of champagne. You,
young sir, being a lily of the field, and this your *début*,
will be exempt from taxation. The honor of your
presence is sufficient in itself."

"It rather reminds one of Mrs. Nickleby and the
love-stricken old gentleman in small-clothes, who
threw the vegetable marrows," says Geoffrey, laughing. "I wonder, Frank, you care to mingle with such
a lot. You really seem to like it."

"And I really do, my aristocratic young friend.
Human nature in all its varieties interests me in the
abstract; human nature, as represented by Miss Lora
Sleaford, interests me consumedly in particular. A
romp with that girl is equal to a boxing-match any
day to put a fellow in condition. Leave all your fastidious notions at Abbott Wood, with your evening
dress; put on a shooting-jacket, and come and be
happy."

They are the latest guests. The old red farm-house
is all alight when they draw near, the scraping of Jud's

violin is their greeting as they enter. Some half-dozen young ladies in gay muslin dresses, gilt brooches and chains, and rainbow ribbons are there, and represent the Sleaford "set" in Brightbrook. The young men are generally of a better stamp, and muster stronger; the lower rooms look filled to overflowing as the two late guests arrive. A momentary hush of awe greets Geoffrey Lamar, but it does not last; the festive group here assembled are not awed easily or long.

"For Heaven's sake do not introduce me to anybody!" whispers Geoffrey, nervously, afraid of a torrent of Frank's "chaff." "Just let me alone, and I'll drift into port myself."

There is one face present that he recognizes, that of George Blake, and he seeks refuge by his side. Blake is a bright young fellow, poor, but of good connections; his mother, a widow, teaches music in the village; George, an only son, is at present beginning life in the office of the Brightbrook *News.* He is about eighteen or nineteen—indeed, none of the gentleman are on the aged side of twenty.

But Mr. Blake is destined for higher duty than playing protector—Miss Liz Sleaford sails up, resplendent in crimson ribbons and cheap jewelry, and claims him as her own. They are all in the parlor—Jud, the musician, is perched on a sort of pedestal in a corner to be out of the way, as there is not an inch of spare room for the coming engagement. The dance is a waltz. Frank is spinning round with Lora, as a matter of course, Mr. Blake is blessed with Liz, five other couples revolve and bump against each other with much force, and great good-humor.

Geoffrey has seen a great many waltzes, but the energy, the vim, the "go" of this one he has never seen equaled. And it is a night in early August. The full harvest moon is pouring its pale splendor over the warm, sweet world without ; the faces of the waltzers are redder in ten minutes than the moon was when it rose. The living whirlwind flashing past him so confuses Geoffrey that he gets up at last, and with some difficulty makes his way into the kitchen. This apartment has but two occupants—Dan Sleaford, and a small, scantily-dressed damsel of twelve, who appears to be assistant cook. Dan is the *chef*. At an early age he developed one talent, a talent for clam chowder ; many years of cultivation, and that talent has soared to the heights of positive genius. No "swarry" at the Sleaford's would be considered perfect without a chowder ; it is indeed the *pièce de resistance* of the feast, and is generally the only dish contributed by the feast givers. So Dan, in a state threatening spontaneous combustion, bends over the steaming caldron, from which odors as of Araby the Blest are wafted out into the silent night. The youthful person with him, in a sulky and slipshod manner, is emptying numerous baskets, and arranging their contents on the two deal tables, covered, at present, with very white cloths, and set out with the blue delf, two-pronged forks, and a miscellaneous collection of knives. It requires some skill on Mr. Sleaford's part to keep one eye on the chowder, and bring it to the pitch of perfection for which he is so justly celebrated, and keep the other fixed sternly on his small assistant, to see that she purloins none of the provisions. On the present occasion the spread is something gorgeous. There is, first of all, the champagne—two silver-throated beauties contributed by Frank. Then a basket of able-bodied little mutton pies, the delicate attentions of Mr. George Blake, who has a weakness that way. Then a plum cake, with sugar coating an inch thick, the luscious offering of the young Brightbrook baker. Then a leg of lamb " with fixins," *anglicé*, peas and mint sauce. A bottle of mixed pickles, a wedge of cheese, a can of sweet biscuits and sundries, the tribute by the representative of the grocery. In addition, a great earthenware pot of tea is steeping for the ladies, while the whisky and other spirituous fluids, together with a box of cigars, adorn a shelf of the cupboard. These delicacies, with the chowder—always with the chowder—comprise a supper fit for Brillat Savarin or the Olympian gods.

Geoffrey takes a seat on the sill of one of the open windows, trying to catch a breath of cool air, and amused in spite of himself by the novelty of all this. Dan Sleaford politely essays conversation, but, distracted between the chowder and his handmaid, the attempts are not brilliant. In spite of his Argus eyes, Joanna manages to filch a mutton pie, a handful of mixed biscuits, and a piece of cheese, and secretes this victual somewhere about her garments. Geoffrey watches the elfish child with curiosity ; she is of a type he has never seen before. He has a chivalrous veneration for all things feminine, engendered by his beautiful and stately mother ; but this changeling—it is difficult to imagine her belonging to the same order of beings as his sister Leo, or Olga Ventnor. This evening her best frock, such as it is, has been donned ; she

wears shoes and stockings, and an effort has been made
to brush down the thick shock of darkly-reddish hair.
He sees the pale, pinched features—features not homely in themselves, but spoiled by an expression of settled sullenness and gloom. She looks uncanny, and
most pathetically unchildlike. When Dan Sleaford
girds at her, she shrinks as if she expected a blow.
Her hard life is written in every line of her downcast
and smileless face.

Inside, the fun waxes fast and furious; peals of
laughter ring out, the house quivers with the tread of
the dancers. Jud's fiddle never falters nor fails. A
schottische follows the waltz, then a quadrille, then a
polka ; then George Blake performs a solo, the High
land Fling—a dance which has more genuine fling
about it, as executed by Mr. Blake, than any of the
company has ever before beheld. Then there is a con-
tre dance. Then Dan Sleaford, crimson of visage,
presents himself at the parlor door, and in stentorian
accents announces the chowder and accompaniments,
and tersely commands them to " come on !"

" What, Geoff, old boy ! taking lessons in cook-
ing ?" cries Frank, wiping his hot face. " Phew ! what
a blazer of a night !—and, by Jove ! what a girl Lora
Sleaford is to spin ! There's more go in her than in any
human being I ever met. She has been dancing every
time, and hasn't turned a hair, while I—I give you my
word, old fellow, I'm fit to drop."

But a bumper of foamy iced lager restores the exhausted one, and the company sit down to supper. A
very noisy company it is, a very hungry company too,
and despite the height of the thermometer, boiling
chowder, steaming tea, roast lamb, and mutton pies

disappear with a celerity that speaks well for the faith the consumers have in their own powerful digestions. Every one helps himself and his partner to whatever chances to be handiest; cheese and pickles vanish in company, lamb and pound-cake, mutton pies and peas. The gentlemen slake their thirst with flagons of lager beer, or the more potent whisky; while the ladies genteelly partake of hot tea and iced champagne, one after the other, and with perfect equanimity.

It is all a wonderful experience to Geoffrey Lamar. For Frank—he and George Blake—they are the choice spirits of the board. He is amused, a trifle disgusted also, it may be, but the hilarity carries him away, and he finds himself laughing almost as noisily as the rest. Once or twice he glances about for the attendant sprite, but she is no longer in waiting; every one helps himself. She is in a corner of the fire-place, as though she felt the heat no more than a salamander, munching her pilfered dainties, and staring, with bright, watchful eyes, at the people before her. No one notices her, or thinks of offering her anything to eat or drink. The dogs get an occasional morsel thrown them—she gets nothing.

Supper over, dancing is resumed with ardor and vigor. There is singing, too, spirited songs with ringing choruses, in which the strength and lungs of the "swarry" is thrown. Miss Lora gives them—to a banjo accompaniment—"Sing, oh! for a brave and gallant bark, a brisk and lively breeze,"—which, having a fine resounding chorus, goes near to lift the roof off. Liz does the sentimental, and warbles "Thou hast learned to love another, thou hast broken every vow." Frank Livingston trolls forth, in a very nice

tenor, "Sarah's Young Man," and the Messieurs Sleaford uplift their voices in a nautical duet. The remains of the plum cake, and some cool lemonade are
passed around among the fair sex. The gentlemen
adjourn at intervals to the kitchen cupboard for a
"modest quencher," a quiet cigar, and Geoffrey Lamar,
growing rather bored, keeps his seat on the window-
sill, and wishes it were time to get out of all this noise
and heat, and go.

His interest in Joanna does not flag. She is a
curious study, and he watches her. After supper she
clears off the things, washes the dishes, puts them
away, sweeps up the floor, all in profound silence, and
with deft, swift hands. Then, instead of going to bed,
although it is past midnight, she produces a tattered
book, and resumes her corner to read. With hands
over her ears, eyes riveted to the page, she is seemingly lost to all the tumult around her. He watches her
in silence for awhile, then he speaks.

"What are you reading?"

He has to touch her to make her hear—then she
looks up. How changed her look! the sullen moodi-
ness has passed away, her eyes are eager, her face
bright with the interest of her book. But in that instant the old look of dark, frowning distrust returns.
She points to the page without a word.

"'Monte Cristo,'" he reads. "Do you like it?"

She nods.

"But the first and last seems to be torn out—that
must spoil the interest, I should think. Do you read
much?"

She purses up her mouth and shakes her head.

"Why?"

"No books—no time."

"You are fond of stories?"

"Oh! ain't I!—just!"

"Would you like me to bring you a book the next time I come?"

She looks at him, wondering, distrustful. He is a young gentleman, and he is taking notice of her—he is speaking to her kindly. No one does that. He is offering her a book—no one ever gives her anything. Her sullen look comes back; she does not know what to make of it.

"I will bring you some books," he says, "and I will ask your sisters to let you read them. Books that will suit you better than 'Monte Cristo.'"

"Sisters!" she repeats. "*I* ain't got no sisters. But if you ain't foolin'——" distrustfully. "You *are* foolin', ain't you, mister?"

He assures her of his sincerity.

"Well, then, don't you go and bring no books here. 'Cause I wouldn't be let to have 'em; old Giles would burn 'em up. But I know what you *could* do——" with a cunning look.

"Well—what?"

"Do you know Black's Dam, and the old mill down there in the woods?"

"Yes, I know them."

"Then—if you ain't foolin'—fetch 'em there, and leave 'em in the mill. *I'll* find them; no one else ever goes there. But I know you won't."

"You will see. You will find one there to-morrow night. What's your name?"

"Sleaford's Joanna," she says, with a shrill laugh, "or Wild Joanna—'tain't no odds which. I'm both."

·" What is your other name ?"

" Got no other name. Got no father, no mother, no friends, no nothin'. I'm only Sleaford's Joanna."

She goes back to her book, and when, hours after, the *soirée* breaks up, she is bending over Dumas' extravaganza still. Geoffrey bids her good-night—the only one of the party who has addressed her the whole evening.

And that brief conversation is the mustard-seed, so small as to be hardly visible, from which all the dark record of the future is to grow. There are many memorable nights in Geoffrey Lamar's life, but none that stands out more ominously vivid than this.

<hr />

CHAPTER X.

GEOFFREY LAMAR.

EOFFREY LAMAR goes to no more Sleaford *soirées*, he has no taste for that sort of revelry, but he does not forget the odd, elfish child who wastes midnight oil over the adventures of Dumas' wonderful hero.

He goes next day to Black's Dam, with a volume under his arm, and places it on a rude seat he finds in the ruined mill. It is a dull, sunless day, and the evil look of the place depresses him. What a strange, hideous retreat this child chooses ; it is like herself, eery and frowning. The dark, stagnant pond lies under the gray sky, green and poisonous, the dull croak of a frog making itself heard now and then. It looks black and bad ; so, too, does the deserted mill, falling dry and tindery to decay. Heavy woods and rank undergrowth shut it in on every hand. There is no path, long ago it was overgrown and forsaken, only a slender line worn by the bare feet of the desolate child. A great pity for the forlorn, ill-treated little creature fills him.

"Poor little wretch !" he thinks ; "all work and no play, ignorance, brutality, starvation—it is hard lines for her."

He leaves the book and returns to the village. He and Leo are due at the villa to-day ; they are to dine with convalescent Olga. It is the first time she has left her chamber, and, robed in the daintiest of all her dainty white robes, she is carried down by papa to where the table is set under the trees, and where she is received with acclamations by Frank, and Geoffrey, and Leo. All the long ringlets are gone, she looks pallid and thin, but very, very pretty. She is the little queen of the feast, she is petted and spoiled to her heart's content. And Olga likes to be petted, and ceases to regret the loss of her lovely long hair, and decides there are worse things in the world than brain fever, after all.

Late that evening, after a hard day's work—for it is wash-day at the farm-house, and she has had to carry water from early morning—Sleaford's Joanna steals out by the back way, and darts off to her castle in the wood.

Some faint hope that the young gentleman who spoke to her last night may keep his word stirs within her, but it is very faint. Joanna is not used to people who keep their word, and why should he ever think of

her again ?   It surprises her when she remembers he
noticed her at all.

· Frank Livingston has been coming to the house
for months, and has never spoken to her a single word.
She has provided herself with a candle in a bottle, and
some matches, in case the book *should* prove to be
there.   And if it does not rain, as it looks very much
like doing, she will stay at the mill all night.

The gray light of the overcast day is dying out
when she reaches her gruesome retreat.   But it is not
ugly or forbidding to Joanna ; the quietest, the happiest, the most peaceful hours of her life are spent
here.   The frogs that croak in the green, slimy waters,
croak at her with the voices of friends ; their ugly faces
uplifted from the ooze are the friendliest faces she
knows.   She has read "Robinson Crusoe" of late, and
wild visions of flying from Sleaford's farmstead, and
taking up her permanent abode here, rise before her
ecstatically.   To live here all by herself, never to work,
never to be scolded or beaten, that would be bliss.   But
it is not practicable, the Sleafords would never let her
go like that—who would fetch water, and carry wood,
and wash dishes, and scrub floors, and make beds, and
see to the dinner, and run errands, if she left?   And
grapes do not grow in Brightbrook woods, nor wild
goats run about, waiting to be caught and eaten, as in
Crusoe's lovely isle.

Still, she has done the best she can ; she has brought
an armful of clean straw, a pillow and a quilt or two,
a supply of candles and matches, and spends many a
tranquil summer night here, watching the stars shining
down on her, through the broken roof.   These nights

are the nearest approach to happiness Sleaford's Joanna knows.

She reaches the mill, enters, and finds a book in red and gilt binding lying on the bench. Her heart gives a bound—she has a passion for reading ; such a volume as *this* she has never before beheld. She wipes her grimy fingers on her frock, and takes it gingerly up. There is still light enough to read the title, the " Old Curiosity Shop." It is full of pictures, she gloats over them, the sentences look short, the print is large and clear.

There seems to be plenty of conversation ; as Joanna expresses it, " it looks open-worky." She hugs the book to her breast, her eyes shine with delight. Oh, how good of him—that nice, pleasant-spoken young gentleman, to remember her—*her!* whom nobody ever remembers ; to come all this way and leave this beautiful book.

A great throb of gratitude fills her, all good is not crushed out of the child ; then a pang swift and sharp follows. If he knew how bad she is, how she has nearly killed poor little Miss Ventnor, would he have been so kind ? No, she feels sure not ; he would shrink from her as from a toad. She *is* a toad, a venomous toad, Liz says so—an imp, Jud calls her—a little devil is Dan's pet name for her—lazy little hussy, Lora says, and Old Giles' names mostly are too bad to repeat. No, if he knew what she was like, he never would fetch her any books.

It is dark now ; she lights her candle and begins to read. She is not afraid of being interrupted, no one ever comes to Black's Dam. More than one wretched suicide has sought its villainous waters, and

it is of evil savor in the nostrils of Brightbrook. It is
a weird picture, the dark, stagnant pond, the dark
woods, the dark night sky, the deep and mysterious
stillness, that glimmering light among the ruined timbers of the old mill, and the strange little creature
crouched in a heap, devouring, with greedy eyes, the
story of Little Nell.

Presently the sighing wind rises, falls, stirs the
trees, wails lugubriously through the pines, and then
great drops begin to fall and plash heavily on the
roof. She neither hears nor heeds ; she is far away
amid the Kentish meadows with Little Nell, held
breathless and enchained by the pathos of the tale.

She has never read anything like this ; she laughs
with Dick Swiveller, she identifies herself with the
marchioness, she is lost in wonder at the goodness and
wisdom of Nelly. It is very late, and she has read
quite half the book, when a large drop falls directly
on the glittering candle, and it splutters and goes out.
It is burned nearly to the end anyhow, it is useless
relighting the fragment. She closes her book with a
profound sigh, and for the first time becomes conscious
that it is raining hard and that a gale is surging
through the woods.

Well, it does not matter ; her truss of straw, and
quilts, are in a dry corner, but she would as soon go
home in the rain as not. But before going anywhere,
she sits for nearly half an hour, her knees clasped in
her arms, her black melancholy eyes staring out at the
wet wildness of the lonesome night.

That story of Little Nell troubles and disturbs her.
How different from Nell is she—how wicked, how
miserable ! But then no one has ever loved her, or

cared for her, or taught her. No nice old grandfather
has ever doted on *her ;* no funny Kit Nubbles has been
her friend ; no Mrs. Jarley has protected and been
kind to *her.*

She wonders what it is like to be happy, to have
father, mother, friends ; a home without cursing, or
drinking, or whipping ; nice dresses, and plenty of
books to read. It would be easy enough to be good
then, but she—a strange, mournful wonder fills her
as she looks back over the brief years she can remember.

She is bad, no doubt ; she is very bad—but what
has she done to have such a hard, hard life? She is
only a poor little thing, after all ; only twelve years
old. Was she born wicked, she wonders, and different
from other children? In a blind, pathetic sort of way
she tries to solve the riddle, but it baffles her. She
gropes in utter darkness of heart and soul. It would
be pleasant to be good, she thinks, but it cannot be ;
no one could be good at Sleaford's. And if she was
born a little imp, as they tell her, it is of no use trying. She can no more be like Little Nell than she can
be like Miss Olga Ventnor, or Miss Leo Abbott, with
their floating, perfumed hair and silk dresses, and fair
faces, and pretty, glittering trinkets. No, and she
will not try ; and so, with another great hopeless sigh,
Sleaford's Joanna gives up the puzzle and goes to
bed.

Three days after this it occurs to Geoffrey Lamar
to take a second look at the odd child at Sleaford's.
So he mounts his horse, and rides slowly into the
woodland path that leads to the Red Farm. It is a
mystery to him, as it has been to others, why Mr. Ab-

bott lets this shiftless lot run riot in the best farm he
owns, but it is a mystery he cannot fathom, unless
Frank Livingston's unpleasant hints have some foun-
dation.

In his secret heart he neither likes nor respects his
step-father ; he distrusts him, he shares his mother's
unspoken shrinking and aversion. All the man's tastes,
and instincts, and ways are low. Geoffrey is a gentleman, lad as he is, and the son of a gentleman ; his
feelings are by nature refined ; he hates coarseness,
vulgarity, pride of wealth ; his intellect is beyond his
years, and his reason tells him Frank's hints are more
than likely to be true. Mr. Abbott is good to him, is
proud of him, is fond of him, is lavishly generous to
him, and the boy fights with his feelings and keeps
them down. He ought to be grateful, and he is, but
despite all that Mr. Abbott can come not one whit
nearer to the son than to the mother.

As he rides along, a sudden joyous caroling overhead makes him pause and look up. Twit, twit, twit—
twee-e-e-e ! A whole shower of silvery notes, but the
bird is nowhere to be seen. Then the warble changes ;
a blackbird whistles, a bobolink calls, it is the chatter of a squirrel, the to-whit-to-whoo of an owl, the
harsh croak of a frog, the shrill chirp of a cricket,
then rapidly the clear, shrill song of a lark.

Geoffrey sits dumbfounded. Has a mocking-bird
been let loose in Brightbrook woods ? Suddenly a wild
peal of laughter greets him, there is a rustle of boughs,
and from a tree under which he stands, a thin, elfish
face looks down.

" It's only me, mister, mocking the birds. I often
do it. I can whistle, too. Listen !" The sweetest,

shrillest whistle he has ever heard takes up the air
"Sweet Home," and performs it as he could not do to
save his life. "There!" says the voice. "I'll sing for
you now, if you like. Didn't know I could sing, did
you? All the Sleafords sing, law bless you! but I
only do when I feel like it. Did you ever hear 'Lanigan's Ball?'"

A sweet, strong voice begins that classical ditty,
and the woods give back the melodious echo. Geoffrey Lamar listens in silent amaze. Why, the elf is a
prodigy!—a musical prodigy! Where, in that small,
starved body has she room for a voice like that?

She finishes at last, and whistles a bar or two of
the air by way of closing symphony.

"That was an awful nice book you lent me," she
goes on. "I've read it through twice. I haven't
soiled it a mite, and it's down at the mill. I—I'm
lots obliged to you, you know. Didn't think you'd
ever fetch it."

She descends a branch or two from her lofty roost,
and brings herself to a level with the rider.

"It *is* Sleaford's Joanna!" says Geoffrey, his breath
nearly taken away. "Why, you must be a witch. Who
taught you to sing and whistle, and twitter like a bird,
in this fashion?"

"Nobody taught me—taught myself. It's jest as
easy as nothin' at all."

"Can you sing anything but 'Lanigan's Ball?'"

Joanna nods.

"Know a hymn. Lora heard your mar sing it at
her meetin'. Goes like this."

The silvery childish treble uplifts and peals out
with a force that fairly amazes him. The hymn, from

5

those lips, amazes him still more. It is "Rock of Ages."

> "Rock of Ages, cleft for me,
> Let me hide myself in Thee!"

How strangely from those impish lips sound the grand, strong words!

> "Nothing in my hand I bring,
> Simply to Thy cross I cling;
> Naked, come to Thee for dress,
> Helpless, look to Thee for grace;
> Rock of Ages, cleft for me,
> Let me hide myself in Thee!"

"Upon my word, you are a marvel!" Geoffrey says, catching his bated breath. "And so you like the book? Would you like another?"

"Oh!" ejaculated Joanna, rapturously; "wouldn't I just!"

"Well, you shall. I will leave it this evening at the mill. Who taught you to read? Have you ever been at school?"

"School!" Joanna echoes, scornfully; "I guess not. Catch Old Giles sending me to school. Not but that I'd like to go, mind you. No, Jud teaches me. He ain't so bad, Jud ain't—don't curse nor hit me like the rest. Teached me some writin', too, but not much."

"And you would like to learn more?"

"You bet! But 'tain't no use. Old Giles would beat me to death if I spoke of such a thing."

"Do you mean to say he really beats and swears at you?"

Joanna laughs shrilly.

"Oh, no, not at all! *He* wouldn't hurt nobody! Look here, mister!"

She uncovers her shoulders by a dexterous hitch, and shows him long black and blue welts purpling the flesh.

"Did that last night; was drunk, you know. Beat me till I couldn't stir."

"What had you done?" Geoffrey asks, sick at heart.

"Nothin' 'tall. Didn't fetch the boot-jack quick enough. Got me into a corner where I couldn't wriggle away, and lashed me till Jud took the whip out of his hand. Says he'll beat my soul out next time. May if he likes. *I* don't care."

She begins to whistle defiantly, but tears of pain and wrath well up in spite of her, and she winks them angrily away.

"Poor little soul!" the lad says, strongly touched. And at the pitying words all her bravado breaks down, and she suddenly covers her face, and sobs wildly:

"I wish I was dead—I do! I wish I was dead and buried!"

"Hush," he says, distressed, "that is wicked. Don't cry; I am going to try and do something for you. I am going to help you if I can. I am sure you would be a good girl if you had a chance. It is a shame—a shame! They use you worse than a dog!"

"Oh, dear! oh, dear! oh, dear!" the poor little wretch sobs. It is the first time in her life the floodgates have thus been opened. She cries wildly now, as she does all things, as if her very heart were bursting. It is the first time any one has ever been sorry for her, and the sympathy goes near to break her heart.

"Do not cry," he says. "Look here, Joanna, I will leave the book for you to-night, and I will come to see you again in—let me see—two days. Now, good-by, and do not get whipped, if you can, till I come back."

With which the youthful knight-errant of tattered damsels in distress turns his horse's head, and rides slowly and thoughtfully homeward, revolving in his mind a decidedly bold project, which, if carried into effect, bids fairs to alter the whole future life of Sleaford's Joanna.

CHAPTER XI.

IN WHICH MR. ABBOTT ASSERTS HIMSELF.

HE light of the August sunset lies low over Abbott Wood, as young Geoffrey Lamar rides slowly up the shaded avenue, still lost in thought. And yet not so deeply absorbed but that the glowing beauty of green glade, and sunny slope, scented rose-thicket, waving depths of fern and bracken, ruby lines of light slanting through brown boles of trees, strike him with a keen sense of delight. It is *his*, all this fair domain, this noble inheritance ; no birthright, but the generous gift promised him often by the master of Abbott Wood. And that sense of proprietorship accents vividly his pleasure in its green loveliness, as he rides up under those tall, arching elms. He is not an embryo artist, as is Frank Livingston. He does not rant of light and shade, of breadth and perspective, of tone and color, and backgrounds and chien-oscuro, or the rest of the art-jargon in which his flighty friend excels, but he loves every tree, and stone, and coppice, and flower, and bird about the place, and means, please Heaven, it shall be his home, wander whither he may, through life.

Mr. Abbott is in the stables, smoking and lecturing the grooms, when Geoffrey resigns his horse to the boy who caters to him. He nods affectionately to his step-son. It has been said he is fond and proud of him—proud, after an absurd fashion, that the lad is a gentleman by birth and breeding, while resenting at the same time the grave reserve the youth maintains between them. But Geoffrey is in a grateful and gentle mood at this moment ; moreover, he is in the character of a suppliant, and returns his step-father's greeting with cordiality.

"I've been deucedly put out just now, Geoff, my boy," Mr. Abbott says, quitting the stables with him ; "not so much with these fellows, though they *are* a set of lazy dogs, who shirk work whenever they can. But I was down at Cooper's this afternoon, and the way that place is going to wreck and ruin under that shif'less lot is enough to turn a man's hair gray. I gave old Job a bit of my mind, let me tell you, and out they go next quarter day, by the Lord Harry ! Mind you, Geoff, when you're master here, keep no tenants on your land like the Coopers. Out with 'em neck and crop !"

"Cooper is not a model farmer," says Geoffrey, coolly, " but in comparison with another of your tenants, his place is a paradise. I mean Sleaford's—the Red Farm."

A dark frown bends Mr. Abbott's brows. He takes out his cigar and looks at the boy.

"Sleaford's!" he growls. "What do *you* know of Sleaford's? What takes you there?"

"Frank Livingston took me the other evening. They had a dance of some sort. But I have passed the place often, and can see. Besides, every one is talking of it, and wondering you do not send them adrift."

"Every one be—every one had better mind his own business! You too," Mr. Abbott would like to add, but he knows the state of haughty surprise Geoffrey's face can assume when it likes, and does not care to provoke it. "I don't explain to all Brightbrook—hang 'em—my reasons, but I don't mind to you. Black Giles Sleaford was a—well, acquaintance of mine out in San Francisco, some fourteen years ago, and he did me—well, a sort of service, in those days. He's a worthless devil, I allow, but what's a man to do? Turn his back on an old fri—acquaintance; and leave him to starve, when he's rolling in riches himself? It's the way of the world, I know; but, by Jupiter, it ain't John Abbott's way. So he's at the Red Farm, and there I mean to let him stay. It ain't the same case as the Coopers, at all.· But look here, Geoffrey, boy, don't you go there. I don't like it. I don't ask many favors; just grant me this one. They're low, dear boy, and it ain't no place for a young gentleman born and bred, like you. Livingston may go if he likes; he's a good-for-nothing rattle-pate at best, but you're not of that sort. Don't you go to Sleaford's, Geoff, any more—to please the old man!"

He lays his hand, in his earnestness, on the lad's

shoulder, and looks with troubled eyes down into his
face. Geoffrey shrugs his shoulders—the old, instinctive feeling of shrinking from his step-father nevei
more strongly upon him.

"I am not likely to go there as Frank does," he
answers, carelessly ; " he likes that sort of thing—I do
not. But once or twice more I believe I must. I have
a little project on hand connected with one of that
family which will take me there again—at least as
often as that."

Mr. Abbott's gaze grows more and more perturbed.
"One of that family !" he repeats. "You don't
mind my asking which one, do you, Geoff ? It ain't
—— " he hesitates ; bully, braggart, bold man that he
is, he has a strong respect for this boy. "It ain't—
excuse me—one of the girls ?"

He fears to meet that icy stare he knows so well
from both mother and son, and resents so bitterly.
But to his surprise Geoffrey only laughs.

"Exactly, sir, one of the girls—the youngest. I
will not tell you what it is just now. You will think
it absurd, I dare say. I will speak to my mother first,
and she will inform you. There ! I see her on the terrace. Excuse me, sir, she is beckoning."

He darts away, his face lighting. As a sculptor
may regard some peerless marble goddess, almost as a
good Catholic may reverence some fair, sweet saint, so
Geoffrey Lamar looks upon his mother. To him she is
liege lady ; to him she stands alone among women for
beauty, culture, grace, goodness. Her very pride
makes a halo around her in his love-blind eyes.

John Abbott does not attempt to go after him.
Neither mother nor son need him or desire him ; he

would be but a barrier to their confidence, a blot on the landscape. He feels it now, as he has felt it a thousand times, with silent, impotent wrath, but his anger is mingled just at present with another feeling —fear.

"His mother !" he says, vacantly ; " he is going to tell his mother ! One of the Sleaford girls—the youngest. I—I don't like the look of this."

Mrs. Abbott stands on the terrace, the crimson western light falling full upon her, and smiles as her son draws near. She is a beautiful woman, tall, slender, olive-skinned, with dark, solemn, Southern eyes, and languid, high-bred grace in every slow movement. She is like a picture as she stands here—like a Titian or a Murillo stepped out of its frame—in her trailing dress of violet silk, the delicate laces, the cluster diamond at her throat, the guelder-rose in her hair. She looks as a queen might—as a queen should—regal, royal, superb.

"I hope you are in very good humor, mother," is Geoffrey's greeting, plunging into business at once ; "because I have come to ask a favor—a very great favor, you may think."

Mrs. Abbott's smile, faint but very sweet, answers. Her eyes rest on her boy lovingly, lingeringly—he is very, very dear to her. She loves her little Leo, too ; but there is this difference—she loves Geoffrey for his father's sake as well as his own.

"Do I ever refuse you anything, I wonder ?" she says, slightly amused. "You are a tyrant, Geoff, and abuse your power. It is one of my failings, but I cannot say no."

"But I am uncommonly afraid you will this time.

It is no trifle. It will be a responsibility, and you may think it derogatory besides."

The smile fades from her face.

" *You* could never ask me to do anything you thought that," she quietiy says.

" Nor do I—you may. It will be a bore, I am sure. The only thing to be said in its favor is, that you will be doing good."

" Doing good can never be derogatory. Go on, Geoffrey, out with this wonderful request. What a philanthropist, by-the-bye, you are getting to be."

The proud, smiling look returns—she takes his arm, and they saunter slowly up and down the terrace.

" Don't call names, madre mio," laughs Geoffrey. "Well—here goes ! But thereby hangs a tale, to which you must listen by way of prologue or argument. The favor come after. Lend me thine ears then—I will a tale unfold."

And then—not without dramatic power and pathos —he tells the story of Sleaford's Joanna.

" She is treated as you would not see a dog in your house treated, mother ; she is in a very hot-bed of ignorance, and vulgarity and vice.· And I am sure she is not naturally bad. She has a love for reading which speaks well for her, and her voice—ah ! well, you will have to hear that before you can believe it. This is the story, mother—the favor is, will you stretch out your hand—this beautiful hand," the young knight exclaims, kissing it, " and save that wretched child !"

" My Geoff !" the lady answers, a tremor in her voice, " how ?"

" Send for her here—make Miss Rice give her lessons in English and singing, lift her out of the slough

5*

of darkness in which she is lost now. Save her body and soul! You can, mother."

There is emotion in the lad's voice, in his earnest face, in his deep, glowing gray eyes. His mother stops in her walk, tears on her dark lashes, both hands on his shoulders.

"My boy! my boy! but it is like you. Oh! I thank the good God for giving me such a son. Yes, what I can do, I will. It is an awful responsibility, an awful thought, that the life, the soul of any human creature may be in our hands. If I can help her, save her, as you say, I am ready. I say nothing in your praise. Heaven has given you a great heart, my Geoffrey—your father's noble soul. To lift the lost, to save the unfortunate, what can be nobler? Yes, I will do it. Send her here when you will."

The outburst is over—she pauses. She seldom gives way to her feelings like this. There is silence for a little; both descend to the lower earth again.

"But she cannot associate with Leo," Mrs. Abbott says, in her usual manner, "such a child as that!"

"Certainly not. What I thought was, that after Miss Rice had finished Leo's lessons for the day, she should dismiss her, and take in hand Joanna. Her name is Joanna. Leo always finishes by three—Joanna could come from three to six. Of course, Miss Rice will be willing, and glad of the extra salary."

"Of course. These people will make no objection to the little girl's coming, will they? They must be very dreadful from what you say. I wonder that Mr. Abbott, particular as he is, allows them on his land."

"Others wonder too," Geoffrey responds, dryly. "The fact remains—he does. I really do not know whether they will object or not. I spoke to no one, of course, until I had spoken to you. If they refuse, why, we can do no more. I will ride over and see to-morrow. Meantime, I suppose it will be necessary to mention it to Mr. Abbott."

"I suppose so"—the smooth brow of the lady con- tracts a little—she does not like mentioning things to Mr. Abbott—"but it cannot matter to him."

"No, but still he likes—— "

"Yes, yes, it shall be done. I see him yonder, and will speak to him at once, if you like."

"Thank you, mother."

She approaches her husband. She walks with the slow, swaying grace of a Southern woman, the lights and shadows from sunshine and trees flecking the vio- let sheen of her dress. Her son watches her, so does her husband, both with eyes that say, "Is she not the fairest of all the fair women on earth?"

Mr. Abbott removes his cigar, and stands with a certain deference of manner, as his wife draws near. If her dark head is lifted a trifle higher than usual, it is instinctive with her when about to ask what sounds to her like a favor. If the voice in which she speaks has a prouder inflection than customary, it is unconsci- ously and for the same reason. In briefest words she tells the story. Geoffrey has taken a fancy to help a poor little village child—may she come here and re- ceive lessons from Miss Rice, when Miss Rice has fin- ished every day with Leonora?

It is not often Mrs. Abbott voluntarily seeks her husband, or asks him for favors. His coarse face quite lights up into gladness now.

"Certainly, certainly, certainly!" he says, "any-

thing you and Geoff wish. Half a dozen village girls
if you like, my—my dear. The lad's the best lad
alive—sensible, steady, good-natured. I'm fond of
him, that I am, Mrs. Abbott."

"Thanks," Mrs. Abbott says, bending her stately
head. She turns to go, has gone half a dozen steps,
when her husband's voice reaches her.

"Nora."

She turns slowly. He seldom calls her by her
name; he stands, looking rather sheepishly now at his
cigar.

"You've never been over to Laurel Hill—the new
place I bought last week. It's an uncommon pretty
spot—eight miles t'other side of Brightbrook. Suppose you let me drive you there to-morrow?"

If he were a suppliant lover he could hardly look
more humble, more anxious. The line between his
wife's straight, dark brows deepens.

"To-morrow I dine with Colonel and Mrs. Ventnor."

"Well, next day then."

"Next day I am going up to New York to do some
very necessary shopping."

"Well, the day after. Oh! hang it, Nora, say yes!
You never go anywhere with me now, and I don't so
often ask you, neither."

"Certainly I will go," she says, but she says it so
coldly, so distantly, that the man sets his teeth. "I
did not know you thought it a matter of any moment.
I will go the day after to-morrow, or whenever you
wish."

"I don't wish," he returns, shortly. "Don't trouble
yourself, Mrs. Abbott, I don't wish for anything.
We'll never mind Laurel Hill!"

He resumes his cigar, turns his back upon her, thrusts his hands in his pockets, and strides away. But half an hour after, as he still stalks sulkily up and down, a thought strikes him, a most unpleasant thought. It turns him hot all over.

"By the Lord!" he cries, taking out his cigar, aghast, "I shouldn't wonder but what it *is!*"

A great bell, up in one of the windy, make-believe Gothic turrets, clangs out; it is the dinner-bell of Abbott Wood. The master is not dressed, a faint odor as of stables hangs about him, but he is in no mood to conciliate his stiff wife, and make a dinner toilet. He is chafed, rubbed over so much the wrong way, and it affords him a grim sort of pleasure to set her at defiance, and outrage her sense of sight and smell, by appearing just as he is. He marches into the dining-room, grisly, forbidding, ireful. It is a beautiful and spacious room—the dinner service is all in the way of plate, napery, crystal, china, that money can do to make that most ungraceful necessity—eating —graceful. Flowers are there in profusion, a golden after-glow fills the apartment, the viands are as nearly perfect as possible, the mistress of the mansion a fair and gracious lady, Geoffrey the most polished of youthful Paladins, little Leo like an opera fairy in pink silk, but the master, stern and unsmiling as the Death's Head of the Egyptian banquets, takes his place, and begins his soup in unsocial silence and glumness. At last he looks up.

"I didn't ask the name of the little beggar you propose to bring here," he says to Geoffrey. "Who is she?"

The youth glances at him in surprise. These

sudden changes of temperature are not uncommon in
Mr. Abbott's moral thermometer, but they are always
disconcerting.

"Her name is Sleaford's Joanna—or more prop-
erly, I suppose, Joanna Sleaford."

Mr. Abbott's spoon drops with a clash in his plate.
As a thunder-cloud blackens the face of the sky, so a
swarthy frown darkens the face of the man.

"I thought so," he says. "It's well I made sure
in time. I withdraw my consent, madam. No brat
of Sleaford's ever sets foot in this house!"

"Sir!" Geoffrey cries, hotly.

It is the tone, the look, insolent beyond measure,
addressed to his mother, that stings him. For Mrs.
Abbott, she does not say a word. She looks once at
the man before her, then back at her plate.

"Ah! sit down, my lad—there is nothing for you
to get your mettle up about. Only Sleaford's Joanna
won't come here. Leo is *my* daughter—I'll know who
she associates with. And, by heavens! it sha'n't be
with a cub out of Giles Sleaford's den!"

The veins in his forehead stand out purple—he
brings his clenched fist down on the table until the
glass rings.

Geoffrey's face flushes crimson, he looks at his
mother, prepared to resent this violence. She is a
shade paler than usual, a little curl of scorn and disgust dilates the delicate nostrils—otherwise she is perfectly calm.

"Do not excite yourself, Mr. Abbott," she says, in
slow, iced tones, "there is really no need. Resume
your dinner, Geoffrey. Of course it shall be quite as
Mr. Abbott wishes."

And then silence falls—such silence! Mrs. Abbott seems slowly to petrify as she sits. Geoffrey's face is rigid with wrath. Mr. Abbott makes short work of *his* dinner, and departs without a word. Only little Leo, of the quartet, dines at all.

But one sentence, at rising, passes between the mother and son.

"You will tell this poor child she cannot come," Mrs. Abbott says, and Geoffrey nods.

But an obstinate look comes about his mouth ; he is not easily baffled ; those resolute lips, that curved chin, were not given him for nothing. Joanna may not come here, but he will go instead to Miss Rice, and arrange with her to give the girl lessons at her own rooms. His pocket-money is abundant ; he will pay for her himself. She *shall* be taught, that is as fixed as fate, if he has to buy Sleaford's consent with his last penny. Contradiction has the effect on young Lamar it has on all determined people—it only re-doubles his determination.

It rains the next day, a steady, drizzling, persist-ent rain. But he cares very little for a wet jacket ; sleeping on his resolution only makes him more resolute. He mounts his "dapple gray" and rides through the dripping woods to Sleaford's. No mock-ing-bird is perched among the branches to-day, to waylay him with its delusive melody. He reaches the house, puts his horse under cover, and enters. Only two of the family are to be seen—Joanna, scrubbing a floor that very much needs scrubbing, and Giles himself, smoking, in the corner, a meditative pipe. He greets his visitor with a surprised nod, and watches him curiously. For Joanna—it is evidently one of

her dark days ; her small face looks cross and cantan-
kerous, she curtly returns his salutation, she scrubs the
boards with ill-tempered vehemence.   The rain beats
against the panes, the house and everything about it
looks dismal and forlorn.

" Well, Joanna," Geoffrey says, in an undertone, " I
promised to come, and I am here.   But my project
has failed for the present.   I intended you to come to
Abbott Wood every day for lessons, but it seems it
cannot be.   We must hit on some other plan.   You
would not mind going up the village every afternoon,
would you ?"

Before Joanna can reply, Sleaford takes his pipe
from his mouth, and breaks in.   He has caught the
words, low as they are spoken.

"What's that ?" he demands, gruffly.

"I meant to tell you," Geoffrey courteously returns, "and ask your consent.   Of course, all this is
subject to your control.   Your little girl is clever, I
think, and has a fine voice.   I intended to have her
taught, and that voice cultivated—always with your
permission.   I thought at first of getting her to come
every day to our house, but——"

" Well, but what ?"

" It cannot be, it seems.   Still, I can manage it.
She can go to Brightbrook and take her lessons there
instead."

" Stop a bit," says Giles Sleaford, resuming his
pipe ; " why can't she go to Abbott Wood ?"

" Well," Geoffrey replies, with that frank regard
for simple truth that is characteristic of him, " the
fact is, Mr. Abbott objects.   Not that it matters at
all—the other way will do just as well."

"Stop a bit !" repeats Mr. Sleaford ; "did you put it to your guv'ner, 'I want to learn a little girl,' says you, 'that don't know nothin' but cussin' and lowness, and make a lady out o' her!' Did you put it like that?"

"Something like that—yes."

"Namin' no names at fust?"

"Exactly."

"And what did he say *then?*"

"Well, he said yes," answers Geoffrey, a little embarrassed, but still adhering to truth.

"And when he found who it was he wouldn't. 'Give her a name,' ses he. 'Sleaford's Joanna,' ses you. 'I'm d—d if you do!' ses he, 'none o' that lot comes here!' That was it, wasn't it?"

"Well, more or less," Geoffrey returns, laughing in spite of himself. "You must be a wizard, I think, Mr. Sleaford. But it really does not matter, you know ; the other way——"

"Stop a bit !" reiterates Giles Sleaford. "Was it your intentions as how your mar should look arter Joanner when she went up to the big house, and kind o' help to eddicate her and that?"

"It was, but as I say——"

"Stop a bit! hold on—it ain't the same no way, sendin' her to the village to a teacher woman. The gal shall go to your guv'ner's house or she shan't go at all. Now you stop a bit, don't do nothin' afore to-morrow, and maybe—I name no names, mind you !—and maybe she can be let to go to your mar."

With which Mr. Sleaford relapses into ruminative silence and slowly refills his pipe, which has gone out. There is a grim sort of grin on his forbidding face as

he does so, and he swallows a chuckle or two as he watches the heir of Abbott Wood rise and go away.

"So Red Jack won't, won't he?" he says, half aloud, with one of these suppressed chuckles; "because she's a Sleaford ! Ah ! well, we will see."

CHAPTER XII.

"NOBODY'S CHILD."

R. ABBOTT is sitting alone in the library at Abbott Wood. For the very great personage he is in some respects, his position is an undignified one. He has tilted back the carved and cushioned chair in which his bulky body reposes, elevated his boots on the low black marble mantel, and is rapidly filling the room with tobacco smoke. A frown still rests on his brow ; he has not forgiven his wife—he is not disposed to forgive her ; it is only one more added to the lengthy list of affronts she has put upon him.

"And if ever I get a chance," he mutters, as he smokes, "I'll pay you back with interest, my high and mighty lady !"

Little Leo has just left him. *She* is his at any rate; he will have her with him when he chooses, in the very teeth of her scornful mother. The child is sufficiently fond of him; he is foolishly indulgent to her, after the manner of his kind ; but now she, too, has quitted him. Nine has struck, and nurse has come and borne her off. At present he is solacing himself with a pipe, the evening paper, and some crusty port, until it shall be time to go to bed.

"A wet night, by jingo !" he says, as in the pauses of rattling the paper he hears the dash of the rain against the glass, and the sough of the wind in the trees.

The room in which he sits is a grand one—a hundred years old to look at, at least : everything in it, about it, is richly hued, deeply tinted, warmly toned. There is an oriel window, where sunset lights fall through on a dark, polished oaken floor in orange, and ruby, and amethyst dyes. A soft, rose-red carpet covers the center of the floor ; a tiger-skin rug is stretched in front of the shining grate. Mellow-brown panels are everywhere where books are not. Books are many ; hundreds of volumes in costly bindings—purple, crimson, white and gold—not a " dummy " among them all. There are bronzes, and a few dark paintings of the literary lights of the world, quaint old furniture, all carved with arabesques and griffin's-heads, and upholstered in bright crimson cloth. Here, too, as in nearly every room of the house, is burned in the panes the escutcheon of his Southern wife. It looks a very temple of culture and learning, and, with the usual fine irony of fate, John Abbott is its high priest. Not one, of all these hundreds of costly volumes, does his stumpy brown fingers ever open ; his literature is confined to the New York and Brightbrook daily papers, and all the sporting journals he can buy.

As he sits and puffs his clouds of smoke, and swallows his wine, there is a tap at the door, and a man-servant enters.

"Well," inquires Mr. Abbott, " what now ?"

"There is a man in the hall, sir, to see you particular. He says his name is Sleaford."

The servant looks at him with covert cunning as he makes the announcement. In a place like Brightbrook there can be no such thing as a secret. The servants of Abbott Wood have heard of the Sleafords, but this is the first time one of that celebrated family has presented himself at the manor. Mr. Abbott drops his paper, and slowly rises from his chair, a gray pallor overspreading the peony hue of his face.

"Sleaford !" he repeats, blankly ; "did you say Sleaford ?"   .

"Sleaford, sir—Giles Sleaford. He is waiting in the vestibule, dripping wet. Told him I didn't know you were at home, sir, but would see. *Are* you at home, sir ?"

"Show him in, you fool, and be quick !"

The man retreats. Mr. Abbott resumes his chair, breathing quickly, that grayish shade still on his face, and tries to resume his usual bluff, blustering manner as well, but in vain. He is frightened—braggart, boaster that he is ; his hand shakes—he is forced to fling aside his paper with an oath. .

"Sleaford !" he thinks ; "this time of night—and such a night ! Good G—— ! what is he after now ?"

◆ The door reopens, and, dripping like a huge water-dog, his hat on his head, his hands in his pockets, Giles Sleaford stalks into the room. "Oh, you *are* to home !" he says, with a sneer ; "the flunkey said as how he didn't know. It ain't the kind o' night heavy swells like John Abbott, Esquire, of Abbott Wood, would be like to go out promenadin'. It's as black as a wolf's mouth, and comin' down like blazes."

"Sit down, Sleaford," says Mr. Abbott, in a tone
of marked civility. He sends one of the carved and
cushioned chairs whirling on its castors toward him,
but Mr. Sleaford only glances at it with profound
contempt. " It is, as you say, the deuce and all of a
night to be out in. But now that you *are* here, if
there is anything I can do for you——"

" Ah ! if there is !" returns Mr. Sleaford, still sar-
donic ; " as if there was anything a rich gent like
Mr. Abbott *couldn't* do for a poor bloke like me. As
if I would tramp it through mud and water a good
three mile for the pleasure of lookin' at your jimcracks, and axin' arter your 'elth. Yes, there *is* some-
thin' you can do for me, and what's more, you've got
to do it, or I'll know the reason why."

The sneer changes to a menace. Mr. Abbott rises
with precipitation, opens the door quickly, and looks
down the long, lighted passage. There are no eaves-
droppers. He closes the door, locks it, and faces his
man. The danger is here, and he does not lack pluck
to meet it.

" What do you want ?" he demands ; " it was part
of our bargain that you were never to come here.
Why are you here ? I'm not a man to be trifled with
—you ought to know that before to-night."

" There ain't much about you, Jack Abbott, that I
don't know," Sleaford retorts, coolly. " Don't take on
none o' your rich-man airs with me. This is a snug
crib—all this here pooty furniture and books cost a
few dollars, I reckon. You wouldn't like to swop 'em
for a cell in Sing Sing, and a guv'ment striped suit ?
What am I here for ? I'm here to find out why one o'

my kids ain't to come to your wife to get a eddication,
if that there young sport, your step-son, says so ?"

The two men look each other straight in the eyes
—fierce, dogged determination in Sleaford's, malignant, baffled fury in Abbott's.

"So ! this is what you want, Black Giles ?"

" This is what I want, Jack Abbott.   And what I'll
have, by the Eternal !   Mind you, I don't care a cuss
about eddication, nor whether the gal ever knows B
from a cow's horn, but the young gent wants it, and
you were willin' till you found out who she was, and
then you wouldn't.   Now, I'll stand none o' that.   My
gal's comin' up here to be eddicated by your wife,"
says Mr. Sleaford, beating out his proposition with the
finger of one hand on the palm of the other, "which is
a lady born and bred, and by your step-son, which he's
what all the gold that ever panned out in the diggins
can't make *you*—a gentleman.   You forbid it yes'day
—you'll take that back to-morrow, and whenever the
young swell says the word, Joanner's comin' up here
for that there eddication !"

All this Mr. Sleaford says, slowly and impressively
—by no means in a passion.   His hat is still on his
head—politeness with Black Giles is not a matter of
hat.   And he fixes Mr. Abbott with his "glittering
eye," while he thus dogmatically lays down the law.
Mr. Abbott, too, has cooled.   Indeed, for two extremely choleric gentlemen, their manner has quite
the repose that marks the caste of Vere de Vere.   The
master of the mansion takes a turn or two up and
down the slippery floor before he replies.   The tenant
of the Red Farm eyes him with stolid malignity.

"I wish you wouldn't insist on this, Giles," he

says, in a troubled tone, at last. "I have a reason for
it. Come! I'll buy you off. I'll give you——"

"No, you won't. I ain't to be bought off. She's
got to come. But I'm out o' cash. I want three hundred dollars."

John Abbott's eyes flash, but still he holds himself
in hand.

"You are joking! Only last week I gave you——"

"Never mind last week, that's gone with last
year's snow. It's no good palaverin'—you know what
I want. All your money wouldn't buy me off. She's
got to come."

Again silence—again broken by Mr. Abbott.

"How old is this confounded girl?" he demands,
and mentally consigns her to perdition. "Your girls
ought to be all grown up, Sleaford."

"Ought they. Well, they ain't. She's twelve,
just."

"Twelve! What nonsense! Why, your wife's
been dead these sixteen years."

"Ah!" says Giles Sleaford.

It is a brief interjection, but the tone, the glare
that goes with it brings back the blood in a purple
glow to the other man's face.

"We won't talk about *that*," says Sleaford between
his teeth, "nor what followed. 'Cause why? I might
forget you was the richest, respectablest gent here-
abouts, and fly at your throat, and choke the black
heart out o' you. Gimme that money and let me git!
The blackest night that ever blowed is better than a
pallis with you in it."

With a cowed look, Mr. Abbott goes to a desk,
counts over a roll of bills, and hands it to his tenant.

"Sleaford," he says, almost in a supplicating tone, "I wish you would go away from here. People are talking. The Red Farm is going to the dogs. It's not that I care for that. I don't care for that, but —but I don't want people to talk. I've been a good friend to you, Giles——"

The wild-beast glare that looks at him out of Giles Sleaford's eyes makes him pause.

"About money, I mean," he resumes hurriedly. "I'm not stingy, no man ever called me that. Name your price and go. Back to San Francisco : you can have a good time there ; and let by-gones be by-gones. I'll come down handsome, by Jove, I will."

Giles Sleaford pockets the money, and looks at him with wolfish eyes.

"I'm a poor devil," he says, "but if I was poorer, if I was a dog in a ditch, I wouldn't take half your millions and leave you. I had work enough to find you, Lord knows ! But I *have* found you, and while you and me's above ground we'll never part."

He turns with the words and leaves the library. No more is said, no good-night is exchanged. Mr. Abbott in person sees his visitor to the door, and lets him out. The darkness is profound, a great gust of wind and rain beats in their faces, but Giles Sleaford plunges into the black gulf and tramps doggedly out of sight.

*   *   *   *   *   *

Next day, as Geoffrey Lamar is leaving the house after breakfast, on purpose to ride to the village and see Miss Rice, the teacher, his step-father approaches, in a shuffling way, and lays his hand on his shoulder.

"If I said anything t'other day at dinner," he

says, gruffly, but apologetically, "I want you to overlook it, dear boy. I was put out, and I showed it.
Let that little girl come whenever you like."

Geoffrey glances at him, rather haughtily. It is one
of his failings that he is slow to forgive.

"It is a matter of no consequence whether she ever
comes here or not. I am perfectly satisfied to let it
drop."

"No, you ain't, dear boy—you know you ain't. You
want her to come, and so does your mother. I'm sorry
—I can't say no more. Fetch her here and forget
my words."

"Very well, sir," Geoffrey returns in his grand
manner—his head thrown back, his mouth somewhat
stern. It is a very natural manner with the lad, and
is exceedingly effective with most people. So it is to
Sleaford's he rides, instead of to the village, and the
result is, that, dressed in her holiday best, Sleaford's
Joanna presents herself on Monday afternoon at
Abbott Wood to begin her education.

Mrs. Abbott looks at the wild creature in wonder
and pity. Out in the woods there is a certain free,
lithe grace about the girl—in this grand room, before
this grand lady, she stands shifting from one foot to
the other, downcast of face, awkward of manner, shy,
silent, uncouth. Even the attempts at civilization, the
shoes and stockings, the smoothed hair, the washed
and shining face, embarrass her by their painful novelty. Miss Rice is there, a little, brisk, old body, with
round, bird-like eyes, and the general air of a lively
robin, in her brown stuff dress.

"My son tells me you can sing," Mrs. Abbott says

6

in her slow, sweet way. "Will you sing something for us that we may judge?"

As well ask her to fly! Joanna stands mute, a desperate feeling creeping over her to make a dash for the door, and fly forever to Black's Dam.

"You cannot?" with a smile. "Ah! well, it is natural. Miss Rice will play something for you instead, and I will leave you to get acquainted."

So Mrs. Abbott, with fine tact, goes, and Joanna draws a free breath for the first time. So much beauty, and condescension, and silk dress, have overwhelmed her. Miss Rice is insignificant—she never overwhelmed any one in her life. She goes to the piano, and plays what she thinks Joanna will like, a sparkling waltz, and a gay polka.

Joanna *does* like it, and listens with rapture.

"Now tell me some of your songs, and I will play the accompaniment," says Miss Rice.

Joanna goes over half a dozen. "Old Dog Tray," "Wait for the Wagon," "Sally, Come Up." Miss Rice knows none of them.

"Here is 'Nobody's Child.' Can you sing that?" she asks.

As it chances, Joanna can, and does. All her embarrassment is gone with Mrs. Abbott. Her strong young voice takes up the air, as Miss Rice softly strikes the chords, and peals out full and clear. There is a mournful appropriateness in every word.

> "Out in the dreary and pitiless street,
> With my torn old shoes, and my bare cold feet,
> All day I have wandered to and fro,
> Hungry and shivering, nowhere to go.
> The night's coming down in darkness and dread,
> And the cold sleet is beating upon my poor head.

Ah ! why does the wind rush about me so wild ?
Is it because I am Nobody's Child ?"

Miss Rice listens, surprised and delighted. And
Mrs. Abbott, just outside the open window, listens too,
and mentally decides that Geoffrey was right. This
girl is worth saving, if only for sake of that charming
voice. She sings with expression, the pathos of the
words find an echo in her untaught heart. She, too,
is Nobody's Child.

" Oh, you have a lovely voice, indeed !" cries little
Miss Rice, enthusiastically, " and after a few months
training—ah, well, only wait ! That will do now ; we
will see what else you know, and get out a few
books."

The " what else " turns out to be nothing at all.
She can read with tolerable correctness, and write a
little. She cannot sew, knit, crochet—knows nothing,
in fact.

" It is virgin soil," says Miss Rice, briskly, to her
patroness ; " plenty of weeds, and no cultivation.
Well, we must pluck up the weeds, and plant the seeds
of knowledge. Good-day, my dear lady."

Miss Rice trips away, and Joanna more slowly follows. She passes the Gothic lodge, and is well out of
sight of that neat little structure, when the master of
Abbott Wood comes suddenly upon her, and stretching out his brawny right hand, catches her by the
wrist. He has been lying in wait.

" You are Joanna Sleaford ?"

She jerks away her hand. Roughness is the atmosphere of her life, and impish Joanna is Joanna at once.
" No, I ain't."

" Who are you, then ? Don't tell me lies !"

" Don't you tell them ! I am Sleaford's Joanna."
" What d'ye mean ? It's the same thing."
" Oh, no 'taint. My name ain't Sleaford, mister."
All Joanna's usual pertness is in her elfish tone and
face.

" What is it, then ?"

"Don't know, and don't care. Sleaford's Joanna
does as good as anything else."

She begins to whistle—then breaks off to laugh
shrilly.

" You'll know me next time for certain. What are
you starin' at? It ain't good manners, old gentleman."

To tell the truth, he is staring as Joanna has never
been stared at before in her life, a blank expression of
new-born consternation in his face.

" Little girl," he says, " I am Mr. Abbott, and I
want you to answer me a few questions. Who are you,
if you are not Sleaford's daughter ?"

" Told you before I didn't know. I don't tell lies.
You mightn't think so, but I don't. It's sneaky.
Picked me up in a gutter, he says. Wish he'd left me
there. Gutter's better than his house any day."

" How old are you ?"

" Jest gone twelve."

"Do you remember nothing of the time before
you lived with Sleaford? Nothing of your father or
mother ?"

" Never. Had none, maybe. Grew in the gutter,
I guess. Say, mister, it's getting late. I want to go
home."

" Go, then," he says, mechanically.

He draws back, and she darts off fleetly as a squirrel. He stands and watches her out of sight, that blank expression still on his face.

"Of all that could happen I never thought of that," he mutters. "I never thought Black Giles was so deep. No, I thought of everything, but I'm blessed if I ever thought of *that*."

She has disappeared, and the dinner-bell is summoning the master of the house. He turns up the avenue, but all that day, and for many days after, John Abbott muses and muses, and is strangely silent and still.

And so it comes to pass, that from that day a new life begins for Sleaford's Joanna.

PART SECOND.

CHAPTER I.

WHAT THE YEARS MAKE OF JOANNA.

T is a December afternoon, and brightly, crisply clear. The last yellow light of the wintry sunset, shining in between parted curtains of lace and heavy crimson drapery, falls upon a young girl seated at a grand piano, touching the keys with flexible, strong fingers, and singing in a full, rich contralto, that makes everything in the room vibrate. It is the winter drawing-room of Abbott Wood, a spacious and splendid apartment, vast and lofty, but the trained, powerful voice fills it easily. She is singing exercises and solfeggios ; she has been so practicing for the past hour, running up in showers of silvery high notes, holding the highest, sometimes, so long and steadily that you gasped from sympathy, and then running down the scale until the last low, sweet tone melted into the chords her fingers struck. The girl is young—seventeen—tall, slight, a little angular at present, but promising well for the future. She is dressed in a black alpaca that has seen service, and which is neither particularly neat nor well-fitting—a rusty garment, that looks distinctly out of place in that glowing room. Her hair, of which she has a profusion, and which is red-brown in hue, but more red than brown, is knotted up in a loose and careless knot, without the slightest attempt at the becoming. Her face is pale and thin, the features good, but the expression set and severe for seventeen.

"What a peculiar-looking girl !" people say of her when they see her first, and are apt to look again with some curiosity. "She is not pretty at all, but it is rather a—a striking face," and the word describes it very well. It is not pretty ; it is far from plain ; and it is a face most people are apt to look at more than once. It is what five years have made of Sleaford's Joanna.

Five years ! They work changes from twelve to seventeen ; this is what five years, much care, instruction, and painstaking on the part of good Miss Rice have made Joanna. A slim young person, with a face that seldom smiles ; an unlimited capacity for discontent with her own life, that increases every day of

that life ; an utter apathy as to dress, tidiness, needlework ; a conviction that she is hopelessly ugly, and
that it is of no use wasting time trying to redeem that
ugliness ; a delicious voice, a tolerable amount of pro-
ficiency as a pianist—that is Joanna.

She sits alone. Voices and laughter—young
voices—reach her from the grounds ; once her name
is called, but she pays no heed. A gay group are out
there, enjoying the windless winter evening, but with
gayety this girl has little—has ever had little—to do.
Wild Joanna she can be called no longer ; she seems
quiet enough ; Sleaford's Joanna she is still—the
household drudge, even as she was five years ago, with
work-reddened, work-hardened hands. She grows
tired of exercises after a little, and begins, almost unconsciously, to sing snatches of songs—English, German, Italian—a very pot-pourri. Then, all at once, she
strikes a few solemn, resounding chords, and begins
Rossini's "Stabat Mater," and the instrument quivers
with force of those grand tones—

"Cujus animum gementum !"

It is a glorious anthem, sung with passion, pathos, and
power.

"Bravo !" says a voice ; "encore, mademoiselle. If
I had a bouquet I would throw it."

She glances round and smiles, and when she smiles
you discover for the first time that this girl might be
almost handsome if she chose. For she has a rare
smile, that quite transforms her sallow, moody face.
She has very fine teeth, too, not in the least like pearls,
but fully equal to those beautiful enameled half circles
that grin at you from dental show-cases.

"Sing 'When Swallows Build,' Joanna," says the new-comer, throwing himself on a sofa near, and looking at her with kindly eyes.

It is Geoffrey Lamar down for the Christmas festivities—Geoffrey at twenty-one, not so very much unlike the Geoffrey of sixteen. Grown taller, though still not tall, looking strong and well-trained, both as to muscle and mind, retaining that resolute mouth and chin, retaining also that slightly haughty air, and those deep-set, steadfast, sea-gray eyes. He retains everything, even that pleasant friendly regard for Sleaford's Joanna, to which she is indebted for her power to-day to make the room ring with the "Stabat Mater."

She turns over the music, and finds the song. "What have you done with the others?" she asks, carelessly.

"Oh ! Livingston is there, and where girls are concerned he is always a host in himself. There were a great many pretty people present at the Ventnors' last night," says Geoffrey, laughing, "but Frank was the belle of the ball. Do you want me to turn your music, Joanna? Because, if you do, I will sacrifice comfort to politeness and get up."

"No, don't trouble yourself," Joanna answers. "As you work so hard all the rest of the year, I suppose you claim the right to be lazy at Christmas. And besides, I am not used to politeness."

"No?" says Geoffrey, and looks at her thoughtfully ; "it strikes me you seem a trifle out of sorts of late, Joanna. You are as thin as a shadow and nearly as mute. Tell me—is it the old trouble? Do these people treat you badly still?"

She shrugs her shoulders, an impatient, ireful look

darkens her face. "What does it matter," she says, in a voice of irritated weariness. "I ought to be used to it by this, but the trouble with me is, I get used to nothing. Do not mind my looks—I am always thin and cross—it is natural, I suppose ; and as to being mute, when one has nothing pleasant to say one had best hold one's tongue. Every one is good to me here, better than I deserve. That ought to suffice."

She begins her song, but the impatient ring is yet in her voice. Geoffrey lies still and watches her. He has the interest in her we all have in the thing we have saved and protected ; he would like to see her repay that interest by blooming looks and bright laughter ; but his power fails, something is amiss. She is educated, refined, cared for, but she is not happy—he has a vague, uneasy suspicion she is not particularly *good*. Antagonistic influences are at work, driving her two ways at once—here all is luxury, refinement, high-breeding, tender care—there all is coarseness, vulgarity, brutal usage. Long ago Giles Sleaford was implored to give her up altogether, but he obstinately and doggedly refused.

"She is not your daughter," Geoffrey has urged. "You do not care for her. Give her to us. She is none of yours."

"How d'ye know that, youngster?" Sleaford says, a cunning look in his bleary eyes. "*I* never said so, an' I'm the only one as knows."

"Well, if she is, then, you should have her welfare at heart. Let her come to us for good and all. She is attached to my mother, and would like it."

"Ah! I dare say ! She's a lazy jade, an' would like to be a fine lady, with nothin' to do but play the

6*

pianny and sing songs. But it won't do, young gent. I don't see it no way. I ain't goin' to give up Joanna."

" If money is any inducement——" begins Geoffrey after a pause. He is exceedingly tenacious of purpose —he hates to give up anything on which he has once set his mind.

"Look a here, young gentleman," says Giles Slea-ford ; "I ain't got no spite agin you. You're a game young rooster, and I respects yer. But let this here come to an end. I won't give up Joanna to you or no living man. That gal's the trump card in my hand, though the time ain't come to play her yet. She may keep on goin' to your 'ouse—I've said so, and I'll stick to it—but back here she comes, rain or shine, every night for life. Now drop it !"

And so, night after night, Joanna turns from the beauty and grandeur of Abbott Wood to the bleak ugliness and disorder of the Red Farm ; from good-natured Miss Rice to scolding Liz, or sneering Lora ; from the stately kindness of Mrs. Abbott to the im-precations of Black Giles ; from the melodies of Chopin and Schubert to the grimy kitchen labor, the wash-board and scrubbing-brush of Sleaford's. It is an abnormal life, two existences, glaringly wide apart, and the girl is simply being ruined between them.

" Ah ! that is fine," says a second voice, and a second face appears at the open window. " My word of honor, Joanna, you *have* a voice ! Sing us some-thing else."

She starts a little, and something—it is so faint you can hardly call it color—flashes into her face. She does not glance round, her fingers strike a discordant chord, she stops confusedly, her head droops a little.

"How like the Grand Turk, surveying his favorite Sultana, Lamar looks!" goes on, sarcastically, this voice; "stretched out there, drinking in all this melody. Luxurious sybarite, bid the Light of the Harem sing us another — She pays no attention to my deferential request."

But before Lamar can obey, Joanna has begun again. Without notes this time, some subtile chord of memory awakened, she sings a song she has not thought of for years, the first she ever sung in this house—*Nobody's Child.*

There is a pause. The trite saying of "tears in the voice" comes to the mind of Geoffrey—pain, pathos, passion, are in the simple words. She feels them—oh! she feels them to the very depths of her soul. Nameless, homeless, parentless, a waif and stray, a castaway of the city streets—nothing more. All the kind charity, the friendly good-nature of these rich people, cannot alter that.

As she sings the last words, two young girls, who have been lingering in the door-way, unwilling to disturb the music, enter. A greater contrast to the words she has been singing, to the singer herself, can hardly be imagined. They are heiresses, both; they have everything this girl has not—name, lineage, wealth, beauty, love. They are Olga Ventnor and Leo Abbott.

They advance. Leo's arm is around Olga's waist; she is one of the clinging, affectionate sort of little people, as addicted to caresses as to *bonbons.* She hardly comes up to Olga's shoulder, though but a year younger. She is a pretty little brunette of fifteen, plump, pale, dark-eyed, dark-haired, dressed in the

daintiest and brightest of costumes. She worships
Olga, and looks up to her; she is her ideal, immensely
wiser, and more grown up than herself—her superior
in every way.

Miss Olga Ventnor, at sixteen, is certainly a very
fair young lady. Tall, slight, erect, graceful, the
delicate head proudly poised, and "sunning over with
curls," still worn girlish fashion, loose on her shoulders,
the "flower face" quite without flaw, a little proud,
perhaps, but very, very lovely. The eyes are more
purple than blue—"pansy eyes" a stricken youth of
eighteen has been known to call them—a thought cold
in expression, but rarely beautiful. She is dressed in
pale gray silk, very simply made, and trimmed with
garnet velvet, a ribbon of the same color tying back
her profuse blonde hair—no rings, brooches, bracelets,
jewelry of any kind, yet looking, from top to toe, the
superb princess her Cousin Frank calls her.

It is the said Cousin Frank who stands at the
window. He saunters in now, and what the years
have done for him is to transform an extremely good-
looking youth of seventeen into an extremely handsome young man of twenty-two, with a most desirable
light mustache, quick, restless blue eyes, a vivacious
society manner, and a pensive way of looking at young
ladies, and bending over them, and holding their fans
and quoting poetry at them, that even at two-and
twenty he has found very effective. That Mr. Frank
is a flirt of the most pronounced male order, and has
been consumed by four grand passions already, is a
matter of history. He has a studio on Broadway, and
paints young ladies' heads very prettily. He is also
celebrated as the best leader of Germans in the city,

and, in short, is an ornament and acquisition to society. He, too, is down for the Christmas festivities, and to make himself agreeable to his Cousin Olga, home from school. Leo does not go to school—masters and Miss Rice fuse knowledge into her at home.

"Why do you sing that, Jo?" Leo says, quitting her friend, and putting that caressing right arm around the pianist instead. "It is a melancholy little thing, and we don't want melancholy little things this happy Christmas time. Do not sing it any more."

She touches the untidy reddish hair with a gentle touch. She is a loving little heart, and she is very sorry for this poor Joanna, who has such a hard life, and such disagreeable relations. It comes naturally to her to love all by whom she is surrounded, to be generous, and unselfish, and impulsive, and without a particle of pride. In this last, she is quite unlike mother, brother, and bosom friend. Miss Ventnor glances across, but does not go near the piano. She crosses to a distant window instead, and Geoffrey Lamar gets lazily up from his recumbent position, and joins her.

"It will certainly snow to-morrow," the young lady says, looking up with those great "pansy eyes" at the twilight sky. "I am very glad. A green yule —you know the proverb. Christmas without snow and sleigh-bells—nature could not make a greater mistake."

"What lovely eyes!" Geoffrey Lamar thinks.

He has thought so often before, but each time they meet after a few months' separation, this girl's beauty strikes him with the force of a new revelation. He looks across at Frank Livingston, devoting himself to little laughing Leo, with that *empressement* he considers this sort of thing needs, and his straight strong eyebrows contract. The sapphire eyes may be never so bright, but they are bespoken.

Other eyes, black and somber, watch covertly Frank's flirtation. Leo is a little girl, he cares nothing about her, he is merely keeping his hand in, it is never well to get out of practice, but he looks at the same time as if Miss Abbott were the only creature of her sex in the universe.

"Do look at Joanna," Olga says; "what a dark and angry face."

"Truly," Geoffrey utters, in some surprise.

Her face *does* look dark, angry, menacing; she strikes the chords of the piano as though it were an enemy's face.

"What is the matter with her? A moment ago she was all right. She is an odd girl—a girl of moods and whims."

"A girl I do not like," Olga Ventnor says, with a very decided uplifting of the head; "a girl I fear and distrust. I wonder how you all can make so much of her, Geoffrey—can think so well of her. I do not wish to injure her, but I could never like her, or treat her as Leo does. Not that there is much in that," she adds, laughing, "dear little Leo loves all the world."

"You do not like her—you do not trust her," Geoffrey repeats; "now why, I wonder! If it is because of your first meeting——"

"*That* was nothing," Olga says, in the same quick, decided tone. "I have forgotten and forgiven that long ago. She was only a wild, half-savage child *then*. It is now I do not trust her. She is quiet, she says little, she is attached to your mother, she likes Leo a little, she studies hard, she sings well, she keeps her place, but——"

"Well," he says, smiling, "go on. What a wise-acre you are becoming. But——"

He likes to hear her talk, to be with her, to look in those deep, purple eyes, to meet that radiant smile. She is a beautiful creature, so brightly beautiful that it is a delight only to look at her. ·

"It is not so easy to explain what I mean. You have read of men who tame animals? They take a young tiger and feed it on milk. It grows up, gentle, sleek, playful as a kitten. One day they give it raw meat, the next it turns on its keeper, without warning or provocation, and tears him to pieces. Joanna is like that tiger—to be trusted no more than the tiger. You look shocked. I cannot help it. I know she is your *protegée*, and that you are bound to defend her, but it is the truth all the same. I do not know it, I feel it. And one day you will see. Now, do not let us talk about her. What are you doing in town? Walking the hospitals? How dreadful! What do you want, studying medicine? As if you ever meant to practice! Being a 'Saw-bones,' a 'Bob Sawyer!'" she laughs, the clear girlish laugh that is sweeter than all Joanna's music to his ears. "I like Bob Sawyer, but at the same time there is no sense in your follow-ing his foot-steps. You know you never mean to be a doctor."

"Indeed, that is precisely what I do mean; what I hope, what I am positively sure I shall be this time next year. Let me write M. D. after my name, and I die happy."

"You will never be a doctor," the young lady re
peats, in her decided way; she is used to having
opinions of her own, and having them listened to with
respect; "that is to say, a practicing doctor. It is
your whim, your hobby, and a very horrid one, I
think. What dreadful sights you must see, what
shocking suffering, what frightful disease."

"Yes," he answers, gravely, "God knows I do—
sights, suffering, I pray you may never dream of.
But to ameliorate all that, to heal the suffering, to
give health to disease, to soothe pain, is not that a
godlike mission, Olga?"

"To those to whom the sight and suffering are
necessary—yes—to you, no. One need not witness
the misery of others in order to alleviate it. You are
going to be very rich; you will not work as a doctor.
There are enough without you, and they need it more
than you do."

He smiles at her, at the fair, earnest, proud young
face.

"You talk like my mother. What a wise little
lady you are, princess! If I thought *you* could really
take an interest in the matter——" he stops, the color
coming into his face.

"I take an interest in all my friends," Miss Ventnor says, with great calm. "Frank, are we going
home to dinner, or are we not? Because I believe we
promised mamma——"

Livingston needs no second bidding. He rises
with alacrity, and is at her side in an instant. Half
an hour of Leo has bored him; the art of flirtation is
one of the lost arts, so far as she is concerned, and
Lamar has monopolized Olga long enough.

"I am *so* sorry you must go," Leo says, plaintively, "but as your mamma is ill, and you have to take her place, Olga, I suppose you must. Good-by, dear. Be sure you come early to-morrow evening."

For to-morrow is Leo's birthday, and there is to be a gathering of the clans and a dance.

The four stand together, a charming group of young heads and fair faces. The fifth looks at them, and holds herself aloof. She is as young as they, she might be as fair under other circumstances, but she is not of them ; unlike them, she has not spoken a word, she has played on steadily, no one knows what. They hear the piano, they see the performer, and one is nearly as much to them as the other. They are kind to her—yes, polite to her always, and there are times when she would rather they struck her. She is Slea-ford's Joanna—they are of the golden youth of the earth, well-born, high-bred. Heaven and earth are not farther apart than they.

Geoffrey and Leo go out with their guests. The windless, mild December twilight, gray and star-studded, is beautiful, as they saunter to the gate.

"And Olga predicts snow," says Geoffrey, laughing, " in the face of that sky."

"If she predicts it you may be sure it will come," says Frank. "The elements themselves dare not oppose the imperial will of the Princess Olga !"

"Look at the new moon !" cries Leo, " and wish. What are you wishing for, Geoff ?—what do you wish for, Olga ? *I* wish for a snow-storm to-morrow, and then a lovely night."

They all look. What do they all wish for ? Geoffrey's eyes rest on Olga, before he looks at the sky.

His wish might be read, if there were eyes to read it.
Olga looks up too—for what does beautiful Olga Ventnor wish ?

> " ' I saw the new moon late yes'treen,
> Wi' the auld moon in her airms,' "

she quotes. "I see her now. Do not come any farther, Leo, in your bare head. It grows chilly ; you
may catch cold."

So they part. All the way back to the house Leo
chatters, but Geoffrey is silent.

"We have left Joanna alone all this time," she
says, as they re-enter, "beg pardon, Jo, but—why, she
has gone !"

She has gone. She has risen a moment after they
left, taken her hat, gone out of a side door, and gone
home. The grand portico entrance is not for her, and
the home she goes to is Sleaford's.

CHAPTER II.

IN WHICH JOANNA ENTERS SOCIETY.

"AMMA," says Leo Abbott, "I wonder why
papa dislikes Joanna so much ?"

They make a pretty picture, mother
and daughter. Mrs. Abbott, gracious
and handsome as ever, sits at her embroidery-frame,
with a basket of silks, and floss, and zephyr, in rainbow shades, beside her. She is making tapestry, like
a mediæval countess in a baronial hall—a huge piece,

with four large figures. It is a Scriptural subject, "Susanna and the Elders," though at this stage of proceedings it is not so easy to tell which *is* Susanna, and which *are* the elders. Leo nestles on a footstool at her feet. She is one of the caressing sort, who always nestle on footstools and cushions, like kittens, and who like to purr, and be petted. There is no affectation about it—it is all very natural and very pretty in Leo.

The lady looks up from her frame, and her dark, large-lidded eyes rest on her daughter.

" Are you not mistaken ?" she says, quietly. " Why should your papa dislike Joanna ?"

" Ah ! why indeed ? I am sure I do not know—*I* think Joanna charming. All the same, papa dislikes her—more, he looks sometimes as if he were actually *afraid* of her !"

" Afraid ! my child, what nonsense you talk."

But the inflection of Mrs. Abbott's voice as she says it is perfectly calm—the faintest of smiles dawns about her mouth, as she takes a fresh needleful of gold-colored silk, and puts a long, slanting stitch in Susanna's back hair. As if anything of this wonderful discovery was new to her !

" Well, perhaps it is nonsense," says Leo, resignedly ; "all I have to say, mamma, is, you watch papa the next time he and Joanna meet, and see for yourself."

Mrs. Abbott's amused smile deepens.

" My dear," she remarks, " I will, if you will tell me this—when *do* they ever meet ?"

Leo looks up at her with puzzled eyes—then slowly a light breaks upon her.

"That is true," she says, amazedly ; " they never do meet. I have never seen them in a room together in all these years ! Now, how is that, I wonder?" '

" Watch and see," replies Mrs. Abbott, enigmatically, taking some bister-hued floss this time, to shade the eldest Elder's complexion. " What has started the subject now ?"

" Why, this. Half an hour ago, after I left Miss Rice, and before Joanna had come, papa called me out to take a walk with him in the grounds. I went, and as we were going down the laburnum walk, Joanna came up—she generally does take that side entrance. The moment papa saw her, he stopped in what he was saying, looking *so* flurried, you cannot think, and drew me with him between the trees. 'I don't want to meet that young woman,' he said. But, mamma, he watched her out of sight with the strangest look ! It was exactly (only that *is* absurd) as if he was frightened —as if he was afraid of *her !*"

" Well, my dear, you do not generally stand in awe of your papa—why did you not ask him about it ?" says mamma.

" Oh ! I said : ' Why, papa, what is the matter ? You do look so oddly ! You are not afraid of our Joanna, are you ?' He gave me such a look—as cross as he *can* look at me, and he says ' Afraid ! that be blowed ! And *our* Joanna, too ! Who made her yours, I wonder ! I don't like her, and I don't like to see her gadding here. She's no fit chum for you—a gentleman's daughter, by Jove !' "

Leo mimics her father's blustering voice so well, that Mrs. Abbott has to laugh.

" Then he told me to run away into the house, and

went off by himself. But it is very odd, I think. I am sure Joanna has the manner of a lady—when she likes—and is good enough to be companion to anybody."

"Ah! when she likes!" repeats Mrs. Abbott, significantly. There is a pause. "Your friend, Olga, seems to share in your papa's dislike, Leo," she says, still absorbed in the Elder's leathery complexion.

"Yes," Leo answers, thoughtfully; "Olga does not like Joanna, and there is not much love lost, I think. Joanna, mamma," laughs Leo, "could be one of the good haters old Dr. Johnson liked, if she chose. I will tell you though who *does* like her more than his mother would quite approve of, I guess, if she knew."

"Who?" demands Mrs. Abbott, looking startled, and letting the "I guess" slip in the excitement of the moment.

"George Blake—Miss Rice's nephew, you know. He comes here sometimes with Frank to play croquet. He is in the office of a New York daily paper, and is quite clever, they say, and he runs down here once or twice a week, to see his mother—he *says!*" Leo laughs.

"You think it is not to see his mother?"

"I think it is to see Joanna. You always send our Perkins home with her when she is here late, and George Blake waylays them, and takes Jo out of his hands. Perkins walks behind until they reach Sleaford's, then he touches his hat, says 'good-night, Miss,' and comes home and tells the others. And then I have seen him watch Jo when we all play croquet."

"It seems to me you see a great deal, little Leo," says mamma, reprovingly. "Fifteen-year-old eyes and ears should not be quite so sharp, and you should never, never on any account hearken to the gossip of servants."

Miss Leo blushes. Her mamma has not permitted her to read many novels, she has seen next to no "grown-up" society at all; all the same her feminine soul tells her George Blake is a victim to the tender passion, and consumed with love for Joanna.

"Does this George Blake make much money?" inquires Mrs. Abbott, after another pause, deserting the Elder and returning to Susanna, her mind projecting itself into the future of her *protegée.* After all, the young man might make a very good husband for the girl.

" Fifteen dollars a week," responds Leo, promptly, " and he pays seven out of that for his board ! And I don't think Joanna would make a good housekeeper, or manage on fifteen dollars a week. And besides, she wouldn't have him."

" My dear !" says her mother, smiling again.

" Oh, no, she wouldn't, mamma," Leo iterates with conviction ; " she treats him with the greatest disdain, scolds him when he meets her, and sometimes makes him go back. But he meets her next time just the same. I wonder what Miss Rice would say ? She is awfully proud of George, thinks he is going to be a Horace Greeley by and by——"

There is a tap at the door. It proves to be Miss Rice in person, who wishes to know if Miss Leo will come and practice that duet she is to sing to-night with Joanna. So Leo goes, and Mrs. Abbott takes another strand of pale gold silk, and looks at Susanna's flowing tresses with a very thoughtful face.

She thinks of Joanna and her husband. What Leo has discovered to-day for the first time is a very old story to Leo's mother. It surprised her at first, it puzzles her still, but she does not object to it—she has found it useful in more ways than one. Mr. Abbott, in words, has never, since that first day, objected in the least to the presence of Geoffrey's ward, as they call her, but in action he has objected to her, all these five years, as strongly as man can. He avoids her as he might a snake ; if they meet by chance he beats a retreat ; if she enters a room where he is, he leaves it ; he breaks off whatever he is saying to listen to her when she speaks. If she stays for dinner, as she has on one or two occasions, he dines in solitude.

This is all very remarkable, but more remarkable still is that look his face assumes at sight of her ; that look is so extraordinarily like one of shrinking fear. Who is this girl ? What is she to the Sleafords ? What to her husband, that all this should be so ? What secret binds him and this man Sleaford together in its dark tie ?

For Joanna, she is evidently unconscious of her power. She sees that Mr. Abbott avoids and dislikes her, but she is used to that, and does not mind. She dislikes him in turn, so they are quits. That she has any further hold upon him, she is unaware. Mrs. Abbott thinks of all this, but she has little desire to lift the vail ; the screen that hides her husband's past life is a merciful one ; she shrinks from ever knowing what lies behind. If she does not wish for the presence of Mr. Abbott, when her children's young friends assemble at Abbott Wood, she has but to keep Jo-

anna by her side—he will not come. She takes advantage of this to see rather more company than was her
wont. Joanna's presence is a guarantee that Mr. Abbott's uncultured remarks will not put her to the blush.

Brightbrook has some very desirable residents now,
very nice people, indeed, who come there for the
summer, and there is abundance of pleasant society
for Leo. Mr. Abbott intrudes not, for Joanna is
always there to sing. Long ago, Mrs. Abbott, who
really likes the girl, would have taken her to Abbott
Wood " for good " had Giles Sleaford not resolutely
refused to give her up.

Those five years have not altered him in any way,
except that he daily grows more besotted with drink
and "dry rot." He lets Mr. Abbott comparatively
alone ; his pockets are always well filled, his girls and
boys well dressed, the old rude plenty reigns at the
farmstead, the old "swarrys" still obtain, it is the
rendezvous of a very lively lot of young men and
maidens. People have grown to accept Sleaford and
his thriftless family, and pretty well ceased to wonder
at his connection with Mr. Abbott. A billionaire is a
privileged being. They are proud of Abbott Wood
and its burly lord ; he has in a great measure made the
place, he is the Seigneur of the soil, owns half the village, and the big white hotel that in summer is so well
and fashionably filled. Hillside breezes, trout streams,
gunning, boating, bathing, fishing (*see prospectus*), all
are here, and city folk come with their wives and little
ones, their maid servants, and man servants (sometimes), and enjoy them.

Mrs. Abbott likes Joanna, and takes an interest in
her welfare. Yes, but Joanna loves Mrs. Abbott,

reveres her, admires her, thinks her the most beautiful, accomplished, and perfect being on earth. Her
worship of this great lady is, to a certain extent, her
religion, her salvation. If she is tempted to do wrong,
to give way to passion, the thought, "Mrs. Abbott
will not like it," is sufficient to restrain her. Her
smile is Joanna's guerdon, her praise the girl's delight,
to please her is the highest ambition of her life. The
lady has tried to teach her, to make a Christian of her,
to give her yet a higher standard, but it is not so easy
to evangelize this young heathen. The leopard does
not change his spots ; Joanna does not change her
nature in spite of beautiful music, painted windows,
embroidered altar-cloths, and the flowery periods of
the Rev. Ignatius Lamb. She listens, and chafes inwardly—and yet, as constant dropping will wear a
stone, so five years of this have subdued the girl, and
made her turn her thoughts, with a certain stricken
awe, to those great truths she reads and hears. There
is a Heaven, and she may go to it, she, Sleaford's
Joanna, quite as readily as fair Olga Ventnor herself.
That fact she has grasped, and it does her good, increases her self-respect, and spurs her on to better
things. She is far less fierce, she gives up bad language, she tries to listen in silence to the taunts and
sneers at home, to rise superior to her surroundings.
But oh ! it is weary work—it is a never-ending struggle ; she falls back again and again, the old bitterness,
the old despair, clutch her hardly at times. Envy,
hatred, and all uncharitableness devour her heart, and
tear it to pieces between them. It is an abnormal life
she leads, two lives, and she is supremely miserable.
She strives to be content, to be thankful—it is impos-

7

sible. She loves Mrs. Abbott, she reveres her, she would do anything in the world to win her praise—the best of this poor Joanna begins and ends there. To her she is passionately grateful ; to the rest of the world her heart is like a stone. Even to Geoffrey, her first friend, she is almost apathetic—she likes Leo, that is all. There is, perhaps, one other exception, but this exception only adds to her unhappiness—it fills her with a gnawing, miserable unrest. She feels wicked and helpless, and all the time she longs to be good, to be noble, to be true. Her good and bad angels war strongly for the soul of Joanna.

Long ago she confessed her first sin—her attack upon Olga Ventnor. She goes to Mrs. Abbott and confesses it voluntarily, looking downcast and ashamed. The lady listens very gravely.

" I feared so," she says: " it is good of you to confess it, Joanna. To be sorry for a fault is to amend it. But I think you ought to apologize to Miss Ventnor."

" Oh !" Joanna says, with a gasp—*That* is quite another thing—to tell this kind, good, gentle lady is easy.

"I think you ought. It nearly killed her. She does not suspect, and she will meet you here. I do not order you to do so—I leave it to your own conscience. But I think you ought."

That is all. There is a struggle in the wild heart of Sleaford's Joanna—the first struggle between right and wrong, and right conquers. She goes lingeringly up to Olga Ventnor, standing for a moment alone, and stammers out her confession.

" It was me," she says, confusedly. " I didn't mean

to hurt you—only to cut off your hair. I'm very sorry.
I hope you—you don't mind!"

"*You!*" Olga exclaims, horror in her eyes. All
the terror of that terrible time returns to her. She
looks at her with fear, with abhorrence, and turns and
flies.

Joanna stands mute, motionless. Half an hour
after, when Olga, her first panic over, and ashamed of
what she has done, returns, she finds her standing
there still.

"I am sorry," Olga says, but her head is very erect
as she says it—she does not look sorry. "I do not
mind in the least—now. I did not think when I ran
away. I hope *you* do not mind."

The black eyes look at her. They are so fierce, so
full of hatred, that Olga recoils.

"I will mind as long as I live!" Joanna says, and
turns from her, striking down the hand she has half
held out.

So ends Joanna's first impulse to try and be
"good." Alas! most of her impulses end in the
same way.

*　　*　　*　　*　　*　　*

There are lights, and flowers, and fair faces, and
music, and feasting in silent, stately Abbott Wood to-
night, for the little daughter of the house is fifteen,
and her friends, and Olga's, and Geoffrey's are down
from the city in force to wish her many happy returns.
She has had her wish. It has snowed all day, and now
the moon, a brilliant Christmas sickle, shines down on
glistening snow, black, bare trees, gaunt hedges and
avenues, but it is windless, and still mild. It is no
green yule, and great fires blaze high in gleaming

grates, for no abomination of pipes or registers dese-
crate winter at Abbott Wood. The "mistletoe
bough" hangs from the drawing-room ceiling, though
the custom of kissing under it is more honored in the
breach than the observance ; holly, and arbutus, and
winter berries adorn walls and windows, and there are
flowers, flowers, flowers everywhere. A tolerably
large company are coming—nearly all young people,
for it is understood it is little more than a girl's party,
after all.

"Remember ! come early, Joanna," is Mrs. Abbott's
last injunction ; "and be in your best looks and voice
to-night."

Joanna shrugs her shoulders.

"My looks do not matter in the least. My voice I
will try and have to order," is her answer. It is for
her voice she is here, she knows, not for herself.

She comes early, and dresses in a little room that
is kept for her use. There is so much envy and
bickering with Lora and Liz, that she keeps but few
of her things at home. Mrs. Abbott provides her
dresses, of course, but simple ones always. Joanna
will have nothing else, and Mrs. Abbott sees that
gayety would not accord with the fitness of things.
She wears to-night a dress of dark-blue silk, but so
plainly made that nothing could be less smart ; a gold
cross and chain ; her abundant reddish hair braided
as tightly and compactly as possible about her small
head, and she is ready. And she looks very well—
"slim and genteel, and quite the lady," Mrs. Hill, the
housekeeper, tells her, condescendingly, "only she
ought to put a bit of pink ribbon or blue flower in her
hair."

Joanna laughs.

"To put pink ribbon in red hair would be to paint the lily, Mrs. Hill," she says, good-humoredly. Of personal vanity she has not a particle ; her red hair does not discompose her in the least.

She goes down, and Mrs. Abbott glances at her approvingly. Quite plain, severely simple, yet well-dressed—it is as it should be ; Joanna does her no discredit.

"If only you sing as well as you look, my dear, I shall be quite satisfied," she says, kindly.

Leo is there, all in white—a costly toilet, white lace over pearl-colored silk, and strands of pearls in her dark, perfumed hair. Her bronze eyes shine, her cheeks flush, her childish face is bright with excitement. She kisses Joanna in childish glee. Mr. Abbott reconnoiters once, sees Joanna, and flees.

The company come early, and come rapidly—it is in the country—city hours do not obtain, and it is only Leo's party. A number of youthful guests are staying in the house, nearly a dozen more come from Ventnor Villa, with Olga and Frank.

Olga is like a vision, like an Undine, like a water-lily. She wears some pale, sheeny silk, half silvery, half green, with quantities of tulle, and bunches of pale pink roses. Even Joanna catches her breath as she looks at her. That gold hair, that clear, star-like face, that imperial poise of head and shoulders, that exquisite water-nymph dress.

"Oh !" Joanna says, " how lovely ! how lovely !"

" How lovely !" a voice echoes.

It is Geoffrey Lamar, whose deep gray eyes glow as they look on this Peri. A second later, and he is by her side. Frank Livingston, looking insouciant and handsome, comes over to present his felicitations to Miss Abbott. The rainbow throng meets, mingles, disperses. Joanna, in the shade of a great *jardinière,* watches it all. Frank engages Leo for the first dance ; Geoffrey has Olga ; others seek partners ; dancing begins almost immediately. Colonel Ventnor seeks out Mr. Abbott in the library, and, with two other papas, enjoys a quiet game of whist.

The band music rings merrily out, the young people merrily dance. Joanna does not dance. Young ladies are in the majority—as it is in the nature of young ladies to be—and no one notices her until it is time to sing. Then she glides to the piano, at a signal from Mrs. Abbott, and her fine voice breaks through the chatter and hum, and talkers stop, perforce, to listen. She sings alone, then with Leo, then alone again, for people crowd around her, and there is soft clapping of gloved hands and gentle murmurs of praise.

" Sing us a Christmas carol," says Mrs. Ventnor ; " to-morrow is Christmas Eve."

She thinks a moment, and then, in a softened voice, a little tremulous, she sings a very old hymn :

> " Earthly friends may change and falter,
> Earthly friends may vary;
> He is born, who cannot alter,
> Of the Virgin Mary."

"Oh ! how sweet !" Mrs. Ventnor says, tears in her eyes ; " please—please sing another. Your voice goes to my heart."

The girl lifts two dark, melancholy, grateful eyes to the lady, and sings again :

> " He neither shall be born
> In housen nor in hall,
> Nor in the place of paradise,
> But in an ox's stall.
> He neither shall be rock'd
> In silver nor in gold,
> But in a wooden manger
> That rocks upon the mold."

Then she rises, and they make way for her to pass with a certain deference and wonder.

" Who is she—that plain girl with the beautiful voice ?" they ask in undertones. As she moves on, Frank Livingston meets her, and holds out his hand.

" It is the first time I have had a glimpse of you to-night, Mademoiselle Cantatrice," he says. " You sing more and more like an angel every day. You always make me want to go into a corner and cry whenever you open your mouth !"

Joanna laughs. The compliment is ambiguous, to say the least, but her somber face lights into moment-ary brightness at his careless words. The next moment he is gone. He has espied Olga standing in a window-recess alone. He bends above her, says something laughingly, encircles her slight waist with his arm. Only for a second—with a most decided motion she frees herself, and waves him off. It is all in a moment, but in that moment every trace of gladness leaves Joanna's face. She turns angrily, frowningly away. She will not sing any more. She goes out of the ball-room, finds her shawl and hat, and sullenly quits the house. She glances back at the lighted windows with a darkling face. Music follows her, dancing is recommencing, she will not be missed. She does not care if she is.

She walks down under the black trees to the gate. There she stops, folds her arms on the top of the low stone wall, and stands still. There is nothing more coldly melancholy than moonlight on snow ; it suits her mood, this steel-cut landscape, all ebony and ivory. As she stands, a figure comes out of the shadow and approaches her. She stares at it, but in no surprise or alarm.

"Oh !" she says, ungraciously enough ; "it is *you !*"

"It is I. I thought you would come out, Joanna. You mostly do, you know. Are you going home ?"

"What are you doing here ?" Joanna demands, still ungraciously, and not moving.

"Oh, you know," George Blake answers. "It is my off-night, and I could not keep away. Try and be civil to a fellow, Joanna. Are you going home ? Let me go with you."

She stands silent. George Blake is in love with her—she is amazed, but not in the least flattered by the fact. Plain Sleaford's Joanna, as she is, she has some nameless fascination for him. He has been in the habit of going to the Sleafords' for years without being in the least smitten by either of the fair Misses Sleaford. Suddenly, without knowing why or wherefore, he is possessed of a passion for this girl, Joanna, that holds him as with bonds and fetters. His mother would not approve ; Joanna snubs him unmercifully— all the same, his infatuation deepens with every day.

"Are you coming ?" young Blake asks ; "or are you going back to the house ?"

She glances over her shoulder once more at those lighted windows, with a frown.

"I will go home. Oh, yes, you may come. They will not miss me—they are too well engaged."

"I suppose all the cream of the cream are there?" he says, gayly drawing her arm through his, quite happy for the time—"the Van Rensselaers, the Ventnors, and the rest. Livingston is there, of course?"

"Of course," she says, shortly.

"And devoted to the lovely princess? Ah, what a match he will make!—beauty, riches, everything—must have been born with a diamond spoon in his mouth—that fellow."

She does not reply. She shivers, and draws her shawl with impatience about her.

"How cold it is!" she says, almost angrily. "Do not talk. Let us hurry. It is nearly two o'clock."

But George does talk, gayly and fluently. He talks so much that he is unconscious she listens in silence. They reach the farm, wrapped in quiet and darkness, without meeting a soul. All are in bed, but Joanna has a key.

"Good-night," she says, "and don't be so foolish waiting for me another time. What would your mother say?"

He laughs.

"My mother thinks I am virtuously asleep in New York. We do not tell our mothers everything. It would not be good for 'em. Good-night, Joanna."

He goes off, whistling, through the white, still, frozen night. Joanna gets in, and reaches her room, but she does not go to bed. She sits there in the chill, ghostly moonlight a long time—so long that the

7*

moon wanes, and sets, and the stars fade out, and the
deep darkness that precedes dawn falls on the earth.
Far off, at Abbott Wood, the gay birth-night party is
breaking up, and good-byes are being spoken, to the
merry music of sleigh-bells. But the dark morning
sky is not darker than the set face of Sleaford's
Joanna.

CHAPTER III.

IN WHICH JOANNA CAPS THE CLIMAX.

T is the afternoon of New Year's Day—a
windy and overcast afternoon. Fast drifting clouds are blown wildly over a leaden
sky, " onding on snaw ;" a gale surges with
the roar of the sea through the pine woods ; far off, the
deep diapason of that mighty sea itself blends its
hoarse roar in the elemental chorus. The marshes lie
all flat and sodden with recent rain and melted snow.
It is a desolate picture on which the girl looks who
leans over the gate at Sleaford's, and gazes blankly
before her, with eyes as dreary as the landscape itself.
She looks flushed and weary, and with reason ; the
long soughing blast sweeps cool and kindly as a friend's
hand over her hot forehead. Her wild hair blows
about in its usual untidy fashion—her dress is a torn
and soiled calico wrapper. No " neat-handed Phillis,"
this, no spotless dimity household divinity, but simply
Sleaford's Joanna resting after the toils of the day.
    The red farm-house behind her lies silent and som-
ber, the bark of one of the many dogs, now and then,

alone breaking the silence. The household are away, except the master, and he is sleeping off a heavy dinner, washed down by copious draughts of whisky, in the upper chamber, sacred to his use. For is it not New Year's Day, and have not Liz and Lora to receive their gentlemen friends ? Neither the weather nor the roads being propitious, and Sleaford's being two or three miles out of the way, the young ladies have accepted the invitation of a couple of their friends, and have gone *en grande tenue* to Brightbrook to receive. Dan and Jud, in their Sabbath best, are "calling." Giles, Joanna, and the dogs are keeping house.

It has been no holiday for the girl ; she has never had a holiday in her life. There has been a dinner party at the farm-house, and she has been cook. The office has been no sinecure—there has been a goose stuffed with sage and onions, a large, vulgar, savory bird, to roast—a turkey, with dressing, to boil, a plum pudding ditto, sundry vegetables, and stewed fruits, to go with these dainties. Yesterday a huge beefsteak and kidney pasty was concocted, and a ham boiled. To these viands a select company of six young ladies and gentlemen, exclusive of the family, have turned their hungry attention. The Miss Sleafords, in brand-new silk suits, have gone to meeting in Brightbrook, and brought their friends back with them. Joanna has cooked, but has refused to wait at table.

"There is your dinner ; wait on yourselves, or go without," she has said, briefly, and they *have* waited on themselves without much grumbling, for everything has been done to a charm. Now they are gone again ; she has washed the dishes and " redd up," and, tired, dushed, heavy-hearted, she stands leaning over the fence, looking with those great black, melancholy eyes of hers, at that low-lying, fast-drifting sky. \

But it is neither the weariness of labor, the dreariness of utter solitude, the loss of a holiday that all the rest of the world is enjoying, that weighs her down. To all these things she is inured ; custom has blunted their edge, she hardly feels their pain. It is something else, something belonging to that other life that is not connected with Sleaford's—that other life that seems to belong to another world.

The changes that have occurred since the Christmas birthnight party are these. The Ventnors have returned to town, their visitors with them. Before going they had given a party, to which Joanna was bidden, in kindliest, gentlest words, by kindly, gentle Mrs. Ventnor. The girl had gone, of course ; it was not optional with her to decline. She is asked to sing, and goes for that purpose. The Abbotts are there, all who were at Abbott's Wood the other night, and many more. Once more Olga, in palest rose silk, looks lovely as a dream ; everything she wears seems to become her more than the last. Once more very young men flock around her as butterflies round a rosebud ; and at this party something has occurred that has stung this poor, sensitive, morbid Joanna to the very heart. Only Mrs. Abbott, and one other, have power enough over that heart to sting it to its core—it is that other who unwittingly has done it.

Joanna has been singing. Some passionate pain at her heart makes the song—a despairing love song— ring out with an intensity of power that thrills all who listen. Mrs. Van Rensselaer, the greatest of all great ladies, has taken the girl's hand in her grand duchess manner, and said some overpoweringly condescending things. It is one of Joanna's innumerable faults that she hates patronage, and all who patronize. Instead of being overwhelmed by the gracious kindness of Mrs. Van Rensselaer, who has patronized the greatest artists in her time, Joanna frees her hand, and cuts the lady brusquely and decidedly short. She turns her back deliberately upon her—her—Mrs. Van Rensselaer!—and moves away. The lady stands petrified. The expression of her rigid amazement and dismay, her stony stare, are too much for Frank Livingston, who witnesses the performance. He retreats into a window recess to laugh. There he encounters Geoffrey Lamar, who, with knitted brows, has also beheld this little scene.

"By Jove!" Frank cries, throwing back his head, and laughing explosively, "it is the most delicious joke! the great Mrs. Van Rensselaer snubbed—snubbed by Sleaford's Joanna! Behold the glare of that Medusa face! On my word, I believe she will have a fit!"

"Mrs. Van Rensselaer deserves it!" Geoffrey says, flushing with anger. "Why cannot they let the girl alone? God has given her an exquisite voice, and such women as that think to uplift her by their patronizing praise. She has served Mrs. Van Rensselaer right!"

"Bravo, Geoff! Set lance in rest, and ride forth in defense of your protegé. Do you know what it reminds me of?—that old story of James the First, the baronet-making king, and his nurse. The old lady asks him, you know, to make her son a gentleman. 'I'll mak your son a baronet, if ye like, Lucky,' says the king, 'but the deevil himsel' wadna mak him a gentleman.' The cases are similar. You may make Sleaford's Joanna a singer if you like, Lamar, but—your mother herself cannot make her a gentlewoman."

He goes off laughing. A figure, standing motionless, hidden by a flower-wreathed pillar, has heard every word. And the white marble of the pillar is not whiter than her face. Livingston is quoting Shakespeare over his shoulder as he goes :

> "Oh, when she's angry she is keen and shrewd;
> She was a vixen when she went to school,
> And though she is but little, she is fierce !"

An hour after he comes up to her, as she stands a little apart, after singing again—a sweet little Scotch ballad, that has touched even him.

"I foresee we are all going to be proud of our Brightbrook nightingale," he says, gayly. "When your biography is written, we will recall—and put on airs in consequence—that we knew and heard you first. By-the-bye, the honor of discovery lies with Lamar. How was it, I wonder, that I, knowing you so long before him, never found you out, or thought what a singing bird you were ?"

She looks at him. To this day he does not understand, perhaps, the fiery wrath and scorn of her eyes. "*You!*" she says, and he winces and stares at her tone. "You ! Why, you never thought of any one but yourself in all your life !"

"Upon my word," says Mr. Livingston, when he recovers a little, "here is a facer ! First she floors Mrs. Van Rensselaer—now me. What have I done, I wonder ? I haven't been patronizing, have I, Olga ?"

Miss Ventnor's beautiful, short upper lip curls.

"She is never very civil, but to-night she is really quite too horrid. Mrs. Van Rensselaer is *very* angry." Then she remembers Joanna is her mother's guest, and stops. "I suppose it is to be expected, poor creature; the better way is to say nothing to her at all. This waltz is yours, I think, Frank, if you wish to claim it."

If he wishes? Frank's blue, speaking eyes answer the question, but Olga only laughs.

"Keep your sentimental looks for Rosa Brevoort, sir," she says, tossing back her sunshiny tresses; "she believes in them—I do not. No, nor your pretty speeches, either—so don't go quoting Tennyson at me! Young men who quote poetry and look as you do at every girl you dance with, ought to be bowstrung, or put in the pillory."

Miss Olga speaks with some irritation. She means what she says. She laughs at Livingston's love-making; she derides his tender glances; she declines being flirted with, but for some cause it annoys her. Perhaps she does not choose to make one in the long litany of Frank's flirtees. Of that family compact, settled five years ago, she has not heard a word.

And this being New Year's Day, as she stands here alone, and untidy, at the gate, Joanna is thinking of all this. Every day of her life she chafes more and more; either existence, perhaps, she could stand, but both are killing her.

"Why have I ever known these people?" her soul cries out in its bitterness. "Better, oh! a thousand times better to drudge in Sleaford's kitchen, to cook dinners, and wash pots and pans, and know no higher, fairer life. I might live as an animal does then—eat, and sleep, and never think. But to know them, to see their life, to mingle with it, to be among them, but never of them—I cannot endure it much longer. It will either end in my killing myself or running away !"

As she speaks, and she speaks aloud—much solitude has taught her the habit—a man comes up the slushy road, and stands near her, unseen.

" Kill myself," she repeats, in a low, tense tone, " and why not ? It is the shortest solution to the difficulty. Perhaps even *he* would care then ! But no," contemptuously, " he would say, ' By Jove, you know —poor Joanna !' and waltz with Olga ten minutes after. Still, I swear, I have half a mind to go down to Black's Dam and do it !"

At this moment she is handsome ; her sallow cheeks flushed, her black eyes shining with unholy fire. She strikes her clenched hand, in her desperate mood, on the bar, so as to bring blood. The strange fascination that has held George Blake from the first, sweeps over him like a resistless torrent now. He leans forward, his face flushing darkly red.

" Don't drown yourself, Joanna," he says ; " do better. Marry me !"

She looks at him. She has not heard him ; he has overheard her, but he does not discompose her in the least. She looks at him a full minute without speaking. It is one of the traits of Joanna's curious character, that she can stare any man or woman alive out of countenance, without winking once.

" Do better ?" she repeats. " Would that be doing better ?" Her eyes never leave his face. " Are you rich ?" she demands.

" No, poor—poor as a church mouse ; a penniless

beggar of a paragraphist. But it would be better than Black's Dam."

" Would it ?" she says again. " I am not so sure of that. Black's Dam would end everything—going with you would not. It would be only exchanging one sort of hardship for another. And I don't want to marry —*you !*"

" I am awfully fond of you, Joanna," the poor young fellow pleads. " I would work for you. We could live in New York on my pay. And you would have a good time. I get free passes to all the theaters, you know, and all the sights, and that. We could board, you know. You would not have to work. And you would like New York. Do think of it, Joanna."

" New York ?" she repeats, and her great eyes light. "Yes, I would like New York. I *will* think of it, George Blake."

She declines further courtship—does not even ask her adorer in, and dismisses him summarily enough.

"I wish you would go. I don't want to talk. I am tired to death—oh, so tired ! so tired !" drawing a long, hard breath. "I was up nearly all last night. I will go in and go to bed."

" And you will think of it, Joanna ?"

" Oh, yes, I will think of it. I would like to go to New York. I cannot endure my life here much longer."

" And I may come soon again ?"

" Come whenever you like," she says, half impatiently, half indifferently. "I suppose I ought to feel pleased, I have so few friends, but I don't. If I ever run away with you, you will be sorry for it all the rest of your life."

It is an ominous prediction, and he thinks of it with
bitterness of spirit in after days. But the glamour is
upon him now ; he would not have his eyes open if he
could.

"I will risk it," he answers, fervently. "I will risk
all things, so that you come."

*   *   *   *   *   *

Three days after this, Mrs. Abbott announces a second change.

"The week after next," she says, "Leo, and my son
and I are going to New York to spend a month with
the Ventnors. The only difference it will make to
you, Joanna, is that you will go to Miss Rice's cottage
for your daily lessons, instead of coming here."

Joanna listens almost apathetically. Yes, the only
difference. And yet she is conscious of a pang in listening to the lady's calmly-kind words. She loves
Mrs. Abbott, and she loves so few—so few.

She goes home that evening, home to Sleaford's, and
no prescience tells her it is for the last time—the very
last time, forever. She has no intention of running
away with George Blake ; she thinks as little of him
as of the dry twigs that snap under her feet.

She feels wearied and aimless—the feeling is growing upon her day by day. She saunters listlessly along,
after a fashion very unlike her naturally swift, strong,
springy walk.

What is the use of feeling sorry Mrs. Abbott is
going away ? What is the use of feeling sorry for
anything—loving anything ? It is only added pain.

It is a perfect January evening—cold, sparkling,
clear. There is snow on the ground, white and unde-
filed, here in this woodland path—feathery snow on

the black, bare boughs. A brilliant sky is above, pale blue, rich with sunset tints, pearl. ruby, orange, opal, paling slowly to silvery gray. There is no wind. It is a sparkling January gem, set in hazy mist. She reaches the house, takes one last wistful look at all that loveliness of sky and earth, and goes in. The family are assembled, all but old Giles. They are discussing some matter with considerable eagerness.

"She won't do it," Liz is remarking ; "not if you offered her as much again. She has got all sorts of stuck-up notions since these people have took her in hand. She won't go a step ; you'll see."

"I *will* see !" growls Dan Sleaford ; "and what is more, I will make her *feel* if she refuses. Set a beggar on horseback, indeed ! The old man ought to knowed better than ever let her go."

"If she hadn't gone, neither you nor Watjen would want her now," remarks Jud.

"Hush !" says Lora ; "here she is !" and the conversation immediately stops.

She glanced at them carelessly, and throws off her jacket and hat. There is always plenty for her to do when she gets home ; but, for a wonder, neither of the girls issue orders now. There is a pause—Dan breaks it.

"Look here, Jo," he begins, in a wheedling tone, "I've got some good news for you. Here's a chance for you to turn an honest penny at last. You'd like to earn some pocket-money, wouldn't you ?"

She looks at him distrustfully, and does not answer. Rough Dan Sleaford, in this lamb-like mood, is a little more to be suspected than in his natural state. He is a younger copy of his father—coarseness, cruelty, drunkenness included.

"You know Watjen's? You've heard of Watjen's?" he says, in the same insinuating tone ; "him as keeps the lager-bier garden and concert hall up the village? He's lately come from New York, you know, and does as they do it there."

Yes, she has heard of Watjen's—a low drinking place, where the roughs of Brightbrook most do congregate, and where the lowest of both sexes perform for the amusement of the smokers, and drinkers, and bummers of the place. She nods shortly.

"Well—he's an out-and-out good fellow is Watjen, and he's heerd of your singin'—how you can tip 'em French and Dutch songs as easy as wink, and play tho pianny like everything. Well—(mind you, the best singers of New York come and sing for him ; the highest-toned sort o' ladies !)—Watjen wants to engage you. He'll give you one-fifty a night, and I'll drive you over and back every evenin'. There !"

Dan closes this brilliant offer with a flourish. To do Herr Watjen justice, he has offered double that amount for each night, with the promise of an increase, should Joanna find favor in the eyes of his patrons. But Dan judges it is not well to dazzle her with the whole splendid truth. Joanna sits mute as a fish.

"Well !" he cries, "don't ye hear ! One-fifty a night to do what you darn please with ! D'ye hear ?"

"I hear."

"Why don't ye answer, then ?" Dan's voice and temper are rising. The girls exchange aggravating, I-told-you-so smiles. "I want an answer. Is it yes or no ?"

"It is no."

She says it so composedly, that for a moment he

cannot take in the full force of the refusal. He gives
a gasp, and sits with his mouth open.

" Wha-a-a-t !"

"I say no. I wouldn't sing in Watjen's beer garden for a thousand dollars a night—for ten thousand
dollars a night ! I wouldn't set foot in it to save his
life and yours !"

There is no mistaking this time. Her voice rings
with scorn, and she turns to leave the kitchen. Dan
Sleaford leaps to his feet like a tiger, and seizes her
by the arm.

"Say that again, d—— you !" he cries, hoarse with
passion—"say it again !"

She looks at him unflinchingly, her eyes flashing
fire—literally flashing fire.

" I wouldn't go to save your neck from the gallows," she says, between her teeth, " where it is due !"

He waits for no more. The array of horsewhips
from which Giles was wont to select for her benefit is
still there. He seizes one, blind with fury and drink ;
there is a sharp hissing through the air, and it descends. It rises and falls again, quick as light. *Then*,
with a scream of passion, pain, rage, that those who
hear never forget, she turns upon him. In that moment a mad power possesses her—she is stronger than
he. She wrenches the whip out of his grasp, lifts it—
the butt-end this time—and brings it down with all
the force of fury across his head. It lays it open—the
whip has a heavy handle ; a rain of blood pours over
his eyes, and blinds him. He relaxes his hold, stag-
gers backward blindly, and falls. There is a simultaneous shriek and rush, Joanna flings the whip into
the midst of them, and flies.

She is beside herself—she knows not what she has done, or whither she is going. She rushes on like a mad thing, heedless of all obstacles, and falls prostrate at last on the edge of Black's Dam. As a hunted animal flies instinctively to its lair, so her feet have carried her here, and here she falls, panting, spent, for the time being perfectly insane. Jud Sleaford has often predicted that she will murder some of them, and Jud's prediction seems to have come true at last.

───── ◆◆ ─────

CHAPTER IV.

IN WHICH JOANNA RUNS AWAY.

OW long she lies she cannot tell. A panic of horror and despair at herself and the deed she has done, fills her. Has she murdered him? She has threatened often enough to kill some of them in her ungovernable bursts of temper, if they will not let her alone. Has she done it at last? It is not sorrow that stirs her, nor fear; it is a panic of darkest despair and misery such as in all her miserable life she has never felt before. She crouches there in the snow, feeling no cold, numb soul and body. A hurried step crunches over the frozen ground. There is an exclamation; a hand touches her shoulder, and strives to lift her head.

"Joanna!" a breathless voice says; "Joanna, what is this?"

It is a friendly voice. She lifts her stricken, despairing eyes to a friendly face. The sight breaks the tor-

por of agony ; she springs to her feet, and flings her
arms about his neck.

"George Blake !" she cries, with a choking sob.
"George Blake ! George Blake !"

The young fellow holds her to him—pity, terror,
blank consternation in his face.

"Joanna, what is all this? What have you been
doing ? What has that—that brute been doing to
you? Do you know they say that you "—he chokes
over the words—"that you have killed him ?"

She gives a gasp, and still clings hold of him. The
whole world seems slipping away ; she seems to stand
in the wide universe alone in her desolation, with only
this single friend.

"I have been to the house," he goes on ; "all is
confusion there. Jud has gone for a doctor. There
is blood on the floor, and on the whip-handle they say
you struck him with. He is lying, bleeding still, and
stunned, on the settee in the kitchen. The girls say
you have killed him. Oh ! Joanna, speak, and tell me
what it is !"

She tries to do so. Her words are broken and incoherent, but he manages to get at the story—the
provocation, the attack, the reprisal. His eyes flash
with honest indignation.

"The brute ! the cowardly scoundrel ! You served
him right, Joanna—you acted in self-defense. Even
if he *is* killed, which I don't believe, you have served
him right. But he will not die. A beast like that
stands a great deal of killing. Don't shake so, my
dear ; don't wear that haggard face—it will be all
right. I tell you it is only what you ought to have
done long ago. The black, sullen dog ! to take his

horsewhip to you!" He grinds his teeth. "I hope he
will bear the mark of your blow to his dying day!"

She slips out of his arms, and sits down on a fallen
log, her hands clasping her knees, after her old fashion, that miserable, hunted look never leaving her eyes.

"I knew you would come here," the young man
goes on, seating himself beside her; "it is always your
sanctuary in troubled times, my poor Joanna. Oh, my
dear, my dear! my poor, ill-used, suffering girl! if I
could only take your place, and endure all this for
you!"

She holds out her hand to him silently. He is so
good, so leal, her one loyal friend and knight. Great
slow tears well up, and soften the blank anguish of
her hopeless eyes.

"I will tell you what I will do," he says, after a
pause. "I feel sure the fellow will not die—these
venomous reptiles are so tenacious of life—still, we both
feel anxious. If you will wait here, I will go back to
the house and find out. I will return and tell you the
truth—the worst certainty is better than suspense.
Only promise me"—he clasps the cold hand he holds
hard—"you will not do anything—anything rash while
I am gone."

He looks toward the pond, lying dark and stagnant
under the evening sky; then his troubled eyes seek her
face.

"Promise me, Joanna," he says, "you will stay here
until I return."

"I promise," she says, and he knows she will keep
her word.

He rises instantly, and without a moment's delay
starts off on his mission.

She keeps her word to the letter. She sits as he
has left her, never even stirring until he returns. The
last opal-tinted gleam of sunset dies away, the frosty
January stars come thickly out, the night wind rises
bleakly, the frogs croak dismally down in the fetid
depths of their slimy pools. She does not stir; apathy
succeeds agony; she hardly feels ; she is benumbed,
stupefied—she neither cares nor fears longer.

Presently, but it is a long time, too, the footsteps
crunch once more over the frozen snow, and George
Blake comes rapidly forward. One look at his face
tells his news—it is bright, eager, smiling ; his step is
alert and buoyant.

"All right, Joanna," he calls, gayly. "It is as I
said; the fellow is going to live to grace the gallows
yet. It is an ugly gash, and has let him a lot of blood
—as much as if he were a bullock—but it is bandaged
up now, and he's asleep. I heard the doctor tell him,"
says George, laughing, "it was the best thing could
have happened to him; it had ‚probably saved him a
fit of apoplexy, and that he ought to keep you as a sort
of family leech, to break his head at intervals. 'It is
very bad blood,' says the doctor, 'and you're the better for losing a gallon or two of it.' "

George's laugh rings out boyishly; the relief is so
unutterable.

But she does not look glad, she does not speak, she
does not smile. She sits quite still, looking straight
before her, at the pale, snow-lit, star-lit landscape.

His face, too, grows grave as he regards her.

"And now, Jo," he says, resuming his seat beside
her, " what next ?"

8

He has to repeat the question before she seems to hear, then the blank gaze turns to his face.

"You cannot go back there," he says, and he sees her shrink and shudder at the thought. "You cannot stay here. Then what are you to do?"

She makes no reply.

In all the wide world, he wonders, as he watches her, is there another creature so forlorn, so homeless as this?

"Perhaps you will go to Abbott Wood?" he suggests. And at that she finds her voice, and breaks out with a great despairing cry.

"Oh, no, no, no! Never there! Never there any more! Oh, what will Mrs. Abbott say? Oh me! oh me! oh me!"

He sits in silent distress. Great sobs tear and rend their way up from her heart. She weeps wildly aloud. He has never seen Joanna cry before—few ever have—and the tortured sobs shake him through and through.

"Don't, Joanna!" he says. "Oh, do not! I cannot bear to hear you. Don't cry like that!"

As well ask the tide not to flow. Repressed nature will have its revenge; she must weep or die. She sobs on and on, until the paroxysm spends itself, and she stops from sheer exhaustion. A jealous pang wrings George Blake's heart—how she loves this Mrs. Abbott! But still the question is unanswered—what is to be done—and the night wears on. George's watch points to ten. He holds it out to her in silent appeal.

"Wait," she says. "Let me think. Let me think!"

The hysterics have done her good; her apathy is swept away; she is fully aroused to a sense of her

situation—to the importance of that question—what
next?

She sits and thinks. Impossible to return to Sleaford's—horror fills her at the thought. More impossible still to go to Abbott Wood after this terrible
deed. Besides, even if she could, even if Mrs. Abbott
would consent to overlook her almost being a murderess, Giles Sleaford would never let her stay. She
would be brought back to the farm by force—then,
what is to be done?

She looks up at last; her black eyes turn to the
face of her companion, and fix there in such a long,
searching stare that he is disconcerted.

"What is it, Joanna?" he asks. "You know
there is nothing in all the world I would not do for
you."

"*Nothing?*" she tersely repeats.

"Nothing that man can do."

"You asked me the other day to marry you. Will
you marry me *now?*"

"Will I?" his face lights up with quick joy—he
catches both her hands; "*will* I? Oh, Joanna!"

"Will you take me to New York to-night, and
marry me to-morrow?"

"Sharp work!" he says, "but even that may be accomplished. I will take you to New York, and I will
marry you! Joanna! Joanna! how happy you have
made me!"

"I!" she says, mournfully, "I make any one happy!
Oh! George Blake, you will hate me one day for this!
I ought not to ask it—I am a wretch—almost a murderess—not fit to be any good man's wife. And you
are good. Oh! I ought not! I ought not!"

"You ought—you must!" he exclaims, alarmed;
"What nonsense you are talking, Jo! Murderess,
indeed! The pity is you did not give the cur twice as
much. Ah! what care I will take of you, Joanna,
how happy I will make you. You will forget this
wretched life and these miserable people. You shall
have my whole heart and life."

"And your mother," she says, in the same mournful voice, "what will she say? And your aunt—good
Miss Rice? Oh! you foolish fellow! Take me to
New York, but do *not* marry me. Let me earn my
own living—I am young, and strong, and willing, and
used to hard work. I will be a kitchen-maid—anything. No life can be so hard, so sordid, as the life I
lead here."

"I will marry you," he says, "I refuse to release
you. You said you would be my wife and you must
—I cannot live without you. Oh! Joanna," the young
fellow cries out in a burst of passion, "you torture me!
Cannot you see that I love you?"

She shakes her head.

"No," she says, "I cannot see it, nor understand it.
What is there in me—plain, red-haired, ill-tempered
Joanna, to love? And I do not care for *you*."

"That will come in time. I will be so good to you,
so fond of you, you will not be able to help it. Say no
more about it, Joanna. I claim you and will have
you."

"Very well," she answers, resignedly; "remember,
whatever comes, I have warned you. Now settle all
the rest yourself. I trust you—I am in your hands."

"And I will be true to your trust," he says, fervently, "so help me Heaven!"

He lifts one of her hands, the red, work-hardened hands, to his lips. And then for a little they sit in silence.

It is a strange betrothal—the hour of night, the gloomy scene, white snow, black woods, dead silence, starry sky, and Black's Dam, evil and ominous, at their feet. All George Blake's life long that picture stands out, distinct from all others, in his memory—he and this strange girl who fascinates him, sitting there, the only creatures, it seems, left in all the world !

"Let me see," he says, returning to the practical, "there is no up-train to the city before five o'clock. That is the one I generally go by, when I spend a night in Brightbrook. It is now past eleven : how are we to get through the intervening hours? You will perish if we stay here."

" And I must have something to wear," says Joanna, glancing at her dress. It is the grimy, well-worn old alpaca. "Let me see. They are not likely to sit up to-night with him, are they ? "

"Not in the least likely, I should say. He is all right ; was snoring like a grampus when I left. Why?"

"I must get into the house, and get something to wear. I cannot go to New York like this."

He see that she cannot, but still he looks anxious and doubtful.

"It is a risk," he says.

"Not at all, if they do not sit up. I can always get in, and once in bed I am not afraid of *that* family. They sleep as if for a wager. It is a risk I must run. I must have a better dress, a shawl and hat. And I can wait indoors until it is time to start for the station."

"An hour will take us," Blake says. "Come then, Joanna, let us be up and doing. I shall get into a fever waiting, if we stay here."

They go—starting on the first stage of that journey, that is to lead—who can tell where?

It is nearly midnight when they reach the Red Farm. No sign of recent tragedy is there—quiet slumber evidently reigns. It is better even than they had dared to hope.

"Where will you wait?" the girl asks. "It will be cold for you."

"I will walk about," he answers. "The night is mild, and my overcoat is proof against frost-bite. Only do not be caught, Joanna, or change your mind, or fall asleep. I will never forgive you if you fail me now !"

"I will not fail," she says, firmly. "Before four I will be with you again."

She leaves him, and admits herself after her old fashion—bolts and bars are few and far between at Sleaford's. All is still. She takes off her shoes and creeps up stairs and listens.

All still.

Now the question arises, what shall she wear ? She does not want to disgrace George Blake. Nearly all the things Mrs. Abbott has given her are in her room at Abbott Wood—Liz and Lora immediately confiscating to their use anything attractive she brings to the farm. She has absolutely nothing of her own fit to put on. No—but the other girls have ! Joanna has not the slightest scruple in the matter. They take everything of hers ; it is a poor rule that will not work both ways. She will help herself from Lora's ward-

robe ! They are of the same height. Lora is a " fine
girl," and stout enough to make two of such a slip as
Joanna, but fit does not signify. She softly opens the
wardrobe, and begins operations. It is a small closet
adjoining their bedroom, and dark as a pocket ; but
she has brought a candle-end with her from the kitchen.
She lights it now and sets to work.

As well take the best when she is about it ! There
hangs the new black silk suit, gotten up expressly for
New Year's Day, and worn on that occasion only. She
takes it down from its peg. Here is Lora's Sunday
hat, a black velvet beauty, with crimson roses and
snowy plume. To twist out this latter appendage is
the work of a second—the red roses for the present
must stand. Now she wants a wrap. Here is a cloth
jacket, handsomely trimmed ; she unhooks it. Then,
as she is moving away, a last article catches her eye.
It is a crimson wool shawl, a rich and glowing wrap,
and the pride of Liz's soul.

Some faint spirit of *diablerie*, more than actual
need, makes her add this to the heap. She returns to
the kitchen, her arms filled with her spoils. She has
already secured one or two little gifts of Mrs. Abbott's
and Leo's. A gold breastpin, a pearl and ruby ring,
and her very last New Year's gift—a little gold watch
and chain—the watch Mrs. Abbott's present, the chain
Geoffrey's, the ring Leo's. And now in the warm
kitchen she arrays herself deliberately in pilfered
plumes, with a sort of wicked zest in the tremendous
uproar there will be to-morrow. Dan's mishap will be
nothing to this—Liz and Lora will go straight out of
their senses.

"It is not stealing," the girl says to herself. "I

have worked for them all my life ; I have earned these
things ten times over.   And they have taken lots of
mine—Mrs. Abbott's gifts.   I have a right to take
what I want."

Whether or no, they are taken, and will be kept.
Once dressed she seats herself, and waits impatiently
for the clock to strike four.   She is eager to be off, to
turn her back forever upon this hated house, these
hated people—to begin the world anew.   A new life is
dawning for her ; whatever it brings it can bring
nothing half so bad as the life she is leaving.   New
York ! the thought of that great city and its possibilities dazzles her.   Of George Blake she thinks little.
He is, perforce, part of that new life, but she would
rather he were not.   She does not care for him ; he
tries her with his boyish fondness and insipid love-
making.   Still, she cannot do without him—so Mrs.
George Blake, willy nilly, it seems she must be.

One, two, three, four ! from the old wooden Connecticut clock.   She draws a long breath of relief,
rises, makes her way out, as she made it in.

The night has changed—the morning is dark,
damp, dismal.   George Blake is waiting, poor faithful
sentinel.   He comes up, his teeth chattering, white
rime on mustache and hair.

"At last," he says, wearily ; "give you my honor,
Joanna, I thought the time would never come.   What
a night this has been !   Shall you ever forget it ?"

She does not speak ; she looks back darkly at the
house she is leaving.

"Good-by, you dreary prison," she says.   "I may be
miserable in the time that is to come, but I can never
again be as miserable as I have been in you."

"You shall never be miserable. Can you not trust me, Joanna?" he says, reproachfully.

"Come !" is her only answer. He draws her hand through his arm, and they are off, walking fleetly, and in silence, along the bleak, windy road.

It wants a quarter of five when they reach the station. It is quite deserted, but there is a fire in the waiting-room.

He takes her in, and sees for the first time the silken robe, the velvet hat, the crimson shawl.

"My word, Joanna !" he says, laughing, "how smart you are ! As a bridegroom cometh out of his chamber ! Where did you raise all this superfine toggery ?"

"It belongs to Lora," answers Joanna, in the most matter-of-fact tone possible, "all but the shawl—that belongs to Liz ! The watch and brooch are my own. I did not want to shame you by being shabby."

He stares at her, then bursts out laughing ; but he is not best pleased, either, at these vague notions of *meum* and *tuum*. There is no time, however, to remonstrate ; the train rushes in almost immediately, and the instant it stops the runaways are aboard.

"Now then !" George Blake exclaims, " we are off at last ; let those catch who can ! In three hours wo will be in New York."

It is a silent trip. The young fellow sits lost in a happy dream. He will marry Joanna. They will board in the city for a little, then his mother will "come round," and his wife can live with her, while he will run down three or four times a week. By and by his salary will be raised, he will become an editor himself, he will take a nice little house over Brooklyn

8*

way, with a garden, a grape arbor, some rose trees and
geraniums, and he and Joanna will live happily forever
after !

That is his dream. For Joanna, what does *she*
dream of as she sits beside him, her lips compressed,
a line as of pain between her eyebrows, her eyes looking out at the gray, forlorn dawn. Nothing bright,
certainly, with that face.

They reach the city. The noise, the uproar, the
throng, the stony streets, bewilder her—she clings to
her protector's arm. He has decided to take her for
to-day to a hotel, and not present her to his landlady—
an austere lady—until he can present her as his lawful
wedded wife. So he calls a "keb," and they are driven
off to an up-town Broadway hotel.

"Is it always as noisy as this ?" she asks, in a sort
of panic. "My head is splitting already." ˙

"Oh, you will get used to it," he laughs ; "we all
do. You won't even hear it after awhile—*I* don't.
Here we are. Now you shall have breakfast, and then
I will start off, and hunt up a clergyman."

He squeezes her hand, but there is no response.
She withdraws it impatiently, and goes with him into
one of the parlors, where George engages a room for
his wife, and registers boldly as "Mr. and Mrs. George
P. Blake." Mrs. Blake is shown to her apartment,
where she washes her face, smooths her hair, straight-
ens herself generally, and then goes down with Mr.
Blake, to breakfast.

"Now, Jo," he says, when that repast is over, "you
will return to your room, and I will go out and get
you something to read, to pass the time, for I may be
gone some hours. I will fetch a parson with me if I

can ; if not, we will go this evening before a clergyman, and be married. Try not to feel lonesome. In a
few hours you will be my wife !"

Joanna does not look as if there were anything in
this prospect of a particularly rapturous nature, but
she goes to her room, and later accepts the magazines
he brings her, to while away the hours of his absence.
But it is a long day. She yawns over the stories and
pictures for awhile, then throws herself on a sofa, and
falls asleep.

It is late in the afternoon when she awakes.
George is there to take her to dinner, waiting impatiently.

"It is all right," he tells her. "The Reverend
Peter Wiley is my friend ; I have explained to him as
much as is necessary, and we are to go to his house at
nine this evening. I shall want some one to stand up
with me, so after dinner I'll run down to the office, if
you don't mind being alone a little longer, and get one
of our fellows."

They dine, and George again departs ; Joanna
once more returns to her own room. And now it is
drawing awfully near—this great change in her life—
she is about to become George Blake's wife. As she
sits here alone, her face buried in her hands, her whole
life seems to rise up before her—her whole dark, love-
less, most miserable life. A dreadful feeling of sullen,
silent anger possesses her as she sits alone here, her
hands clasped around her knees, her eyes staring
straight before her, after her usual crouching, ungainly
fashion. All the wrongs of her lifetime rise up before
her, a dark and gloomy array. Fatherless, motherless,
what had she done to be sent into the world banned at

her very birth? Hard fare, hard words, hard blows, oaths, kicks, cuffs, constant toil, half naked, half frozen, jeers, scorn, forever and forever! There it stands, the bitter, bad catalogue, never to be forgotten, never to be forgiven. A long life-time of reprisal will be too short to wash white the score her memory holds against almost every human creature she has ever known.

And yet, stay! Not quite all—not George Blake, poor foolish fellow, who has run away with her, or rather with whom *she* has run away. The tense lines of brow and mouth relax a little. It is too bad to have made him do it; he will never know what to do with her all the rest of his life. He will be sorry for it presently—she feels that, although, perhaps, *he* does not just now. But she has not thought of him, only of herself; it has been her one chance of escape from that earthly hell, and she has taken it. What is *she* that she should spare any one! After all, George Blake has asked her once, let him "dree his own weird," she will alter no plan of hers out of pity for him; he is useful to her, and when his day comes let him——

She stops. A quick footstep passes her door, a man's step, a man's voice whistles a gay air. Both are familiar; they strike on her heart like a blow. She springs up and flies to the door. Down the long passage a tall figure goes. A lady passes him; the whistle ceases, he uncovers as she goes by; then he too is gone.

For a moment she stands stunned, her face quite white, her eyes all wild and wide, in a sort of terror, her heart beating thick and fast. Then she darts to

the window, and but just in time. He is passing out
the last light of the evening sky falling full upon him
—handsome, as usual, carelessly elegant, as usual—the
dazzling image that has always appealed so powerfully
to this wild girl's imagination—that has made him
from the first, in her eyes, unlike any other man she
has ever seen. What is the charm? He is only a
well-looking, well-mannered, well-dressed young gentleman, the type of a class that in after years she meets
"thick as leaves in Vallambrosa," and yet, to the last
day of her life, something stamps Frank Livingston
as a "man of men" among them all. In one flashing
glance those quick eyes take in every detail of face,
and figure, and dress, even to the rosebud and gera-
nium leaf peeping out from under his dark paletot, the
white vest, the kid gloves. There is but time for a
glance. He lights a cigar, beckons a coupé, springs
in, and is gone.

She sits down as she has been sitting before, but in
a dazed sort of fashion that frightens even herself.
She tries to take up her train of thought where she has
dropped it—in vain. A swift, incomprehensible revulsion begins within her. She will not marry George
Blake—no, no! never, never! She springs up again,
and puts out her hands as if to keep even the idea off.
She will not marry George Blake—she will die first!
How has she ever thought of such a thing? Why has
she ever come here? Why is she staying here now?
If she stays he will come back and make her marry
him. Make her! She laughs a scornful little laugh,
all by herself, at the thought. But then his pleading
face and wistful boyish blue eyes rise before her. And
he is so fond of her, so ridiculously fond of her.

"Pshaw !" she says aloud, impatiently, "he is a fool to want me. He will get over it."

But she must not stay—it will not do to meet him. She must have been mad with misery ever to think of marrying him—*him!* Alas, for George Blake ! The haughty head erects itself, the straight throat curves. In one moment her mind is made up, beyond power of change. And all by one fleeting glimpse of Frank Livingston going to the opera.

She puts on her hat—Lora's hat—pulls it well down over her face, throws the heavy crimson shawl over her arm, and is ready to go. She writes no line or word of farewell—what is there to say ? And she is not romantic. George will see that she has gone— that is enough. Where is she going ? She does not know—only—not to marry young Mr. Blake. She opens the door, walks quickly down the long corridor, her head defiantly erect, prepared to do battle with George Blake should they meet. But she meets no one. The elevator is just descending ; she enters and goes down. A moment later and she is out, under the sparkling New Year stars, alone, homeless, penniless, in the streets of New York.

———◆•◆———

CHAPTER V.

IN WHICH JOANNA SEEKS HER FORTUNE.

HE yellow-tinted twilight has given place to silvery dark, lighted by a broad full moon. All lamps in the great thoroughfare are alight, windows are blazing like great jewels. Her spirits rise, the fresh night wind is like

strong wine, the old gypsy instinct of freedom awakes
within her. It is well! She is strong, she is *free!*
Oh! blessed freedom, boon beyond all boons of earth!
And for one whole day and night she has thought of
resigning it for life-long bondage to George Blake!
Free to do what she chooses, go where she likes; the
world is all before her, a great city full of infinite
possibilities is around her! No man is her master;
no man ever shall be!

She walks on and on, her blood quickening, her
heart rising. She could sing aloud in this first hour
of her exultation. She is free! her old life lies behind
her, with its shame, its pain, forever and ever. She is
here in the city of her desire, the world all before her
where to choose!

How brilliant the scene is to those country eyes;
how the lamps shine, how the great windows flash
out! But the roar, the rush of many people and
vehicles dizzies and bewilders her. Will she indeed
ever get used to it, as George Blake says? But she
puts away the thought of George Blake; a hot, swift
pang of remorse goes with it. How cruel, how ungrateful he will think her, and "ingratitude is the vice
of slaves." She will not think of him; it is all she can
do to keep from having a vertigo, amid all this light
and noise.

Presently she becomes conscious that curious eyes
are watching her. She does not know it, but she is a
conspicuous object even on Broadway. Her great
amazed black eyes, the unmistakable country stamp
about her, something out of the common in her eager
face, the brilliant shawl, render her a distinct mark in
the moving picture.

And then all at once she realizes that she is being followed, that a man is close at her elbow, has been for some time, and is looking down at her with a sinister leer. He is a big, burly man, with a red face, a mangy, purple mustache, all nose and watch-chain, like a Jew. She glances up at him angrily; he only returns it with a smile of fascinating sweetness.

"You was waitin' for me, my dear, wasn't you?" he says, insinuatingly.

She does not reply, only hurries on, her heart beginning to beat. A policeman passes and eyes the pair suspiciously, but Joanna does not know enough of city ways to appeal to him. She takes these tall men, bound in blue and brass, to be soldiers, and is afraid of them. She walks rapidly—so rapidly, with that free, elastic step she has learned in treading the woods, that her pursuer anathematizes her under·his breath. She has got off Broadway now, and takes corners and streets as they come, and still, with a perseverance worthy a much better cause, her tormentor follows. He has no breath left for conversation. He is stout, his wind is gone, he is gasping like a stranded fish; he lags a step or two behind, and a stern chase is always a long one. Joanna is as fresh as when she started. Suddenly she turns round and faces him, and something in her eyes looks so wicked, so dangerous, that the fellow stops. The next moment she has flown round a corner and disappeared. There is nothing for the owner of the mangy mustache but to get on the first car and go back.

She wanders on and on, glancing about her suspiciously now, lest the florid gentleman should have successors, but no one troubles her. She wonders where

she is.   Up here the streets are quiet ; long rows of
handsome brown houses, as much alike as pins in a
paper, are on either hand.   Pedestrians are few and
walk fast ; the blue and brass soldiers pass her now
and then, but say nothing.   Lights gleam from base-
ment windows.   She pauses and looks wistfully at the
pictures within.   Long tables, laid with white damask,
glass and silver sparkling as at Mrs. Abbott's, servants
moving about.   Sometimes it is a parlor interior, a
long, glowing room lit with great glass globes, a young
girl at the piano, the music coming to where the homeless listener wearily stands ; mamma with a book or
work, papa with his paper, little children flitting about.
A great pain is at her heart.   Oh ! what happy people
there are in the world !   Girls like her, with bright
homes, happy, cherished, beloved, *good.*   She is not
good ; she never has been, she never will be—it is not in
her nature.   She has been born different from others—
more wicked, sullen, fierce, vindictive, and now, last of
all, ungrateful.   A great sob rises in her throat ; she
moves hurriedly on.   She is cold, and tired, and home-
sick—she, who has never had a home, who, more than
ever before, is homeless to-night.   The hard pavement
burns and blisters her feet, used to tread elastic turf.
It is growing very late, and very cold.   Where shall
she stay until morning ?   She cannot walk much longer ; her wearied limbs lag even now.   What shall
she do ?

    The quiet of these up-town streets begins to fright-
en her.   The blinds are all closed now ; the sweet
home-pictures can dazzle her no more.   She must get
back to where there are light and life—to that brilliant, gas-lit, store-lit street she found herself in first.

But she cannot find it; she is in another bright thoroughfare before long, but it is not the same—it is the Bowery.

A clock somewhere strikes ten. Her head is dizzy, a mist is before her eyes, her feet fail, a panic seizes her; she grasps a railing to keep from falling. She can go no farther, come what may.

A little ahead there is a building that looks like a church. She moves toward it, goes up the steps, and sinks down in a heap. A pillar screens her partly; she crouches into the farthest corner, shuts her eyes, and tries to rest.

What shall she do?

The question beats like a trip-hammer through her dazed brain. She has no money, not one penny; she does not know one living soul of all these restless hundreds who flit by. And yet it is characteristic of her stubborn resolution that she never once repents having run away from George Blake, nor thinks of making her way back to him. She knows the name of the hotel she has quitted; it is probable she might find it again, but the thought never occurs to her. Whatever comes, all that is past and done with; she will never take a single step backward to save herself from the worst fate that can befall.

What shall she do? She feels she cannot stay crouched here on the cold stones all night. Whither shall she go?—to whom appeal? She has spent many a night in the open air before—nights as cold as this —but the old mill was her safe shelter, the familiar croak of her friends, the frogs, her welcome, the solemn surge of the forest her lullaby. Here there are men more to be feared than wild beasts, pitiless

people, who look at her with hard, staring eyes, the
"car rattling o'er the stony street," noise, light,
danger. She has spent no night like this in all her life.

Soon what she fears most comes to pass—the
gleam of that fatal red shawl catches the quick eye of
a passer-by. He stops, pauses in the tune he is whistling, peers for a moment, then bounds up the steps,
and stands beside her.

"Sa-a-y, you, hullo !"

She looks up. It is only a boy, a gamin of the
New York streets, with a precocious, ugly, shrewd
little face—a boy of perhaps thirteen. The infinite
misery of her eyes strikes this young gentleman with
a sense of surprise.

"Sa-a-y," he repeats, "dodgin' a cop ?"

The tone is questioning ; the words, of course, are
perfectly incomprehensible. She does not reply.

"Sa-a-y ! Can't yer speak ? Dodgin' a cop ?"

The tone this time is sympathetic, and is meant to
reassure her. If she is performing the action in question, he wishes to inform her he has performed it himself, and that she may count on his commiseration.

"I don't know what you mean," she says, wearily.
"I am from the country ; I have lost my way in the
streets. I have no home, no friends. I was very tired,
and I sat down here to rest."

Her head drops against the cold pillar. She is utterly spiritless and worn out. He stares at her for a
moment, says "Golly !" softly to himself, and slowly
resumes his whistle. He is debating whether to believe
what she says or not.

"Sa-a-y !" he drawls, after a little, "got any
money ?"

"Not a penny."

He resumes his whistle once more. Once more the keen eyes of the boy of the streets goes over her, takes in the silk dress, the gleam of gold, the crimson shawl, the weary, weary face.

"Sa-a-y! what brought ye up to York?"

"I came with a—friend. But I did not want to stay. I came out and lost myself. You need not ask me questions. I cannot tell you more than that. I do not know what to do. I have no money to go to another hotel."

"*Another* hotel! Cricky! We've been in a hotel —Fifth Avenoo or the Windsor, I shouldn't wonder. Sa-a-y, I'm blessed if I don't believe you're tellin' the truth!"

She looks up at him indignantly. The cute, boyish face is a good-humored one, and his youth gives her courage.

"I wish you would tell me what to do," she says, piteously. "You belong here, and must know. I cannot stay here all night."

"Should think not. Well, you might go to the station for protection."

"The what?"

"The station—*pol*iss, you know."

"Why should I go there?" she exclaims, angrily. "I have done nothing wrong. How dare you suggest such a thing!"

"Blessed if you ain't a green un!" the boy says, grinning. "If you won't go there, and get lodgin' free gratis for nothin', where will ye go? *Sure* you got no money?"

"Certain. Not one penny."

"Well, what's that a shinin' so—a gold chain? If it *is* gold—the real Jeremiah, mind—you might put it up the spout, and get money that way. *I'll* show you your uncle's."

She looks at him with such bewildered eyes that he grins again.

"Oh! she's a green un, and no mistake. Looky here," he says, adapting his conversation to his company, "if I get you a lodgin', a clean, comfortable, 'spectable lodgin', will you pawn your jewelry to pay for it? 'Cause if you will, I guess I can help you."

"Oh! most willingly!" she says, relieved.

The brooch and chain are gifts she hates to part with, but anything is better than risking a night here. She rises at once, and hastily begins to divest herself of them.

"Don't you take 'em off now," the boy says, good-naturedly. "To-morrow 'll do. Come along. It's a goodish bit of a walk. We might take a car, but you've no money, and I haint earned salt to my porridge to-day."

"Do you work?" Joanna asks, eyeing the box and brushes he carries.

"You bet! Sells papers in the mornin' and shines boots the rest o' the time. Haint done a stroke worth a cent to-day. Times is awful bad," says this man of business, despondently. "Gents that always took a shine before, goes muddy now, sooner'n part with a blamed nickel!"

"Where are you taking me?" the girl inquires. She is in some trepidation, although the lad's face is not a bad one, and she is dead tired.

"Home, to our house—my old woman's, you know.

Laundress *she* is ; does up gents' and ladies' fine linen.
We've got a spare room in the attic, and now and then
we lets it for lodgin' to girls out o' place—help, ye
know. Mother knows 'em by dozens. They pays a
dollar and a half a week and grubs theirselves. It's
empty now, and I guess you can have it. You look
the right sort, you do. Mother don't take no other,
mind you. 'Taint much farther—up four pair, but the
roof's handy for dryin'."

Joanna is too spent to talk, so in silence they presently reach the place. It *is* up four pairs, and very
long pairs at that ; she feels as though she could never
reach the top. They do reach it, however ; the boy
opens a door, there is a flood of light, a gush of
warmth, and they are "there."

It is now after eleven, but late as is the hour, the
boy's mother is still pursuing her avocation. Upon a
stove glowing red-hot, stands an array of smoothing-
irons; at a long, narrow table in the middle of the
floor the woman stands, polishing the bosom of a shirt.

The room is perfectly neat and clean, two lamps
light it brightly. The woman herself is in a spotless
calico dress and long white apron, and looks both respectable and, like her son, good-natured. On a trun-
dle-bed, in a corner, two children lie asleep.

"Bless us, Thad, how late you are!" she begins.
Then she sees his companion, and stops inquiringly,
but in no surprise, and smiles a welcome. "Good
evening, miss. Come in, and take an air of the fire.
You look half froze."

Joanna advances. The mother takes in, as the son
has done, the silk dress, the golden trinkets, the fine crimson shawl, and her face grows first puzzled, then grave.

She turns to her son, with something of a frown, and motions him into an adjoining room.

"Who is this you have brought?" she asks. "*I* don't know her."

"No more do I," Thad rejoins; "but she's all right—bet you ten cents on it! She ain't no help—no more she ain't a street-tramper. She's a country gal, and greener'n grass. Cut away from her friends, I guess, and come to New York to seek her fortune. They all do it! Don't she hope she may find it !"

"Where did you pick her up?" the mother asks, still dissatisfied.

Thad explains at some length. Thad's mother listens, neither satisfied nor convinced.

"I'd rather have my room empty forever, you know that," she says, with some asperity, "than harbor half the ruck that's going. If I thought she *wasn't* all right, I'd bundle her off again, and let her go to the station, and box your ears into the bargain! I won't have girls picked up from the streets. I only lodge respectable young women out of place."

"Well, *she's* a respectable young woman out o' place," says Thad. "S-a-y, mother, don't let us stand here jawin'. Give a fellow his supper, can't you, and let him go to bed."

"And you say she's got no money?" says the woman.

"No ; but she's got a gold chain, and the best o' clothes, and is willin' to put 'em up the spout first thing to pay you. Say, mother, you can't turn her out, so cheese it all, and give us some supper."

He returns impatiently to the kitchen, where Jo-anna still sits in a cane rocker near the stove. The warmth, the rest, the silence, have lulled her into sleep. Her head lies against the back, her hat is off, her pale, tired face has the look of a spent child.

The woman bends over her, and gradually the perturbed expression leaves her face. No—on that brow the dreadful brand of the streets has never rested. She is little better than a child in years; the story she has told Thad must be true. She is one of those foolish, romance-reading country girls who run away from home and come to New York to seek their fortunes. There are so many of them—so many! Poor souls! the fortune they mostly find is ruin and sin for life, and a death of dark despair. This girl has evidently been well off; her dress is of rich silk, handsomely trimmed and made, she wears a gold chain and watch, a breastpin, and ring. And the shawl on her lap; the woman's eyes glisten as she lifts it. All her life it has been her ambition to own a shawl like this, all wool, deeply, darkly, beautifully red. All her life it has been an ambition unattained.

"I will keep her a fortnight for this shawl," she thinks, replacing it, "if she's a mind to make the bargain."

Thad is calling lustily for his supper. It is soon set before him—some slices of cold corned beef, some bread and butter, and coffee. The lad falls to with an appetite, and his mother gently awakens Joanna.

"You must be hungry," she says; "take some supper and go to bed."

But Joanna is not hungry; she dined late, and fared well. She is very, very tired, though, and will go to bed, with her hostess's permission.

"My name is Gibbs," suggests the matron, taking

one of the lamps, "Mrs. Gibbs. Will you tell me yours?"

For a moment there is a pause. She has no name. The hated one of Sleaford is not hers; she would not retain it if it were. Blake, she thinks of giving; but no, she has no right to poor George's name. The only one that belongs to her is Joanna—Wild Joanna. Then it flashes upon her—she has only to reverse that, and she is now christened for life.

"My name is Wild," she says, "Joanna Wild."

"And you look it," thinks Mrs. Gibbs, going on with the lamp; "wild by name, and wild by nature, I dare say. But you're not a street-tramper, and that's a beautiful shawl, so it's all right."

The room is a tiny attic chamber, with a sloping roof, and lit by only two lights of glass. The bed is wide enough to lie down on, but certainly to turn in it would be a serious risk. Still it looks perfectly clean, and that is everything. The floor is bare; one chair comprises all the furniture there is space for.

"I hope you will sleep well," says Mrs. Gibbs, kindly. "There's a bolt on the door, if you've a mind to, but you're quite safe up here."

"Thank you," Joanna says. "Good night."

Mrs. Gibbs returns to her son and her work—two is her general hour for retiring.

"Gone to roost, has she?" inquires Thad, still going into his supper with energy and appetite. "She's a rum un, she is. Wonder if her mother knows she's out?"

And so, by the mercy of Heaven, Joanna is saved from the streets, and sleeps deeply, dreamlessly, and long, in her hard little attic bed.

9

CHAPTER VI.

IN WHICH JOANNA FINDS HER FORTUNE.

ITH the rising of the next morning's frosty sun, Joanna's new life may fairly be said to begin. It is rather late when she descends to the room with the cooking-stove, which is kitchen, parlor, dining-room, and children's sleeping-room, inclusive. The little black stove so superheats it that the windows are open, and two or three pots of hardy rose geraniums flourish on the sills. They make a pleasant spot of color to the girl's country eyes, with their vivid green leaves and pink blossoms. Sunlight finds the room as tidy as lamplight. Mrs. Gibbs stands over a tub in a corner, washing, a little boy and girl of five toddle about, each with a doll made out of a bottle. This is the home scene that greets Joanna.

"Good morning," Mrs. Gibbs says. "How did you rest, my dear?"

Mrs. Gibbs' language and manners are superior to her station, and Mrs. Gibbs greatly prides herself thereon. She is a person of literary tastes, and has seen better days. The better days were in the lifetime of the late Mr. Gibbs, when she had but little to do, and a great deal of time to read romances, of which she is exceedingly fond.

Mr. Gibbs was by profession a mason's assistant, in other words, a hod-carrier, and one day, overcome by sun-stroke, fell off a scaffolding and was instantly

killed.   That was four years ago, and since then Mrs.
Gibbs had adopted the occupation of laundress, and
wisely eschewed romance.   But what she has read has
left its mark.   Her eldest son making his appearance
about the time she completed "Thaddeus of Warsaw,"
was named after that hero.   After a pause of seven
years, twins arriving almost simultaneously with a copy
of "Alonzo and Melissa," these innocents were christened after that romantic pair.   It is Alonzo and Melissa who are now pressing to their chubby bosoms two
root-beer bottles, and pausing in their play to stare
with round, wondering eyes at the new-comer.   Thaddeus has departed to retail the day's news, and after-
ward "shine" gentlemen's boots.

"I slept very well," Joanna answers, and holds out
her hand with a smile to the little ones.

She loves children, and her eyes brighten at sight
of them.   Many good traits are in the girl's character
that have never had a chance to come out—this is one
of them.   She has never known a child in her life.

Alonzo and Melissa look at her, and, with the in-
tuitive instinct of children and dogs, see in her a friend
at once.

"Perhaps you won't mind getting your own breakfast?" says Mrs. Gibbs.   "I'm busy, as you see.
There's the teapot on the stove, and the dishes, and
bread and butter are in the pantry.   Set the table
yourself and take your breakfast."

"I feel as if I were a burden to you," Joanna says,
"but I hope it will not be for long.   I have no money
now, but the very first I earn I will give you."

She says it with an honesty and earnestness her
hostess sees is very real.   Mrs. Gibbs finds she "likes

the looks of her" by daylight, though she is an un-
common-looking young woman somehow, too.

"What do you intend to do?" she asks, rubbing
away at the shirt she is at work upon.

She smiles a little to herself as she asks—she knows
so well what the answer will be. All these girls who
run away from their friends seem to have but one idea
—to go on the stage and dazzle the New York public
as full-fledged Lady Macbeths. They may leave home
plain and unattractive enough, but something in the
air of the great city is to make them beautiful and
talented, and send them home to their relatives in a
few years, dazzling visions of loveliness, fame, and
wealth. It happens like that to their favorite heroines,
why not to them? But Joanna's reply is not to order.

"I intend to work," she says steadily ; "there is no
kind of housework, I think, I cannot do. I am very
strong, and very willing. I can wash, iron, cook—I
have done it all my life."

Mrs. Gibbs is so astonished that she pauses in her
washing, and, with suds up to her elbows, gazes admir-
ingly at the speaker.

"Well! upon my word!" she says. Then she
laughs, and vigorously resumes her rubbing. "I didn't
expect that, you see," she explains. "Work is the
last thing girls that run—come up from the country—
seem to think of. I have known lots of 'em, and I
never knew one yet who wanted to work. They can
get enough of that at home. They want to go on the
stage, and be ballet girls, actresses, what not. They seem
to think the New York flagstones are made of gold.
Poor things, they soon find out their mistake! Sometimes they go back ashamed and half starved, some-

times they stay on, and—ah ! dear me, the city is a
bad place for a friendless country girl. And *you* want
to work. Oh, well ! you will get that fast enough ;
always plenty to do for willing hands and hearts. And
housework's easier got than most things, than places
in stores, or sewing, or genteel things like that. But
I wonder, seeing it's a hard life, that you came up for
that. By your dress you should have been pretty well
off down there—wherever it is. You won't make
enough at housework, let me tell you, to buy silk
dresses like that, and gold watches and chains."

Joanna glances down at her silk robe and smiles,
wondering what good Mrs. Gibbs would say if she
knew the truth.

"You must have had a good home," continues the
widow, "and kind friends. Take my advice, Miss
Wild, and go back before it is too late. The city is
not what you think it. Go back to your good home,
no matter how hard you may have to work, and thank
the Lord you've got it."

"It was not a good home," Joanna says, steadily.
"I had not kind friends. It was a bad, cruel place to
live in. Yes, bad, and they were bad people. I had
no friends in that house."

"And yet your dress, your jewelry——"

"Oh ! the dress ! that is nothing !" the girl says,
with a touch of her old impatience ; "the watch and
chain were New Year gifts from a lady who *was* kind
to me. But I cannot go back—I never will go back.
I am willing and able to work ; you may recommend
me without fear. The jewelry I will sell and pay you
—the watch I should like to keep for the lady's sake,"
her voice falters a little. "You have been kind to me

—you have saved me from the streets.   As sure as I
live, you will find me grateful."

There is silence.   Mrs. Gibbs rubs away, Joanna
clears off the breakfast service.   Suddenly the widow
breaks out :

"Look here, Miss Wild, I don't want to take no
mean advantage of you, but, of course, I can't afford
to keep you for nothing.   But I will keep you, board,
and everything, for—say a fortnight—that will give
you time to look about you and get used to town, for
that red shawl of yours.   There ! I like that shawl.
If you think it a fair exchange, say so."

She looks eagerly as she makes the proposal, evidently fearing a refusal.   That any one can possess
such a beautiful garment, and be willing to part with
it, is what she does not expect.   But Joanna's face
lights with relief at the offer.

"The red shawl !" she exclaims, laughing, and again
wondering what honest Mrs. Gibbs would say if she
knew how she had come by it, "why, certainly.   I am
glad to be rid of it—*I* could not wear a red shawl if I
wanted to.   I am sure I do not know why I bought it.
Take it and welcome."

The widow draws a long breath—the desire of many
years is attained at last.

"Well, I'm sure, I'm much obliged.   It's a beautiful shawl, all wool, soft as silk, and such a lovely color.
I will tell you what I'll do," cries Mrs. Gibbs, in a
burst of gratitude, "you shall stay for three weeks, if
you've a mind to, and Thad shall take you about Sundays, and I'll find you a nice easy place in a small family, as waitress, or nurse-girl, or something of the sort
Would you mind wearing a cap, and white apron ?"

It appears, upon explanation, that Joanna *would*
mind those badges of servitude, although otherwise
preferring the situation of children's nurse.

" Well, then, it must be general housework, I suppose," says Mrs. Gibbs, " but never mind. I'll find you
a nice, easy place, with only two or three in the family, and every Sunday out. You must come to see me
often, and look upon this as your home whenever out
of place."

Amicable relations of the warmest kind being thus
established through the medium of Liz's brilliant red
shawl, no more is said. But fate has decreed that Joanna is not to get that " nice, easy place," or begin life
as a maid of all work. Her voice and her five years'
steady training stand her in stead at last, in the very
way she least expects.

It begins by the cordial friendship that springs up
in the bosoms of Alonzo and Melissa for Miss Wild.
They take to her, and she to them, in a way quite wonderful, considering the brevity of the acquaintance.

On the evening of the third day, as Joanna sits in
the rocking-chair before the glowing stove, with Melissa and her " bottle baby " in her lap, it chances that,
half unconsciously, she begins to sing. It is that little
Scotch song Frank Livingston used ,to like, " My ain
ingle side."

Mrs. Gibbs is ironing. Outside a wild night is closing in, with high wind, and lashing sleet, and rain.
As Joanna sings and rocks, she is thinking how this
fierce tempest is surging through the pine woods, rattling the timbers of the old mill, troubling the frozen
depths of Black's Dam. She shudders to think that
but for George Blake—oh, poor George Blake!—she

might be lying at this hour dead in. its foul waters.
What are they doing at Sleaford's ?—what at Abbott
Wood ? What does Mrs. Abbott, Geoffrey, Leo, think
of her ? Is George Blake seeking her through the vast
city in vain ? Is Frank Livingston going to the opera,
or the theater, or a ball somewhere up in these stately
brown-stone streets ?

As she thinks she sings, and as she sings, Mrs. Gibbs
gradually ceases work, and listens with open mouth.
The Scotch song is finished ; she begins another, a
German cradle song this time, a crooning, sweet sort
of lullaby, that Leo used to like at this hour. The
iron in the listener's hand has grown cold ; she stands
lost in wonder at this singing bird she has caged.

"Lord bless me, Miss Wild !" she says, when Joanna ceases, "wherever did you learn to sing like
that ?"

The girl looked up at her vacantly, not yet returned
from dream-land.

"Eh ?" she says ; "singing ? Was I singing ? I
did not know it. I was thinking of something else."

Mrs. Gibbs stares.

"Upon my word, Miss Wild," she exclaims, "you
are a strange young woman ! Why, you sing like a
—like a—like Mademoiselle Azelma herself !"

"Who is Mademoiselle Azelma ?"

"She's a singing lady—a German. Who learned
you to sing in German ? I declare, I never was more
surprised in my life !"

"Indeed ! Because I can sing ? Oh, yes, I can
sing—I can play, too, although my hands do not look
like it," Joanna says, smiling.

"You're the most wonderful young girl I ever

came across !" repeats wondering Mrs. Gibbs. " Who would ever think you could sing like that ? Do sing another—out loud this time. Never mind Lissy—she's asleep."

Joanna obeys. She uplifts that fine, pure, strong contralto of hers, and sings " Roberto o tu che adoro," and the Italian, and the compass of voice, and the thrilling sweetness of the song itself, completely confounds good Mrs. Gibbs. She gives up utterly, and sits down.

" Well, I never !" she says, and stares blankly at the girl. "I never in all my life !"—another stare. "I do declare I *never* did !" says Mrs. Gibbs, and gets up again with a gasp.

Joanna laughs outright. She has a delightful laugh—merry, girlish, sweet—but its sound is so unusual it startles herself.

" Is it so very wonderful, then ?" she says, still laughing. " I know I sing well ; I was well taught."

" Tell me this," says Mrs. Gibbs, almost angrily— " why did you say you had no friends, when you have the education, and manners, and dress of a lady ? Why, your musical education must have cost a sight."

" I suppose it did. I told you I had one friend— the lady who gave me my watch. When I was a little, half-starved, ill-used child, she heard me sing, and thought my voice worth cultivating. She has educated me ; I owe her everything. She would have taken me for good, long ago, only those I lived with would not give me up."

" Why did you not go to her when you ran away ?"

" I would not have been allowed to remain. There

9*

were other reasons besides. But you need not be afraid ; I will work just as well when you get me that place, as though I could not sing a note."

" *You* work !" retorts Mrs. Gibbs, almost contemptuously ; " with such a voice as that ! I will get you no place. I will speak to Mr. Ericson about you instead."

Joanna looks inquiringly.

"Mr. Ericson is a German," says the widow, resuming her work—"a teacher of music and singing. I do up his linen. His brother is proprietor of a theater—a little German theater—and Mlle. Azelma sings there, and makes ever so much money. But Mlle. Azelma is a very difficult lady to get along with ; whenever she is out of temper, it flies to her throat, and she cannot sing that night. Professor Ericson swears at her awful in Dutch, and says if he could get any one to take her place, he would send her about her business. Now, I have heard her, and I do think you sing better than she does ; and then you have been trained to singing, which is everything. To-morrow I am going to take his shirts home, and you shall go with me, and sing for him. If he takes a fancy to you your fortune is made."

" But I don't want to go on the stage," Joanna says, blankly ; "I could not. I never was in a theater in my life. I never thought of such a thing."

" Then you had better begin, for it's the very thing to suit you, with that voice. You will earn ten times as much as in any other way, and if you know how to take care of yourself, it's as safe as any other life. It's a most respectable little theater, only not first-class, of course. Fashionable people don't go there. Mr

Ericson has given me and Thad tickets often.   Make up your mind, my dear, that that voice wasn't given you for nothing, or all that teaching either, and earn your living in the easiest way.   Come with me to-morrow, and let Mr. Ericson hear you."

Joanna is startled ; the idea is new, but she is open to conviction.   She goes with Mrs. Gibbs on the morrow, and is presented in due form to Herr Ericson, a little, yellow man, with a bushy white mustache and a frowning brow.

" You can sing ?" he says, scowling under his eyebrows at the girl.   " Bah !   Mrs. Gibbs does not know singing when she hears it.   You can play?   There is a piano—while I pay for my shirts, sit down and sing a song."

His brusque manner sets Joanna more completely at her ease than any civility.   He looks at her contemptuously.   She will show this cross little man she *can* sing.   She seats herself, plays a prelude, and begins one of her best German songs.   The little professor counts out his laundress's money, stops suddenly, fixes his spectacles more securely on his nose, rises hastily, crosses to the piano, and scowls a scowl of intense surprise.

" Good !" he says ; a trifle more snappishly though, if possible, than before.   " You can sing.   And you have been trained.   That is a very good song, and rendered with expression.   You want to go on the stage ?"

Joanna shrugs her shoulders.

" I really do not care about it, Herr Professor.   I never thought of such a thing until Mrs. Gibbs suggested it."

"Humph ! If I get you a place will you accept it ?"

"A place ?"

"A situation—an engagement to sing at my brother's theater. The salary will not be much at first.
You can go on in the chorus, and so get used to the
stage. And I have a project in my mind. Yes, a project——"

He breaks off, and walks rapidly up and down, his
hands in his pantaloons' pockets, frowning horribly,
and biting his mustache.

"Look you here !" he says, "you can sing. You
suit me. · You are the sort of a young woman I have
been looking for for some time. Plenty can sing.
Bah ! that is nothing ! A voice without cultivation—
that is the devil ! You have been trained. In a week
you might go before an audience and make your *debut*.
You shall go before an audience. You shall make
your *debut !* Tell me this—who are your friends ?"

"I have none, Mr. Ericson."

"Good ! Better and better ! Friends are the very
deuce ! Now listen to me. Hundreds would jump at
the offer I am going to make, with voices as good as
yours, only not the cultivation—mind you ! You have
a voice—yes ! You will make a success—true ! You
will never be a great cantatrice !" shaking one nervous
finger at her ; "do not think it. Not a Nilsson, not a
Patti—nothing like it—but a fair singer, a popular vocalist, that you will be. And you shall make your
debut at my brother's theater, and you shall be paid,
and you shall be my *protegee*. Mlle. Azelma shall go
to the devil ! But you will make no engagement with
my brother, for I have another project in my head,"
tapping that member. "Later you shall hear. To·

day I will speak to my brother ; to-morrow night you shall go on in the chorus. Good day !"

He turns them out of the room, then flies after, and calls back Mrs. Gibbs. For Joanna, she is fairly bewildered with the rapidity of all this.

"You take care of that girl, Madame Gibbs !" the professor says, frowning fiercely. "Mark you ! she has a fortune in her throat."

It all comes to pass as the professor wills. He is a sort of human whirlwind, with no idea of letting any other living creature have a will of his own where *he* is. He does speak to "my brother"—a large, mild man of true German stolidity. He provides a costume for the *debutante*, and sends her on in the chorus. It is a small theater ; the performance is German, the actors, the singers, the audience are all German. Joanna goes on and goes off with a phlegm that even Professor Ericson admires. She is nothing daunted by all the faces, and is used to drawing-room performances.

After a night or two, she begins to enter into the spirit of the thing, and to like it. The professor loses no time ; he begins at once to drill her in Mlle. Azelma's principal roles. She hears that popular primadonna, and feels convinced she can equal her, at least. A spirit of ambition, of rivalry, arises within her. The first time Azelma's temper flies to her throat, she, Miss Wild, is to take her place.

That time is not long coming. Mlle. Azelma's latest costume fits badly, her larynx is at once affected ; that evening she is too seriously indisposed to sing— something else must be substituted. Nothing else *shall*, swears the Herr Professor. And in a beautiful costume, Miss Wild, to the surprise of everybody,

takes Mlle. Azelma's part, and sings better than that
lady ever did in all her life. The audience applaud
—they, like the management, are tired of the leading
lady's caprices. Herr Ericson glows with delight.
He fairly clasps Joanna in his arms when she comes
off.

"You sing like an angel," he cries, in a rapture.
"Mlle. Azelma may go hang herself! Ah! I foresee
my project will be a grand success."

Next day the project is unfolded. It is to travel
through the country, with Joanna, and another *protege*
of his, a young Italian tenor he has picked up and in-
structed, and give concerts. Madame Ericson, who is
also a vocalist of no mean ability, goes with them.
They will be a company of four; and they will storm
the provinces! They will make their fortunes! They
will see life! They will cover themselves with im-
mortality!

It suits Joanna exactly. Already she is anxious
to leave New York. Twice she has passed Frank Livingston on the street, and once on horseback in the
park. On neither occasion has he noticed her, but the
rencontre has set her heart beating wildly. Riding in
the park, with a young lady by his side, he has looked
like a demi-god in Joanna's dazed eyes, something so
far above and beyond her, that she wonders to remember
she has ever spoken to him at all. And her last words
to him were a bitter rebuke. She is not safe in New
York; he, or George Blake, may meet and recognize
her, any day. To all who have known her, she wishes
to be forever lost.

Early in May the little company are to start. All this
time Joanna has gone on living with Mrs. Gibbs, whom

she has paid and repaid, over and over again. The rest of her earnings are swallowed up by a wardrobe, which the Herr Professor insists shall be handsome and abundant. She is to sing songs in character, and many costumes are needed to fit them all.

The winter days fly by. May comes, warm and sunny. From Brightbrook she has heard nothing. She does not want to hear. That life is dead and done with, it holds no memory that is not of pain. Sleaford's Joanna lives no more. Miss Wild does, and her new life seems to open pleasantly and promisingly enough. About the middle of May they leave New York, and Joanna is fairly launched in her new life.

CHAPTER VII.

THE TRAGEDY AT SLEAFORD'S.

AND at Brightbrook? It chances that Mr. Giles Sleaford is absent from the bosom of his family while all these disastrous affairs are going on. Mr. Sleaford is a patron of the ring, and a pugilistic encounter for the championship of a town some forty miles away takes place about this time.

In company with some other congenial souls, Giles is on the spot, betting heavily, drinking deeply, swearing roundly, and using his own fists—mawlers, Mr. Sleaford terms them—freely when occasion offers. And so it falls out that for nine days after the flight of Joanna, that flight remains a secret to Black Giles.

On the evening of that ninth day Mr. Sleaford re

turns to his home and family, blacker than usual, more
savage than usual, a sadder, though by no means a
wiser man, cursing his luck, his eyes, the road, the
weather, and prefixing the British adjective "bloody"
to each, as he jogs along.

The road is certainly rutty, the weather especially
gloomy and raw. A keen January wind is blowing,
and driving the sleet in fierce, slanting lines into Mr.
Sleaford's inflamed and whisky-bleared eyes.

A great bitterness is upon him ; the vanity of all
things earthly, of P. R. set-to's in particular, has been
forced upon him rudely. The man he has backed has
been beaten, shamefully and hopelessly, and put in
chancery in three rounds. Put not your trust in prize
fighters, has been sadly brought home to Mr. Giles
Sleaford.

He ambles on, on his jaded horse, stopping at every
"pub," until, as the black and sleety winter night is
closing in, he reaches the Red Farm.

The cheery light of fire and lamp streams far out
over the iron-bound road ; warmth and the savory
smell of supper greet him. But Mr. Sleaford's pater-
nal greeting is growled out, strongly impregnated with
whisky fumes, and is a gruff command for Joanna to
come and pull off his boots. His (adjective) hands are
so (adjective) froze that bless his (adjective) eyes, if
he can do it himself !

There is a pause ; Jud and the two girls exchange
glances. They are all afraid of their father, except
Dan, and Dan at the present moment is not there.
Neither is Joanna, Mr. Sleaford sees, but in her place
is a strapping country lass of fifteen or so, whom he
eyes with surly amaze and disfavor.

"Well, bless my (adjective) eyes!" repeats Mr. Sleaford, ferociously, "what the —— do you mean, by standin' there like a passell of stuck pigs, and starin'? Why the —— don't you call that gal?"

"Looky here, dad," says Jud, to whom the girls mutely appeal, "it's no good making a row, but Joanna ain't here. She's cut and run—there!"

"Hey?" roars Giles Sleaford, staring in fierce amazement at his son.

"True as gospel, dad—cut and run a week—nine days ago—with George Blake."

"And stole all our things—my new silk suit and hat, and Liz's shawl!" chimes in Lora.

"Went off at break of day, to New York, with Blake," continued Jud, plucking up heart of grace to face his formidable father. "Cut Dan's head open with a horsewhip first, and all for wanting her to sing at Watjen's."

Giles Sleaford's jaw drops; his eyes start as if about to fall from their sockets. He is still "far wide" —he only takes in the one blank fact that Joanna has run away.

"This is how it was," goes on Jud, seeing his parent's mystification.

And thereupon gives a dispassionate and perfectly correct version of the whole proceeding. He does not spare Dan; in his heart Jud exults in the pluck Joanna has shown, and chuckles inwardly whenever he looks at his brother's wound. He, himself, has never lifted his hand to the girl.

Giles Sleaford listens in dead silence. Even after his son has done, he sits staring with open mouth and eyes, quite rigid and mute.

This is so unexpected and thrilling that the Misses Sleaford exchange apprehensive looks ; they have ex- pected an outburst of rage and red-hot oaths—they hear neither.

With a snap, Black Giles's jaws come together again, as the chops of a dog close over a bone. Then he takes down his short black pipe, and slowly begins to load it to the muzzle—all without a word of com- ment. He lights up, fills the kitchen with volumes of smoke, always in awful and ominous silence.

Presently Dan comes in, and his father eyes in a peculiar way the longitudinal strip of plaster that adorns his brow. No greeting, except a grumbling sort of grunt on Dan's part, is exchanged.

Mr. Sleaford sits buried in profound reflection. Supper is announced, strong and savory, as it is in the nature of the Sleaford repasts to be. Fried beefsteak smothered in onions and grease, mashed potatoes, hot buckwheat cakes and tea. Giles takes out his pipe, and falls to, with the sharp-set air of a man who has traveled forty miles, and who does not permit the loss of two hundred dollars, and a household drudge, to impair his appetite. But the Sleaford family are, one and all, valiant trenchermen and women.

Seen through the lighted windows, it is a cheerful picture enough of rough, homely comfort and abun- dance—the bountifully spread table, the five healthy, dark-skinned, highly-colored faces—but the repast is eaten in perfect silence, except a few whispered re- marks between the girls.

Outside, the sleet is still lashing the glass, and the night has fairly closed in, in dense darkness and storm. This is the subject of the whispers, and a matter of some concern to the Misses Sleaford, who are due at a dance some few miles up the village, and the unpleasant weather is something of a damper to their expected enjoyment.

After supper, still without a word, Giles gets up, buttons his rough coat, puts on his fur cap, twists some yards of red scarf about his neck, and leaves the house. The young people look at each other uneasily.

"Did you tell the old man?" asks Dan.

"Jud did," says Lora, "and he never said a word —not one single blessed word. I wonder where he's going?"

"What d'ye bet it ain't to Abbott Wood?" says Jud, carefully putting his beloved fiddle in its case. "That old red rooster up there knows more about our dad than any one else. He's going for money. He's been pretty well shook, for I know he backed the Brightbrook Beauty heavy, and he's gone for another supply of the needful. I thought he'd raise the roof when he heard of Joanna's bein' gone, but bless your eyes, he took it like Mary's little lamb! I wonder where Jo is, to-night?"

"Yes, I wonder!" says Liz, viciously. "I wish I had her here for about ten minutes, I would pay her out for my beautiful new red shawl."

If they could have seen Joanna at that moment, they would have seen her "going on" in the train of Mlle. Azelma, and facing a New York German audience for the first time.

"If you gals are coming, come," growls Dan. "I am going to get round the sleigh, so be ready, as I won't wait—mind that."

The young ladies hurry off, giving sundry directions

to Joanna's successor, the stout-limbed rustic maiden, at present supping off the fragments of the feast. They will not be home until morning ; she need not sit up for father, and she is to have breakfast for them, hot and hot, when they return in the morning about six. Then they ascend to their chamber to adorn themselves for the dance, envelop themselves in shawls and " clouds," and finally stow themselves away in the back seat of the sleigh, and are driven through the white whirling storm to their destination.

Their father, meantime, has reached his, which proves to be, as Jud has predicted, Abbott Wood. He still maintains that ominous composure which has so surprised his family, but there is a fierce light of dogged determination in his sinister eyes. It is something more than common that takes him to Abbott Wood. Since he first became the tenant of the Red Farm, fully six years before, he has only entered that house once—one other stormy night. He is going there again, through darkness, and tempest and wind, and this time, too, its master shall do his bidding, or he, Giles, will know the reason why. As before, Joanna is the cause that brings him.

He reaches the house, a huge black bulk in the darkness, but few lights to be seen. He grinds his teeth, and shakes his fist at it, as he rings a peal that brings two startled men-servants hurriedly to the door.

" Is your master in ?" he surlily demands.

The men stare, but the fierce, black-bearded face commands civility, and an answer.

Not in. At Brightbrook. Dinner party. Will be back to-night, but do not know when.

"You're *sure* he ain't in?" says Giles, eyeing the men in a way that makes them step hurriedly back. "'Cause why? You'll save him some trouble if he is, by tellin' him Giles Sleaford is here, and wants to see him, uncommon particular."

He is not in, both men assure him, with the earnestness of personal alarm.

"Hah! Werry well, then. When he does come in you tell him this : 'Giles Sleaford's been here,' ses you. 'Giles Sleaford,' ses you, 'come through all this here bloomin' storm a-purpose to see you to-night, and he *must* see you to-night. Giles Sleaford,' you ses, 'left them words—*must see you to-night.* He can't wait, leastways he won't, not here, but he'll wait for you at his own place,' you ses, 'till after one o'clock, and *you'd better come !* Them,' you ses, 'was Giles Sleaford's own expressions.' You tell your master them words, my man, when he comes from that 'ere dinner-party."

With which Giles Sleaford turns away, remounts his horse, and rides back to the Red Farm.

The girl has not retired ; she is nodding stupidly over the kitchen stove. With an oath she is dismissed to bed, and goes. She is a dull, lumpish creature, and is frightened to find herself alone with the rats and black beetles, and this savage man.

She has Joanna's little room under the rafters, adjoining Giles's own, and opposite the two occupied by the Sleaford boys and girls. She gets into bed, and falls fast asleep in a moment.

She does not know how long she sleeps. All the events of that dreadful night are blurred and confounded in her dull brain. She awakes suddenly to the sound of the fiercely-beating storm, the rain, freezing as it falls, lashing the windows like lines of steel, the wind roaring dismally through the woods. It is very cold, too, and she shivers on her hard bed.

Other sounds reach her from below, the sounds of voices talking—loud and angry voices. Can the girls have come back ? No, these are not girls' voices, they are the harsh, strong voices of disputing men. More and more frightened, she tries to hear—there are two, and both seem to be talking together. Now she recognizes the voice of her master—the other is unknown.

" You don't believe me ! " She hears these words distinctly, shouted rather than spoken by Sleaford ; " by —— ! then you *shall* believe me ! I have them upstairs in my room unbeknown to any in this house. Come along ! by —— you shall see them, you shall believe me ! I have them, by the Eternal, and what's more, I have *you*, and I'll not spare you ! No, may I be everlastingly —— if I do ! "

The imprecations with which this apostrophe is interlarded turns the blood of the young person who listens, as she ever after informs her audience, into a mask of ice. The sound of heavy footsteps stumbling up-stairs follows, two men enter the adjoining room.

There is a fumbling noise as of a search, a smothered mumble of threats and curses in the amiable tones of Mr. Sleaford—silence on the part of the other man— then an exclamation of triumph.

" There ! " cries Sleaford, " look there ! Don't you touch 'em, or I'll let daylight through you. Just look at 'em. Here's the first—you've seen *that* afore. Here's the second—look ! that's new. Maybe ye believe me now? Keep off—keep off, —— you, or by all that's great I'll have your blood! D'ye think I'll let them go, after keeping 'em these eighteen years? Ha! you would, would you?"

There is a crash—it is a falling lamp, an explosion —a fierce struggle—some dreadful oaths. *Then*—over the crash of the storm, of lashing sleet and howling wind, there is a shriek, a dreadful, unnatural scream of agony, then a heavy fall, a hollow moan, then silence.

The girl in the bed huddles up in a heap, frozen with terror. There is a stamping sound ; it is one of the men stamping out the flame of the oil, then a pause, then rapid footsteps rushing down the stairs. A door opens, shuts, then again there is the darkness, the tumult of the storm, and silence in that awful inner-room.

It is a dreadful silence, dreadfully broken. A groan falls on the strained ear of the poor terrified girl.

"Help!" a faint voice calls, "I am stabbed."

She does not dare stir, her teeth chatter, the bed shakes beneath her with fright.

"Help!" says that failing voice once more, "for God's sake!"

She cannot move, she seems frozen fast to the bed wherein she crouches. That terrible cry comes no more—profound stillness reigns in that frightful next room.

How the hours of that night pass this frightened creature never can tell. Her hair does not turn white, which speaks well for its stability of color. She never moves—she has buried herself in a heap under the bed-clothes, and lies there, shivering and quaking.

With the first gray streak of dawn she rises, numb
and stiff, puts on her clothes, opens with shaking
hand the door, shuts her eyes fast, lest they should
light on some horrible specter, and bolts down stairs,
out of the horrid house, far over the soaked and sodden fields, as fast as her legs can carry her, away, away,
anywhere, anywhere, out of that horrible place !

It is a wild, blusterous morning ; the storm is not
yet spent; jagged clouds frown on the earth, sur-
charged with rain ; the wind beats her fiercely ; the
pallid, blank day has hardly begun.   But at the nearest house the goodman has risen, and is opening his
doors and windows, when a flying figure comes leaping
toward him, flings open the house door, and falls prostrate on the threshold.   He picks her up, puts the panting creature into a chair, and, in gasps, and incoherently, she tells her tale.   It is brief—murder has been
done at Sleaford's.

The man sets off, rouses some few of the neighbors,
and starts for the house.   On their way they meet the
double sleigh holding the jaded sons and daughters of
the house, and to them the tale is unfolded.   Five
minutes brings them to the farm.   They hurry in, up
stairs, and pause involuntarily at that closed door.
Even Dan stands for a moment, afraid to see what
is on the other side.

"Oh, go on !" cries Lora, with a hysterical sob.

" Open the door, man," says somebody ; " it may
not be as bad as you think."

He obeys.   A shocking sight meets their eyes.   The
signs of a struggle are everywhere ; the broken lamp,
the charred floor, the overset chairs, and blood—everywhere blood !   It has crept under the bed, it has smear-

ed the furniture ; it dyes to the hilt a long, curved, murderous-looking knife lying near. Prone on the floor, on his face, a man is lying—a big, broad-shouldered, burly man—his hands and clothes crimson with the terrible tide that besmears everything.

" It is father !" says Lora, with a terrible cry.

They lift him up, and Liz falls backward at the ghastly sight, and faints dead away. His face is rigid and besmirched ; from his left side blood still flows in black, coagulated drops. It is the master of the house, destined never more to swear, or drink, or fight, or horsewhip, while his name is Giles.

CHAPTER VIII.

GEOFFREY HEARS A CONFESSION.

T is the forenoon of the day after.

Mrs. Abbott sits alone in her favorite sitting-room—a dainty apartment in white and gold ; a carpet like snow, covered with purple and yellow-hearted pansies ; chairs like ivory, upholstered in pale, creamy tints, that harmonize well with the calla-lily hue of the lady's complexion. There are flowers in abundance—in pots, in vases, in crystal cups ; they fill the air with summer fragrance. There are but few pictures, in heavy gilt frames, and these are portraits—her own, her son's, her daughter's, one or two world-wide celebrities, and one lovely, sunlit, Southern landscape. There are books everywhere, in choice bindings ; an open piano ; rich draperies of

10

creamy silk and lace ; and last, but by no means least, a fire burning brightly in the grate.

Mrs. Abbott herself, in a white cashmere morning-gown, trimmed with Valenciennes, sits back in the puffy depths of a great chair, her book lying idly on her lap, her dark, dreamy eyes on the fire, her thoughts anxious and perplexed. Like all the rest of the world of Brightbrook, she is thinking of the Sleafords.

It is not yet eleven, but ill news flies apace ; it was brought to Mrs. Abbott by Leo an hour ago. The servants never gossip in their lady's presence, but they do not mind Miss Leo, and Miss Leo runs with the news to her mamma. For Joanna's sake, a certain amount of interest attaches to these people, and deeds of violence and bloodshed like this are rare in this peaceful community. Some unknown man had visited Sleaford's late last night, had had a quarrel with Slea-ford, had stabbed Sleaford. That is the vague version that has reached the mistress of Abbott Wood, and that has set her thoughts wandering painfully to a subject she would fain forget.

She has been inexpressibly shocked by the girl's conduct. She had hoped to do her so much good, to lift her above her surroundings—a doubtful sort of good, always—had hoped to refine and subdue her, had thought that task accomplished, and now——! She has heard the whole disgraceful story—how for little or no provocation the girl had set fiercely upon one of the young men, and laid open his head with a blow of a loaded whip-handle, how she fled to the woods, how she entrapped foolish young George Blake into running away with her, how she has added robbery to attempted murder, and gone to New York.

But the sequel is strangest, wildest of all ; it almost exceeds belief. When George Blake's frenzied mother and maiden aunt rush up in pursuit of the fugitive pair, what do they find ? A deserted bridegroom ! What do they hear ? An incomprehensible story ! She has run away with him—yes ; but she has also run away *from* him ! When Blake, with his friend, reached the hotel some two hours after his quitting it, they found an empty room, and a lost bride-elect. Poor George, like a man demented, has been hunting the city ever since, but in vain. If the pavement had opened and swallowed her she could not more completely have disappeared. She has threatened suicide often—has she escaped Black's Dam to find death in the North River ? Mrs. Blake is jubilant, but hides her feelings, and returns with the tale to Brightbrook.

And it is over this Mrs. Abbott is painfully pondering, as she sits and looks at the fire. Geoffrey, too, is on the track ; he scouts the idea of suicide. He maintains that Joanna must have been insulted and goaded beyond endurance. He has faith in her innate goodness and gratitude. In running away from George Blake she has acted for his good. He does not, will not, give her up. " If she is above ground I will find her !" he says, in that quiet, inflexibly determined way of his ; but as yet even he has not obtained the faintest clew.

Down in the servants' hall two tall footmen stand aside with very grave faces, and whisper mysteriously. They know rather more of the affair Sleaford than most people, but they have an excellent place, little to do, good wages, and they judiciously only whisper.

Very late last night, in all that storm, the man Sleaford was here, and left a peremptory order for master,
when master returned. Master rode home about
eleven, was given that message, swore roundly at the
giver, turned his horse, faced the sleet and wind, and
rode off again. About two this morning he returned,
pale as a corpse, drenched, frozen, staggering, *stained
with blood!* Stained with blood—his vest spotted,
one of his hands cut, his face bruised, as if in a struggle. All this is seen at a glance. Then he went to
his room, locked the door, and has not been seen since.
His man left his hot shaving-water and a cup of coffee
in the dressing-room. He did not appear at missus'
breakfast. It has a very ugly look; the two men
have reason to whisper gravely over it, and hold themselves apart.

But the birds of the air carry news of bloodshed.
It is being rumored already, in awe-stricken tones,
through the village, who Giles Sleaford's midnight
visitor was.

Mrs. Abbott throws aside her book at last, with a
heavy, impatient sigh, and rises, and goes to a window. She draws aside the draperies and looks out.
A storm of wind and wet is sweeping past ; the "January thaw" has set in in pouring rain. The landscape
looks all blurred and blotted out, the sky black and
low, the trees twisting and rattling in the gale. Where
is that unfortunate Joanna, this wild winter day? the
lady thinks, with a shiver. Poor creature! it seems of
no use trying to do anything with this sort of people ;
they are true to their own reckless natures, and under
that light outer coating of varnish are tameless and
reckless to the end.

As she stands and gazes at the drifting rain, she sees coming through it the figure of a man. He approaches the house—some one of the servants, she thinks. But a moment after there is a tap at the door, and one of the tall men enters, looking flurried and startled.

"Well?" his mistress says, in some surprise.

"It's—it's a young man, ma'am," the man stammers, "to see you, if you please. A young man by the name of Sleaford."

"Sleaford!" she repeats the name, almost startled herself; it has been in her thoughts all the morning so persistently, and is so associated with tragedy now.

"Yes, ma'am, he wishes to see you most particular, he says. It's a matter of life or death."

"To see me?" more and more surprised. "Are you sure you have not made a mistake? Are you sure it is not *Mr.* Abbott?"

"He said most particular my missus. I put the question to him wasn't it master, and he said *no*, Mrs. Abbott, and a matter of life and death."

"Show him in."

She moves back to her chair before the fire, and the young man by the name of Sleaford is shown in. He casts one careless glance around the beautiful white and gold boudoir, and stands, hat in hand, dripping, dark, strong, weather-beaten, a handsome, gypsy sort of young fellow, my lady thinks, not without a sort of admiration, as if he were a fine or a well-painted picturesque brigand in a Salvator Rosa picture.

"You wished to see me?" her slow, sweet, *legato* tones break the silence. "Will you sit down?"

He looks at the frail, pretty, white and amber chair, and shakes his black head.

"No, lady, I will stay but a minute. My name is Judson Sleaford, my father was stabbed last night. He is dying to-day, and he has sent me to you."

He addresses her with perfect ease of manner, entirely unembarrassed by his errand, her stately presence, or the splendors around him.

"Yes," she says, wondering more and more, "to me?"

"To you, lady—most particular to you. He didn't say so, but I think he would rather Mr. Abbott knew nothing about it. He says it is a matter in which you are concerned, and he wants to make a dying confession to your son."

"To my son?"

"To young Mr. Lamar. Mr. Lamar can tell you later. Is he at home?"

"My son is in New York," Mrs. Abbott replies, turning very pale ; "he is in search of Joanna."

" *That's* unlucky," says Jud, with perfect coolness, "because dad—I mean father—can't hold out much longer, and he says it's important. As well look for last year's partridges as our Joanna—he won't find her. Couldn't you send for him, lady? He could get a dispatch and be here in five hours."

"Certainly," Mrs. Abbott says, "if it is necessary. But——"

"Dad wouldn't take all this trouble if it wasn't. It's of importance, you'd better believe, lady, and worth hearing, whatever it is. You'd best send for him, and tell him to look sharp, if he wants to see the old man alive. He's sinking fast. The doctor says he would be dead now from loss of blood if he wasn't as strong as five ordinary men."

"I will send for him at once—at once," the lady says, rising ; "but I cannot imagine——"

She stops, looking pale and puzzled.

"No more can I," says Jud. "All the same, dad can't die easy with it on his mind—so he says. I'll tell him, then, the young gentleman will be telegraphed for, and will come ? Put it strong, please, lady, so that there may be no mistake."

"He will come the instant he gets the dispatch," Mrs. Abbott says, and Jud Sleaford, with a bow, departs.

"Come down at once. Go straight to Sleaford's."

These are the words she writes and sends to the village by a mounted messenger, which flash over the wires to New York, and find Geoffrey rising from a midday luncheon.

He knits his brows perplexedly as he reads—an odd message, signed by his mother. A moment later his face clears. It concerns Joanna—she has returned, or there is news of her. He looks at his watch—it wants an hour of train-time. He will get to Brightbrook at 4.30, to Sleaford's at 5. If Joanna is back, by fair means or foul, he will compel Giles Sleaford to give her up. His interest in the girl he has befriended is deep and strong—he can hardly understand its depth and strength himself.

The dim afternoon is fast darkening into night, as, by the swiftest conveyance he can find at the depot, he drives through the rainy woods to the Red Farm. All the rest of his life the memory of that drive never leaves him—it is like no other that has gone before, or that comes after. His whole life is changed from that hour. The picture of the desolate scene will never leave him ; in after years he starts from his sleep often, in disturbed dreams living it over again. It is always dark, that picture, with the melancholy drip, drip, of the rain, the forlorn trees, the desolate flats and marshes. It has been said that we die many times before we are laid in our coffin. Looking back, it always seems to Geoffrey Lamar that on that evening he died first.

He reaches the farmstead—a strange stillness and gloom rest upon that noisy household. He has crossed its threshold but twice before ; this is the third and last time. The thought of that somber red house can never return to him again without a thrill of the pain, and shame, and horror of this night.

In the kitchen he finds the girls and their youthful handmaid, huddled together, a shrinking group.

They have feared their harsh father in life, they fear him more in his grisly death. They will not go near his room : a superstitious dread holds them back ; death, and such dark death as this, appals them. Jud is nurse and companion. Dan has deserted the house, and hangs moodily about the premises. A chill strikes Geoffrey—something more than news of Joanna is here.

"What has happened?" he asks. "Why have I been sent for, and told to come here?"

"Don't you know?" Lora asks, in wonder. To her it seems as if all the world must know, as if it had happened months ago, instead of but a few hours. "Father's been murdered, and has sent for you."

"Your father—murdered!"

He stares as he pronounces the horrible word, quite aghast.

"Murdered! and sent for him!"

"Oh! he ain't dead yet," the girl says, beginning to sob hysterically. "He can't die, he says, until he sees you. But he is dying, and there is not a moment to lose. Jud said to call him as soon as ever you came. Liz, go and call him."

"Go yourself!" is Liz's whimpering retort. "I—I'm afraid."

"You go, Beck," Lora says to the girl; and Beck, possessing plenty of stolid stupidity, which stands in good stead of moral courage sometimes, goes.

Jud appears directly.

"It's lucky you've come," he says. "He won't hold out till morning. He's awake and ready to see you. Come up. Look out for the stairs. It's dark, but dad, poor old chap, don't want a light. Here! come in."

The chamber of the tragedy is but dimly lit by two pale gray squares of twilight, but it is sufficient to show the grayer face of the dying man. Geoffrey is a physician; at a glance he sees that death is there. It is a question of very few hours. He is a ghastly sight, black-bearded, bloodless, with staring eyes, and gasping breath. Some of the old fierce light lingers in these glazing eyes; they kindle at sight of his visitor.

"You go, Jud," he says. "I'll speak to this young gent alone."

The wonderful strength of the man is in his voice yet—the old imperious ring in his tone.

Jud obeys.

"If you want anything," he says to Geoffrey, 10*

"knock with your heel on the floor. I'll go down and take a smoke, and I'll hear you. There's the stuff he takes, on the table. Don't let him talk too much ; the doctor says 'tain't good for him."

" Will you go and hold your jaw ?" interrupts the dying man with a glare.

Jud shrugs his shoulders and goes, and Geoffrey is alone with Giles Sleaford.

*   *   *   *   *   *

Nearly an hour passes.

Down stairs the group sit and wait. They wonder what their father can have to say—something about Joanna, they infer. Dan slouches uneasily in and out of the house, the girls cling together in silence. Outside the night and rain fall, the wind sobs feebly.

" Show a light, can't ye ? " Dan growls, stumbling in, and Beck obeys.

But even the bright lamp cannot dispel the gloom, the awe. In that upper chamber there is silence—no telegraphic boot-heel has summoned aid. Can they be talking all this time ?

" It must be awful dark up there," Lora whispers. " Jud ought to go with a light."

But Jud will not go until summoned, "if he knows himself," he asseverates. And he is not summoned for still another half hour.

It is nearly seven when the bedroom door opens, and a footstep slowly descends the stair. Very slowly, unsteadily, it seems, and then the door opens, and Geoffrey Lamar comes in.

They start to their feet, one and all, at sight of him. What has happened? Is father—dead ? For death only should change any face as Geoffrey Lamar's is changed. So white, so haggard, the eyes so wild, so vacant, like the eyes of a sleep-walker, fixed in a blank, sightless stare.

"Oh! what is it?" they all cry out. "Is father dead? Is father dead?"

His dry lips part, he makes an effort to speak, shakes his head, points upwards, and turns and goes. Still in that same blank way, as if dazed or stunned by a blow. The conveyance in which he came is waiting, but he never thinks of it; he plunges on through the rain, across the sloppy fields and marsh land, under the dripping trees—straight on, with the blind, un-erring instinct still of the sleep-walker.

And, strangest of all, he does not go home. He goes on to the village, to the hotel, asks for a room, and locks himself in.

And then he falls, rather than sits, in a chair, covers his face with his hands, and so remains motion-less a long time. He is trying to think, but his brain is spinning like a top—heart, soul, mind are in con-fusion. His thoughts are chaos—no order comes. A great, nameless horror, of sin, and shame, and dark-ness, and ruin has fallen upon him. Past and future are blotted out—the present is only a hopeless whirl of sudden despair. He sits for a long time; then he starts up, and begins pacing the room, as a madman might; his teeth are set, his face blanched, his eyes full of infinite misery, his hands locked. Walking or sitting, he still cannot think. The blow has been too sudden, the agony too great. Later, he will think, until thought becomes almost insanity; to-night he is wild, distraught, master of himself no more.

He sits again, starts up again, and walks until ex-

hausted. Then he flings himself down, his folded
arms on the table, his face resting on them, with one
great heart-wrung sob, and so lies, mute and prone.
And when morning dully and heavily breaks, it so
finds him. He has not slept for a moment the whole
night through.

CHAPTER IX.

A LONG JOURNEY.

HAT night Giles Sleaford dies.
A little group surrounds his bed—the
doctor, the clergyman, a magistrate, his
son Jud, and Dan just within the door.
And the last words of the dying man are these :
"Nobody done it. It was—a accident. He's
acted—all square with me—and—it sha'n't be said—
Giles Sleaford—played it—low down—on him. I've
told the truth—to the young gent—— Nobody done
it. I fell—on the knife. You—gents all—remember
that when I'm—toes up."

With many gasps he says this—the gray shade of
death on his face, its clammy moisture on his brow.
There is a prolonged death-struggle, the strong life
within him fights hard, but the rattle sounds, he
stiffens out with a shiver through all his limbs, and
lies before them—dead.

And John Abbott is vindicated ! It is the doctor
who brings the news to the master of Abbott Wood—
the doctor, who is also the family physician of the
Abbotts. He rides with a very grave face, yet curious
to see how the man will take it. Yes, the servant said,

dubiously, his master is in, but he doesn't know whether he will see any one. Dr. Gillson scribbles a line or two, folds it up, sends it, and the result is he is shown at once to Mr. Abbott's study. There, Mr. Abbott, unshorn and haggard, with blood-shot eyes and disordered dress, sits and looks at him with sullen suspicion as he comes in.

"What is this message of yours?" he demands, surlily. "I am not well to-day. I did not wish to see any one. I——"

"I came from Sleaford's," interrupts the doctor, regarding him covertly. "The man Giles is dead."

"Dead!" John Abbott says. "Dead!" The last trace of florid color leaves his face, and leaves it perfectly livid. "Dead!" he repeats, with a dull, vacant stare.

"Dead!" reiterates Dr. Gillson. "I have just left his death-bed. Mr. Abbott," he says, his hand on the millionaire's arm, "it is known throughout the place that *you* were the man who visited him at midnight or the night before last!"

John Abbott turns his inflamed eyes upon the physician's face, still in that dazed, vacant way. "Well?' he says, moistening his dry lips.

"It is known you had a struggle with him, that violent words passed. It is known that for years he has held some secret power over you. Pardon me for repeating all this, but it is public talk now in Brightbrook. You have been suspected of—killing Giles Sleaford."

"It—it isn't true," Mr. Abbott answers, still in that dull, slow way, so unlike his usual furious manner over even trifles. "I didn't kill him."

"No," the doctor says; "although your own assertion would not vindicate you.   But he has."

"What?"

"On his death-bed just now, his last words were
a vindication of you."

John Abbott gives a great gasp—whether of
amaze or relief the doctor cannot tell—stares at him
a moment, grasps the arms of his chair, sits erect, and
waits.

"His last words vindicate you," repeats the medical man, emphatically.   "'Nobody did it'—I repeat
what he said—'it was an accident.   I fell on the
knife.'   Mr. Powers and the Rev. Cyrus Brown were
both listening, as were also his sons.   My dear sir, I
congratulate myself on being the first to bring you this
good news."

Dr. Gillson feels no particular regard for the man
before him, beyond the regard that all well-constituted
minds must feel for a man who can sign a big check
with the easy grace of John Abbott.   He has signed
more than one for the doctor.

There is a moment's deep silence—the blood comes
back with a red rush to Mr. Abbott's face.   A carafe
of water stands on the table ; he fills himself a full
glass and drinks it off.   Then he rises, thrusts his
hands in his trousers pockets, and begins walking excitedly up and down.

"Have you told my wife this?" are his first words,
and the surly tone of his previous greeting has returned.

"Certainly not, Mr. Abbott.   I should think Mrs.
Abbott would be the very last to hear anything of this

disagreeable nature. It is hardly a topic fitted for a delicate lady's ears."

Mr. Abbott resumes his quick march, his forehead frowning, his glance sullen.

"Look here !" he says ; "this must seem a fishy sort of business to you, and I know there has been a deuced deal of talk about it. Brightbrook is such a beastly talkative little hole, and every man makes his neighbor's business his own. I knew Giles Sleaford years ago—ay, a round score of them, and in the past he did me some—well—services, that I haven't forgot. No, it ain't my way to use a dirty tool, and then fling it aside. I've befriended him, poor beggar, since he came here. And I *was* with him that night, by his own request, and we *did* have a dispute. He had something belonging to me—I wanted it, and he drew a knife. There was a brief struggle for the possession of the property—mine, mind you, by every right—and in that struggle his foot slipped, and he fell forward on the weapon. There is the whole story, so help me. I don't mind owning I've been uneasy about it, for if he hadn't spoken before he died, things looked ugly for me. But he *has* spoken, you tell me, like a trump, and told the truth, by Heaven ! Well !—and so poor Giles, poor beggar, is gone ! Well, we must all go when our time comes. Will you have a glass of wine, doctor ? It's rawish sort of weather, and the roads are beastly."

Dr. Gillson knows what the Abbott vintages are like, and accepts. Mr. Abbott rings, issues orders, and resumes his march.

"I'm glad you haven't told my missis. She's nervous, and, as you say, it ain't quite the topic for a lady,

I hope she won't hear anything of it. A man don't want his family to know everything. And so poor Giles is gone! Well, well! he was a desperate fellow in his time, and strong as an ox. It's a little hole lets a man's life out, ain't it, doctor? Here's the wine, doctor. Help yourself."

"I saw young Lamar last evening," the doctor remarks; "fine young fellow that, and an honor to a noble profession. Capital port this, Mr. Abbott—will you try it yourself?"

"Saw Lamar? Saw Geoff? No, did you though? Didn't know he was down. Yes, I'll take a thimbleful, my mouth feels parched to-day. Yes, a fine young fellow, as you say, doctor—no call to learn your business. *I* provide for him as if he was my son. No need for *him* ever to look at tongues, or feel pulses. But he would do it, sir. Amuses him, I suppose. This house will be his when I pass in my checks. I love that boy, sir, as if he was my own."

From this moment Mr. Abbott's spirits rise, until they are at fever heat. He drinks his own wine, he snaps his fingers at imaginary foes, he clears the Red Farm from the rabble who infest it, he holds up his head, and feels he is a man again. He has never breathed quite freely in the lifetime of Giles Sleaford. It was like standing on a volcano, that might split open and vomit fire at any moment. And now Sleaford has gone, and cleared his character. "Bully for old Giles!" is Mr. Abbott's somewhat inelegant inward exclamation, his eyes sparkling, the fluid color deep in his vinous cheeks. Joanna, too, is gone—it is a blessed relief to be rid of both. He has nothing to fear now.

"Even if they find them—them things," Mr. Abbott muses, "those loggerheads of boys won't be able
to make top or tail of 'em, and there were things no
living soul knew but Black Giles himself. Tisn't
likely he told those louts of his. He bled me pretty
freely in his lifetime, and he wasn't the sort to be
overburdened with family affection, or to care too
much for them he left behind him. But I wish I had
—I had those things."

He ponders over it a good deal, and the result is,
he takes his courage in his two hands later in the day,
and rides over to the house of death. A large and
motley assemblage are there, indoors and out. There
is to be a sort of "wake," of a somewhat festive character too, for copious refreshments for the watchers
are in course of preparation. But the great man
of Brightbrook is met on all hands by such dark looks,
and sullen and sinister glances, such angry, ominous
silence, that he prudently does not press the matter
that has brought him, but rides away again as he
came. Dan Sleaford, in particular, eyes him with so
much latent malevolence, that he breathes more
freely, although no coward, when half a mile of marsh
land lies between them. It only confirms him in his
resolution, however, to sweep, without loss of time, all
this evil-disposed vermin off his land.

Mrs. Abbott is reading a note when he enters his
own drawing-room, with a surprised and perplexed
face. It runs:

"BRIGHTBROOK HOUSE, Jan. 29, 18—.
"MY DEAR MOTHER : I am pressed for time, and
so shall not visit the house before returning to the

city. An important matter calls me away for a few
weeks, so do not be anxious if I am not with you for
some little time. Most affectionately,

"GEOFFREY LAMAR."

Such a strange note—so short, so curt, so incomprehensible. To go without calling to see her, to be
absent for some weeks, to say not one word about his
summons to Sleaford's, or what passed there. Mrs.
Abbott sits fairly puzzled, and a trifle displeased. It
is not in the least like Geoffrey, this brusqueness, this
mystery.

"Has Geoff come?" Mr. Abbott asks, entering in
high good spirits, red, bluff, breezy.   •

She glances at him in surprise, folds her note, and
puts it in her pocket.

"Geoffrey is not here. How did you know he was
down?"

"Oh! old Gillson told me—met him last night at
the station. You don't mean to say, Leonora, he
hasn't been here at all?"

It is a token that Mr. Abbott's spirits are at their
highest, when he calls his wife by her name, or gives
her the loving glance he does at this moment. And
both name and glance from him are particularly odious
to Mrs. Abbott. She rises coldly as he approaches.

"My son has not been here, Mr. Abbott. He did
come down, but he has again gone."

She turns to leave the room, but the seigneur of
Abbott Wood, in his new-born happiness, interposes.

"Oh! hang it all, Nora, don't run away, as if I
was the plague! Sit down and let us have a cozy
talk. A man might as well be married to an iceberg,

blessed if he mightn't. I don't see you hardly from
one week's end to t'other. No man likes to be kept
off at arm's length that way, blessed if he does. It
ain't nature. I don't complain, mind you—I'm proud
of you. You're the handsomest woman, the best-
dressed woman, the highest-stepping woman *I* ever
see—dashed if you ain't! And all the men say so.
And I love the ground you walk on. I wouldn't have
you different if I could. You suit me to a T! Only
don't be so stiff and stand-offish *all* the time. Do sit
down, Nora, and let us have a cozy chat."

"You have been drinking, Mr. Abbott," his wife
says, in cold disgust : "keep off! Do not come near
me! I cannot talk to an intoxicated man."

"No, I ain't drunk—had a glass or two, but bless
you, I ain't drunk. I tell you, you're a stunner, Nora,
and I love you, by George I do, and I love your son,
and half I have shall be his. There! I can't say no
fairer than that. It was the best day of my life, the
day I married you ; only you *are* so high and mighty,
and won't sit down as a wife should, and have a
cozy——"

But Mrs. Abbott waits to hear no more of this
tipsy, uxorious maundering. As he comes toward her,
she swiftly leaves the room, retreats to her own, and
locks the door. Leo is there drawing, and she looks
up in alarm to see her mother's white face, and burning
dark eyes.

She starts up.

"Mamma! what is it ?"

Some vague resemblance to the man below looks
at her out of Leo's eyes, and she puts out her hands to
keep her off.

"No!" she cries, "do not! It is nothing." She
sinks down and covers her face. "Oh!" she thinks,
with a bitterness that is greater than the bitterness of
death, "what a wretch I am! How richly I deserve
my fate! For his money I sold myself, degraded myself! Shall I never get used to my foul bondage? I
try, I pray, I strive, but in spite of myself I am growing to loathe that man."

  *   *   *   *   *   *

Little more than a week later, and Geoffrey Lamar
is in San Francisco. Jaded, travel-worn, pale, he goes
about the business that has brought him there, giving
no time to sight-seeing, or study of life occidental.
That business takes him to a church in the suburbs, to
the search of a certain register, where he finds what
he fears to find, what he has hoped he will not find.
It takes him to still another and similar errand, and
with similar result. He has been fatally successful in
both quests. One more visit remains to be made, then
he returns, with every hope of his life crushed out, it
seems to him, forever. It is to a public building, a
dingy brick edifice, with barred and grated windows,
high spiked walls, and watchful sentinels, but, saddest
of all prisons, a lunatic asylum. He sees the resident
physician and states his errand, and the name of the
person he has come to see. The doctor eyes him curiously.

"It is an odd thing," he says, smiling, "but you
are the first visitor in thirteen years who has asked to
see that patient. Yes, she is here, and she is well, that
is, physically. Mentally, of course——"

The doctor taps his frontal development, and shakes
his head.

"Is she a violent case?" Geoffrey asks.

"Oh, dear, no ; quite the reverse. Gentle as a child, and, seemingly, as sane as you or I, except at intervals. But, of course, it is all seeming. It is a hopeless case. She will never be any better."

"What do you know of her history?"

"What do *you* know of it?" the doctor retorts. "Pardon me, but I never betray trust."

"I know everything. She has been here for fifteen years ; she has lost a child ; her brother placed her under your care for temporary aberration, thinking she would recover. She has not recovered. She grieves for her child, and it is part of her lunacy that she must wait here until that child—now grown up—comes for her. Her husband is a rich man. Your orders are, every care and comfort compatible with close confinement. Her name is Mrs. Bennett."

"All correct," the doctor answers. "I see you know. But her child is dead. You are a relative, I presume?"

"I am not a relative. I ·have been sent here by one. But you mistake in one point. Her daughter is not dead."

"No? You surprise me. I certainly was so informed. Mr. Bennett's remittances from New York are regular as clock-work. She has every care and attention, as you will see. If you are ready, I will accompany you now."

They ascend some flights of stairs, traverse sundry corridors, and enter at last a pleasant, sunny little room. There a woman sits sewing. A carpet is on the floor, a canary is in a cage, some pots of roses and geraniums are in the windows, but the windows themselves are grated like the rest.

"A visitor for you, Mrs. Bennett," the doctor says, cheerily, "a young gentleman from the States."

Mrs. Bennett rises, and makes an old-fashioned little courtesy. She is a thin-faced looking woman, with-dark, wistful eyes, and black hair, thickly threaded with gray. Once she must have been rather pretty, but that once was long ago.

"I do not know you, sir," she says, slowly scanning his features. "Perhaps you bring me news of my child?"

It is difficult to imagine her insane—so gentle, so collected are look and tone.

"I do," Geoffrey answers, with emotion, and he takes the poor creature's hand. "Your daughter is alive and well, and I believe will come for you before long."

"I have been waiting a long time, a very long time," the poor soul says, wiping her eyes. "I get so tired sometimes, so tired; and then I think perhaps she will never come at all. And it is a little lonely here," glancing deprecatingly at the doctor, "although everybody is very kind to me, very kind indeed. But, oh, I want my little Joan—my little Joan!"

The pathos of her tone touches his heart.

"Your little Joan will come, I promise you that, and very soon," he answers.

"And will she take me away?" with a wistful, tearful glance, "for I want to go away. I have been here so long—so many, many years. I would like a change now. I never make a noise, do I, doctor? nor make trouble, like the other people here. I am very quiet.

And I will do everything she tells me if she will only take me away."

"She will take you away, I am sure of that."

"I get so tired, you know," she goes on, piteously. "No one ever comes to see me. My husband is busy working, and sends money to pay for me, and, of course, he cannot leave his business to come. And Giles has gone away. Giles is my brother, but I am afraid of him; he is cross, and he curses. So did my husband, but he was good to me. I have been here a long time, and I have been very patient, and now I want to go away, for I am tired of this house, and so many noisy people."

Geoffrey reassures her, and makes a sign to the doctor to go. Her plaintive voice, her sad, weary eyes, pierce his heart. They bid her farewell, and leave her wiping her poor dim eyes, and murmuring softly that she will be very good if Joan will only come and take her away.

Three days later Geoffrey Lamar starts on his return journey to New York. A great change has come over him. That old look of invincible resolution has deepened to gloomy sternness; he has aged in three days—he looks ten years older than on the night he sat by Giles Sleaford's death-bed. All the youthful brightness has gone—care-worn, haggard, silent, he sits the long days through, while the land whirls by him, seeing nothing of all that passes, hearing nothing of all that goes on. Wrapped in himself and his somber thoughts, thinking, thinking always—so the time wears, and at last the long overland journey is at an end, and he treads the familiar New York streets once more.

He makes no delay in the city. What *must* be

done is best done quickly. All his plans are formed
beyond possibility of change—new plans for a new
life. The past is dead and done with, a wholly new
existence must begin for him at once.

He goes down to Brightbrook, and reaches the village late in the afternoon. The sunset of a sparkling
winter day is paling its crimson fires, and tinging with
its ruby glow the trees, the urns, the western windows
of the great house. He enters the avenue on foot, and
walks up under those noble trees with a quick, firm
step. "For the last time," he thinks, as he looks
around. And it was to have been his—his home—this
fair domain, this goodly inheritance. For *its* loss he
feels no pang—a far heavier blow has fallen upon him.
The loss of fortune can be borne—the loss of honor is
all. And all is lost—even honor.

He asks for Mr. Abbott, and is shown into the library where that gentleman sits, perusing the evening
paper and smoking a cigar. He smokes and drinks a
great deal. At sight of his stepson he starts up,
throws down the paper, turns with radiant face, and
holds out both hands.

"What—Geoff! Back? Dear old boy, how we
have missed you. And where have you been all this
little forever?"

He stands with those welcoming hands outstretched,
a glow deeper than the glow of the sunset, streaming
through the painted oriel, deeper than the port wine
he drinks, on his rubicund face—the glad glow of
welcome. But Geoffrey Lamar, pale, stern, avenging,
draws back from those eager hands.

"No," he says, "we have shaken hands for the last
time. I stand in this house, and speak to you for the

last time. It is the bitter blight and disgrace of my life, that I have ever spoken to you at all ! "

The man falls back from him, his hands drop, his eyes start, he stands staring stupidly at his stepson.

" What—what—what d'ye mean ? " he stammers at last.

" What I say. On his death-bed Giles Sleaford sent for me, and told me his story—and yours. I know the black secret that has bound you two guilty men together. I hold the papers that cost him his life. I have been to San Francisco, and have verified the proofs of your guilt. And John Abbott, scoundrel and BIGAMIST, I have returned to denounce *you !*"

CHAPTER X.

LEO'S BALL.

HE last light of the fair, frosty day, gleaming in myriad hues through the stained glass, falls on the picture within the library—the darkly-polished floor, with its great rose-red square of carpet, its pictures, bronzes, books, and on the figures of the two men. On John Abbott, millionaire and magnate, sitting huddled together in his arm-chair, his face covered with his hands, his guilt brought home to him, unable to look for one second into the fiery eyes of Geoffrey Lamar. On Geoffrey Lamar, standing haughty and wrathful, with gleaming eyes, compressed lips, and knotted forehead. On that high, pale brow the veins stand out,

11

swollen and purple, with the suppressed passion within him. And yet, little has been said, and that little in a tense, repressed tone, lower even than usual.

It is only on the stage, perhaps, that people in these supreme moments of death and despair make long speeches, only in fiction that the dying lie among their downy pillows and make exhaustive confessions of romantic lives. In real life, in the hours of our utmost need, we are apt to find ourselves mute.

John Abbott has not spoken one word. He has attempted no denial, no vindication ; he has fallen into his chair, and crouches there, crushed by the tremendous blow that has fallen upon him. Geoffrey speaks at intervals, in a harsh, unsteady voice, very unlike his own, but the fiery wrath that consumes him is so deep, so deadly, his hatred and abhorrence of this man so utter, that all words fail and seem poor and weak.

"I have little to say," he says, in that low, concentrated voice of passion. "I was a child when the wrong was done. I am a man now, and I do not strike you dead before me, and nothing less can atone. This is the last time I will see you or speak to you while I live ; the last time I will ever set foot in this accursed house. I go from you to my mother, to tell her the truth—the horrible, shameful truth, that may strike her dead while she listens. But if I knew it would, I would still tell her."

He breaks off ; all this he has said in pauses and gasps. He puts up his hand to his throat ; he feels as though he were strangling. For the cowering wretch before him, he neither moves nor speaks.

"If she survives the blow, she will go with me. If I know my mother, you have seen her, too, for the last

time in your life. For your wealth, your doubly-ac-
cursed wealth, she married you ! She has paid the
penalty of that crime. She will renounce you and
it within this hour. If she should not——"

He stops, that strangling feeling of fury that he
is repressing chokes the words he would utter.

"If she should not," he resumes, "she shall see
me no more. But I know her. She will go with me.
Leo, too—she is yours no longer. I will make a home
for them, far from here, where *your* vile name will
never be heard. I will search for Joanna—she, too,
shall know the truth—shall know your crime—shall
know her rights and her mother's wrongs, and to
her and God I leave vengeance. Do you think she
will spare you, John Abbott ? Do you know the penalty of the crime you have done ? Six months hence,
in a felon's cell, condemned to years of labor, I fancy
your millions will avail you little. I am willing that
my name, stainless hitherto, should be dragged
through the mire, so that you are punished. To your
daughter, and to heaven, I leave our wrongs. I go
now to find my mother."

"Stay !" John Abbott says. He lifts his head, and
even Geoffrey, in his whirl of rage and shame, is struck
by the ghastliness of that face. His voice, too, is
hoarse and guttural. "Stay ! I have no right to ask
favors—I don't ask any. But—don't tell to-night."

Geoffrey stares scornfully a moment, then turns
to go.

"I don't ask it for myself—to be spared. I don't
want to be spared. But there is a party to-night—
Leo's." All his words come thickly and with a slow
effort. "The house is full of people down from New

York—her friends and your mother's. All is ready. Spare the little one for one more night—only one. Let her be happy with her friends until to-morrow. Come to-morrow—come as early as you like. It is all true, I deny nothing. Take them away. Only not to-night—for little Leo's sake!"

He says it all in brief, broken sentences; then his head droops, and he is silent again.

Geoffrey stands a moment. For Leo's sake! That is a powerful appeal. And only until to-morrow. The house full of guests too; the exposure would be horrible. And for Leo's sake. Yes, he will wait.

"For Leo's sake," he says frigidly, "I will wait until to-morrow. To-morrow at noon I will send for my mother to the hotel. I enter this house no more."

He goes with the words, and the master of Abbott wood is alone. Alone! with hell in his heart, with despair, and remorse, and agony, and loss, and love, and fear, all tugging at his heart-strings together. It has come—the crash he has always feared. The thunderbolt has fallen and riven his hearth. Giles Sleaford, in his grave, has risen to revenge his sister's wrongs.

The last yellow glimmer of the wintry twilight fades out in gray; darkness falls on the world. Many feet pass his door; a servant enters to light the gas— the library will be needed to-night. John Abbott stumbles past him in the dark, and goes to the room that is sacred to himself alone—the room called his study, where he sees his tenants, transacts business, signs checks, pays help, and smokes pipes. Here he will be undisturbed by his servants, his wife, his daughter, or their butterfly friends.

This party of Leo's is in honor of a young Southern beauty, a friend of Olga Ventnor's, on the eve of
her departure for Europe. It is called Leo's ball, but
in reality it is not merely a young girl's party ; many
distinguished people are present—her mother's friends,
besides the great folks of Brightbrook. The Ventnors,
of course, are down—Olga from her finishing school,
tall and imposing, even at sixteen, with proudly-poised
head, delicate, lovely face, perfect repose of manner
—more beautiful than her most sanguine friends ever
predicted. A trifle imperious, certainly, as though she
were indeed a Princess Olga, looking with blue, dis-
dainful eyes on the slim-waisted, slightly-mustached
young dandies who adore her. They write sonnets to
her eyes and eyebrows, her smile, her form ; they paint
her picture ; they toast her at clubs ; they dream of
her o' nights ; they grow delirious with the promise
of a waltz ; they kiss her gloves, her finger-tips ; they
are ready to shoot each other for a flower from her
bouquet—and she laughs at them all, with girlish, joyous indifference, and tyrannizes over them with right
royal grace. That compact in which Frank Livingston is concerned has not been mooted to her yet, and
the family conclave begin to have their doubts as to
how it will be received.

A young lady who has such pronounced opinions
of her own at sixteen, as to the color and make of her
dresses, and hats, and gloves, will be apt to have pronounced opinions, also, on the more important subject
of a husband. Frank at present is abroad on a sketching tour, it is understood, through Italy and Switzer-
land, and sends her long, racy letters by every mail.
But she laughs at the letters, as she does at the ador-

ers, and flings them aside as indifferently. Whether she walks in "maiden meditation" or not, she is certainly "fancy free." To-night, in white silk embroidered with pink rose-buds, with real pink rosebuds and lilies of the valley in her hair and corsage, it is needless to say she is a vision of beauty. That goes without saying at all times.

Leo, too, in rose silk and illusion, looks like a rose herself, her bright black eyes shining after their old joyous fashion with the delight of the hour.

The rooms are flooded with light, flowers are in profusion everywhere, the guests are numerous, the supper and band down from the city, and Mrs. Abbott in pearl moire and those fabulous diamonds that might rival Lady Dudley's own—quite an ideal hostess for high-bred beauty and grace. Outwardly, that perfect repose seems above being ruffled by any earthly *contretemps*, but inwardly she is ruffled nevertheless. For Leo has just told her, with wide-open, wondering eyes, that Geoffrey has been and is gone.

"Impossible!" Mrs. Abbott says, incredulously. "Why on earth should he do that? There must be some mistake."

"No mistake, mamma; Davis let him in. He went to papa in the library, stayed half an hour, and went away."

"Without word or message to me! And after six weeks of absence! Oh, this is intolerable! Geoffrey never used to act so. What can it mean?"

"*I* don't know, mamma," Leo says; "it is very odd, certainly. Perhaps, hearing there was to be a party, he did not wish to stay. But it is not a bit like Geoff."

"Here is your father now."

A slight frown contracts Mrs. Abbott's smooth forehead—her husband has given her to understand he will not put in an appearance at this party, and now—— She misses Joanna as much, perhaps, for this reason as any other—she was a most useful sheepdog to keep this wolf at bay. These people are nearly all strangers to him—why should he want to join them? It is his own house certainly, but——

"I wanted to see you a moment, Nora," he says, approaching, and even she notes with surprise the livid, leaden pallor of his face, the trembling of his hands, the husky break of his voice, "a moment alone."

"There is nothing the matter?" she demands, in sudden alarm. "Geoffrey, it is nothing about *him?*"

"It is nothing about him."

"But he has been here, and is gone. What does it mean? *You* saw him—why did he not come to me?"

"On account of this party. He's coming to-morrow—at least he intends to see you. I—I don't feel well, Nora; I am going to my room—the study. I shall stay there all night."

"Yes," she says, indifferently, "you had better. You do not look well. Excuse me—I see a new arrival."

"Shake hands, Nora, and say good-night."

She draws back from him, intensely annoyed. Has he been drinking more than usual? Shake hands with him before all these people! What a preposterous idea! She draws decidedly back.

"There is no need of hand-shaking, Mr. Abbott. I have no wish to excite my friends to laughter—nor make a scene. You had better go to bed, as you say,

and as quickly as possible. You really look extremely
ill, and are attracting the attention of the guests."

His hand drops ; he takes one last, long, look as she
moves away to meet the new arrival. She is like a
queen, he thinks—so stately, so graceful, so fair.
Among all the women present, there is not another so
regal. Then he turns away, and at a little distance
encounters his daughter.

"Why, papa," she exclaims, quickly, "what is the
matter? You are looking awfully pale—for *you*.
Are you sick?"

"I ain't well, Leo. I'm going to my room, the study,
you know. I came to say good-night. That's a
pretty dress, my girl, and you look as fresh and pink
as a rose. I'm glad to see you so handsome and happy.
You—you are a little fond of your poor old dad, ain't
you, Leo?"

"Why, papa —— "

"Oh! yes, I know. I ain't like your mother, or
those heavy swells around, but I've been a good father
to you, now, haven't I? I don't think I ever refused
you anything in my life, now did I? And you'd—you'd
be sorry if anything happened me, now wouldn't you?"

Leo looks at him anxiously. The same thought,
alas! crosses her mind as her mother's—has he been
drinking? Mr. Abbott is apt to be maudlin in his
cups, so his pathos is always open to doubt.

"You had better go to bed, papa," says Leo, as her
mother has done. "You look very badly. And perhaps you had better send for Dr. Gillson."

"I don't want Dr. Gillson, my girl. I know what
you're thinking of, but it ain't that. I'm not drunk.
Good-night, little one—kiss your old dad."

Miss Leo's pink lips touch daintily the cold cheek
of her father. Then she, too, flits away to meet her
partner for the first dance. Mr. Abbott is not a subject to be sentimentalized over, even if he is a little
pale. Much drinking has alienated from him even the
respect and affection of his daughter, although she is
fairly fond of papa, too. But it is not in the same way
or degree·in which she is fond of mamma and Geoff.

Mr. Abbott goes to his study, followed by the⁓
crashing, brilliant music of the band. Ladies and gentlemen glance at him, and wonder who he is. His face
strikes them all with a sense of tragedy and discord,
that jars upon the scene. But he disappears and is
forgotten. He shuts himself in, but he does not shut
out the triumphal swell of the music, nor the sound of
the dancers' feet. The joyous tumult of the ball
mocks him in his seclusion. He has shut out the world
with its brightness, its gladness, its joyous life, and the
world goes on just as merrily without him. It comes
well home to him in this hour. He has been something
—he is nothing—he will never be anything in this
world again.

He sits down and has it out. It does not require long
thinking. To-night ends everything. To-morrow he will
stand alone, wife, son, daughter, home, friends—gone.
And he has loved them all. After to-morrow all who
have known him will fall off from him, his name will be a
by-word and a reproach, his memory a thing to be exe-
crated. He will be denounced—is the girl Joanna likely
to spare him ? There will be a trial through which his
wife, his daugh'er will be dragged, and their name de-
filed. There will be the sentence—the prison walls,
the prison dress, the prison labor, the prison fare, the

11*

prison life, the chain, the lash, the prison death—that
will be the story. All his wealth is powerless here.

He goes to a drawer in a desk, unlocks it with slow
deliberation, and takes out one of the articles it con-
tains. It is a revolver, a handsome weapon, silver-
mounted, perfect of its kind. He examines the cham-
bers, reloads carefully, and with a face that seems cut
in gray stone. And still, as he labors at his ghastly
task, the dance music swells and sinks joyously, the
sound of the dancers' flying feet, the echo of their
laughter reach him, and he listens as he works. Then
he goes to the window, opens the closed shutter, and
looks out.

It is a lovely night, following a lovely day. The
deep blue sky a-sparkle with frosty stars, the moon
flooding lawn, and terrace, and copse with crystal
light. Never has Abbott Wood looked more beautiful, never has he loved it so well. He is taking his
last look at it, at the cold, far-off, shining sky, at the
fair white earth, at his home that has been his pride
and boast so long. He is hearkening to the sweet
crash of the band—the wild music of a waltz will be
the last sound of time he will take into eternity.

For the end has come. The wages of sin—death
—is here ; the coward's cure for all ills of earth—suicide—is at hand. He will never see the scorn, the
hatred in his wife's eyes, the shrinking horror of his
daughter's face, the abhorrent gaze of all men. For
him there will be no felon's cell, or lash. His sin has
found him out, and the retribution is now.

He lifts the pistol. A gay burst of laughter just
outside his door greets him on the moment. Over that
merry peal, over the last soft strain of the waltzers,

another sound breaks—a dreadful sound. But it reaches no ear, and only the solemn eyes of the stars look into that silent room.

CHAPTER XI.

AFTER THAT NIGHT.

T is close upon noon of the next day. Sunshine floods the charming breakfast-room of Abbott Wood, glints on crystal, on silver, on egg-shell china, and on a group of gay guests, on the lady of the house in exquisite morning-robe and cap, on her pretty daughter in amber cashmere, rich with golden floss embroideries. The guests have had a brief nap, a cozy cup of tea, and now "booted and spurred," are saying farewell to their gracious hostess and her bright little daughter. The party last night was delightful. All are departing in fine spirits, making appointments for the coming summer and country meetings. They go at last, and with a tired sigh Mrs. Abbott sinks into her chair. She is not very strong, and last night's fatigue tells upon her after her quiet life. Besides, she is worried about her son. Here it is high noon, and he has not put in an appearance to explain his singular conduct. As she sits musing about it her maid approaches with a note. It is from the culprit, and is very brief.

"BRIGHTBROOK HOUSE, Thursday Morning.

"MY DEAR MOTHER :—I am especially anxious to

see you, but I cannot go to Abbott Wood, so, I suppose, I must ask you to meet me here at your earliest
convenience. I will remain in all day expecting you.
Love to Leo.   Ever affectionately,

"G. V. LAMAR."

Mrs. Abbott knits her brows in direst perplexity
over this enigmatical note. "Cannot go to Abbott
Wood!"   But he was here last night. "Must ask
you to meet me here!"   How very odd ; how extremely unpleasant. What can it mean? Is Geoffrey.
losing his senses? She will go at once and find out.
Her hand is on the bell, when her maid again hurries
in, pale, scared, horror-stricken.

"Oh! Mrs. Abbott!   Oh! madam! something
awful has happened !" The girl drops into a chair
panting with sheer affright. "Oh ! ma'am, I don't
know how to tell you."

Mrs. Abbott looks at her a moment and grows
white.

"Is it—anything about my son ?" she asks, almost
in a whisper.

"Mr. Geoffrey ? Oh ! no, ma'am, nothing about
him. It's master, please. Oh ! how shall I tell you !
It's dreadful—dreadful !"

Mrs. Abbott draws a long breath, and stands erect
again, pale, composed, a trifle haughty. There is
nothing about Mr. Abbott that can very greatly surprise or shock Mr. Abbott's wife.

"Do not be an idiot !" she says, sharply. "What
is it ? Say what you have come to say, and go. I am
going out."

"Oh ! no, ma'am, you can't go out to-day. Oh ! I

beg pardon, but you don't know. Prepare yourself—
oh! please do—for—for the worst. Mr. Abbott is
very—very ill."

Mrs. Abbott recalls his looks, his incoherent speech
last night, and slightly shrugs her graceful shoulders.
It has happened to Mr. Abbott to be very—very ill
before, of—delirium tremens!

"Have you sent for Dr. Gillson?" she says, coldly,
and moving away as if to go.

"Oh! my dear lady, wait! It—it isn't what you
think. Dr. Gillson was here hours and hours ago, but
he can do nothing. Nobody can. Oh! ma'am," with
a burst, "master's dead!"

"Dead!" Mrs. Abbott repeats the solemn word,
awe-stricken, and gazes incredulously at the girl.
"Dead!" that strong, burly, red-faced man. The
thought of death in connection with her husband has
never come near her—he and the idea have been so
entirely antagonistic. "Dead!" she repeats for the
third time, mechanically, in slow, wondering tones.

"Davis, his man, found him early this morning,
ma'am," the girl says, with a hysterical, feminine sob,
"and sent for the doctor at once. But it was too late.
He had been dead many hours then. The doctor knew
the house was full of people, and would not let Davis
tell until they were gone. He is in his study still,
ma'am, where they found him, a-lying on the sofa,
dressed. And, oh! if you please, there's to be an inquest."

Mrs. Abbott sits down, feeling suddenly sick and
faint. A passion of remorse sweeps over her; she
covers her face with her hands, and her tears flow.
Idle tears, no doubt—not tears of sorrow certainly.

She has never cared for this dead man—she committed a sin against herself and her womanhood by marrying him. Life by his side has been but " dragging a lengthening chain." She has held him in utter contempt, and has let him see it. But "he who dies pays all debts ;" and now, for all this, a very passion of pain, of remorse, of humiliation, fills her. And, last night, he came to her in some great need, and she rebuffed him ! Now he is dead ! But moments of weakness are *but* moments with this woman, whose life for many years has been one long, bitter self-repression. She lifts her head and looks at the girl again.

"It is very sudden—it is dreadfully sudden. Was it—apoplexy ?"

The maid resumes her weeping as her mistress leaves off. It is not sorrow on her part either—simply, the shock has unnerved her.

"Oh ! ma'am—Mrs. Abbott—that is the worst ! No, it isn't apoplexy—is isn't anything natural. It was suicide !"

"Suicide !" The lady recoils a step in pale horror, and puts out her hands.

"Oh ! dear lady, yes. That is the awful part. It was suicide. He shot himself. While everybody was dancing and enjoying themselves last night, he went into his study and done it. Davis found him all cold and stiff this morning—shot through the head. Oh, dear ! oh, dear ! Oh ! Mrs. Abbott, don't faint ! Oh ! here is Mr. Geoffrey. Oh ! thank the Lord ! Mr. Geoffrey, sir, come and say something to your ma !"

For it is Geoffrey who hurries in, pale, excited, with startled face, and hastens to his mother's side.

" My dearest mother, the news has but just reached

me. Dr. Gillson brought it, and I have hastened here at once. It is very shocking. Mother, do not give way so! Mother, mother, what is this?"

"I have killed him," she whispers, and her head falls on his shoulder, her arms encircle his neck, and she lies white and speechless with horror and remorse.

"Nothing of the sort!" her son says, energetically. "Mother, listen to me—I know what I am saying—you had nothing to do with this tragic death. It was I. I saw him last night—a terrible secret of his past life has been made known to me, and I came and accused him of his crime. I threatened him with public exposure. This is the result. I do not regret my part in it; I simply did my duty; I would do it again. I repeat—with this ghastly ending you had nothing to do. And, mother, he deserved his fate; he merits no pity—from you. He was a villain—dead as he is—I say it! Look up, shed no tears for him, except in thanksgiving that you are free."

All this the maid hears as she hurries from the room. She sees the stern, white face of the pitiless young Rhadamanthus, and wonders what nameless crime it can be poor master can ever have done.

*   *   *   *   *   *

Four days later they bury the master of Abbott Wood in that vast gray stone vault over in Bright-brook Cemetery—that gray mausoleum bearing the name ABBOTT over its gloomy front, and which, until time ends, John Abbott will occupy alone.

It is a very large and imposing funeral, and Mrs. Abbott, in trailing crapes and sables, looks pale but composed, and handsomer than ever. Leo's tears, people note, are the only tears that fall. There has

been an inquest, but no cause, except that useful and
well-worn one—temporary aberration of mind—can be
assigned for the rash deed.

Business has summoned Geoffrey Lamar to the city
on the day before, and among the melancholy cortege
he is conspicuous by his absence. All the Ventnors are
down to console the widow and orphan. But Mrs.
Abbott's high-bred calm stands her in as good stead
now, as in all the other emergencies of life—consola-
tory platitudes would simply be impertinences here.
As yet she knows nothing, only—that she is free !
After a very dreadful and disgraceful manner truly,
but still—free.

They bury the dead man, and his will is read. The
widow is superbly dowered, her son inherits Abbott
Wood and half the great fortune the millionaire has
left. Servants and friends are handsomely remembered.
No fairer or more generous will was ever made.

People begin to find out his good points ; he was
rough-and-ready, certainly, says Brightbrook, but an
off-hand, whole-souled fellow, free with his money always, and if he swore at a "help" this moment, he
was just as ready to tip him a dollar the next. He
wasn't such a bad sort of man. Brightbrook owes
him everything—he has made the place, built churches,
schools, town halls, jails, almshouses, laid out the park,
donated the fountain, erected model cottages for his
tenants, was a capital landlord, if he *was* a little strict.
' So, in spite of the suicide, he is after a manner canon-
ized in the village.

As to the death itself—people rather shirk that—
he did not live happily with his wife—she and her son
looked down upon him from first to last. And he

drank to excess. And he had had D. T., and in one
of these fits the deed was done, and that was all
about it.

The day after the funeral Geoffrey Lamar returns.
He wears no mourning, and settled sternness and
gloom rest on his face. The first inquiries he makes
are for the Sleafords, and he learns the Sleafords are
gone, driven away, the farm deserted, the house empty.
Lora has married a love-stricken butcher, and gone to
live in the next town ; Liz has drifted away to the city,
the boys have disappeared, loneliness reigns at Sleaford's.

The Red Farm is for rent, Geoffrey rides over and
looks at it—already it has the air of a deserted house,
already desolation has settled upon it, already the
timid avoid it after nightfall, already it is hinted Sleaford "walks."

It is very strange that these two men, connected in
some way in their life-time, should so quickly and awfully follow each other to a violent death.

"They were ugly in their lives," says a ghastly wit
of the village, "and in death they are not divided."

No news of Joanna as yet, and of late the search
has rather been given up. George Blake, poor faithful, foolish fellow, still mourns and searches, Geoffrey
proposes soon to recommence, but he has another and
sadder duty first to fulfill. He has yet to tell his
mother the frightful truth, that she has never for one
hour been John Abbott's wife—that Leo is "nobody's
child," that neither he nor one of them have any
shadow of rightful claim on all this boundless wealth
the dead man has left.

As the night falls of that day, that day never to

be forgotten in their lives, he tells her. They sit alone
in her darkening sitting-room, with closed doors, looking out at the falling winter night, the red gleam of
the fire flickering in the snow, and gold, and amber of
the bijou room.

Infinitely. gentle, infinitely tender are his words ;
he holds her hands, he breaks it to her, this revelation
that is to drag her pride in the very dust. For a long
time it is impossible to make her comprehend, the horror is too utter—she cannot, she will not take it in.

Then suddenly a shriek rings through the house,
another and another, and she starts up like a woman
gone mad—she breaks from him, she beats the air with
her hands, her frenzied cries resound. For the moment she *is* mad. What was John Abbott's suicide, a
hecatomb of suicides, to such horror as this ! Then
she sways and falls—almost for the first time in her
son's knowledge of her—headlong in a dead faint.

After that, there are weeks, that in all the future
time are blank.

She lies very ill, ill unto death, frantic, delirious,
burning with fever, talking rapidly, wildly, incoherently ; shrieking out at times that she will not believe it,
that she cannot believe it, that John Abbott, with that
pistol hole in his head, is pursuing her, and that Geoffrey is holding her until he comes up.

Her ravings are continuous, are frightful. Night
and day her son is beside her ; Leo is kept out of the
room by force—it is too shocking for her to see or
hear. Every one, doctors included, think she will die ;
but her superb, unbroken health hitherto saves her
life now.

Slowly the fever subsides, slowly life and reason

come back, and pale, spent, weak as a babe, white as
a snow spirit, she looks out one May day, and sees the
green young world, the jubilant sunshine, the sweet
spring flowers once more.

In two or three weeks she is to be taken away—for
her health. Abbott Wood is to be left in charge of
Mrs. Hill and one or two of the servants. Mrs. Abbott, her son, and daughter may be absent for years.
After all, says Brightbrook, that cold, proud woman
must have cared a little for her plebeian husband to be
stricken with fever in this way by the shock of his
death. And Brightbrook has thought her especially
cold and heartless at the funeral. So easy it is to be
mistaken.

Early in June they depart. Nothing is said to Leo
—time enough to tell her later, and then only part of
the miserable whole. She must learn that they are
poor, of course, that another claimant with a better
right exists for Abbott Wood, that they must look to
Geoffrey and his profession now for their support.

For it is needless to say that neither mother nor
son can touch one penny of that man's money—the
money that is rightfully Joanna's. They are not going
abroad to travel, as all the world thinks ; they are
going to a little house in one of the suburbs of New
York for the present, while Geoffrey begins his new
life of hard labor, heavily handicapped in the race.

For obvious reasons his mother retains the name of
Abbott, loathsome to her ears, but Leo must be considered first now. No one—not even the Ventnors—
are to know of them or their plans ; *that* world and
all in it has gone forever ; nothing but poverty, seclusion, anguish, shame remains.

For the Ventnors—Olga finds it very lonely, that
vacation at the pretty rose-draped villa, and mourns
disconsolately for her friends. She is nearly seventeen now—"a fair girl graduate, with golden hair,"
glad that the thralldom of her fashionable school is
over. But this fall and winter she is to go on, under
the best masters, with music, painting, and languages ;
live very quietly at Brightbrook, and early in April start
with papa and mamma for that two years' European trip.

Some American heiresses have lately been marrying
brilliantly abroad—marrying both fortune and title—
and every day Frank Livingston's chances grow fewer
and farther between. His mamma's anguish breaks
out whenever she thinks of it. She writes him agonized
appeals to meet the Ventnors, and try, try, try with
Olga, before one of those all-fascinating British officers
and nobles carry off the prize. But Frank, smoking,
sight-seeing, church-visiting in Rome, seeing statuary,
and paintings, and frescoes, a great deal, going to
cozy little artist reunions, sketching and painting
after a desultory fashion, and having a good time,
does not concern himself very greatly about his fair,
far-off cousin. Art is his mistress at present, storied
Rome the idol of his heart, his big brown meerschaum
rather more to him than all the heiresses and beauties
in wide America. If Olga has a mind, and is pleased
to approve of him when next they meet, *he* has no
objection. If not—he shrugs his shoulders, and hums
that couplet that has consoled so many when the
grapes were sour and hung beyond reach,

"If she be not fair to me,
What care I how fair she be!"

*   *   *   *   *   *

And now this record has come back to the beginning—to that wet October evening when Miss Ventnor drove past the Red Farm in the pony carriage,
and pointed it out to her friend. Giles Sleaford is
dead, Lora is married, Liz has gone cityward, the
"boys" have disappeared, Joanna has run away with
George Blake, and is not to be found. Sleaford's is a
"haunted house." At Abbott Wood silence and loneliness reign. It, too, is a deserted mansion. Its master has died a tragic death, Mrs. Abbott, Leo, Geoffrey,
are abroad, traveling for health and forgetfulness.
At Ventnor Villa Olga practices, sings, paints, reads
French, German, Italian, rides, drives, blooms a rose of
the world,

> "Fair as a star, when only one
> Is shining in the sky."

And so, with sweet, slow voice, she tells her friend, in
brief, this wet October night, the story of the
Sleafords.

PART THIRD.

CHAPTER I.

AFTER THE STORY ENDED.

"AND now, my dearest Hilda, having nar-
rated all the incidents of the voyage, I
propose to answer your very artful question about a *certain person*. Well, yes,
le beau cousin, as you term poor Frank, is still here,
still hovering as the moth around the flame, to quote

your rather hackneyed simile. He followed us down
here from New York, a week ago, and is poor mamma's
cavalier servant, and to me, the most devoted of
friends and cousins. Friends and cousins, I repeat.
You need not smile—he will never be more. All that
you say of his good looks, and charming manners, and
sunny temper, I admit. Still looks, and manners and
temper, are not *all* that one requires in a husband.
You perceive I put your delicately-vailed hints into
plain English. I am not a sentimental person. I read
my Tennyson, and my novels, and dimly, and as in a
dream, I realize what it is all about—this grand passion writers make the burden of their song. But I
have never felt it, and for Frank Livingston I never
will. I like him too well ever to love him. And yet,
my Hilda, I have my ideal——"

The pencil—she had written this with a slender
golden trinket, suspended from her chatelaine—pauses
here, and the writer looks out before her with dreamy
azure, half-smiling eyes. She sits on the low sea wall
of Abbott Wood, her sketch-book on her lap, and
scribbles, on thin foreign paper, this letter. The sea
lies below her, dimpling and sparkling in the lovely
light of a June afternoon. A great willow bending
over the wall droops its feathery plumes nearly to her
fair head. Her hat is on the grass beside her, she
has been sketching, but nothing in the view is lovelier than herself. She sits here, a tall, slender, most
graceful figure, dressed in light muslin, her pale golden
hair plaited about her head. There is not a touch of
brown in the perfect tinting of that pale gold, and
her eyebrows and lashes are fairer than her hair. Her
eyes are really wonderful in their limpid sapphire blue.

Her complexion is colorless, but has the vivid warmth of first youth and perfect health. A little gold cross clasps some creamy white lace at the throat, a white cashmere wrap, embroidered in gold, lies with her hat. As she sits there, she is a vision of radiant youth and dazzling blonde beauty.

She sits for a little, watching with that misty, far-off look the tiny waves, slipping up and down the white sands, then she takes up her pencil and resumes.

"I have my ideal, and he is not in the least like Frank. Beauty shall by no means be an essential, nor a perfectly cloudless temper either—we might weary of perpetual sweetness and sunshine. But, oh! my Hilda, he shall be noble, he shall be capable of self-sacrifice, he shall be a king among men to *me*. He shall be above me in all ways——"

A second time she breaks off, this time she crumples up the flimsy sheet of perfumed French paper, and thrusts it into her pocket. For a step comes quickly down the path behind her, and a man's voice sings, as he comes, with mellow sweetness, "La Donna e mobile." She glances round, half petulantly, as he draws near.

"You are like a shadow," she says, in a tone that suits the glance; "like a detective on the trail. How did you know I was here?"

"Don't be cross, Olga," says Frank Livingston, throwing himself on the grass beside her. "How can I tell? Some spirit in my feet—how is it Shelley goes?—led me to the charmed spot. What are you doing—sketching?"

"I came with that design, but I believe, unlikely as it may sound—I have been thinking."

"Ah ! dare I hope——"

"No, Frank, it was not of you, so do not put on that complacent look. Did mamma tell you to bring me home ?"

· "Your mamma is asleep, my dearest Olga, and does not need you in the least. Do you know, I find it difficult to realize after all our wanderings that we are home once more. And here! This place seems haunted. The last time I was here was with Geoffrey Lamar."

He takes off his hat, and the soft sea wind stirs his dark curly hair. It is a new Frank Livingston, bronzed, bearded, mustached, muscular, improved almost out of knowledge by years, and travel and cultured association. He looks handsome as a latter-day Adonis, in his gray tweed suit, and with a dash of his old Bohemian *insouciance* upon him still. Lying here, with the flickering sunshine sifting through willow plumes on his upturned face and uncovered head, he is wonderfully good to look 'at, and the half smile comes back into Olga Ventnor's eyes as they rest on him.

"You look like a picture as you lie there, Frank," she says, in an amused tone. "Do not stir, please—I want to sketch you. You are a thing of beauty and a joy forever, when you fall into picturesque attitudes, and hold your tongue. You spoil everything when you open your mouth. You ought to go through life posing, and never destroy the illusion by speaking a word. I shall send this to Hilda Stafford in my next letter. Do you know, Frank, she admires you immensely ?"

"Lady Hilda does me much honor," says Livingston, composedly. "You, too, my dear cousin, with your more than doubtful compliments. The role of barber's block which you so kindly assign me——"

"Turn a hair-breadth this way," interrupts Miss Ventnor, "and please be silent. I never can sketch and talk. I will have you in black and white in a second, and I know Lady Hilda will wear you next her heart."

Livingston laughs, but with a vexed look, and obeys. His blue eyes, very like Olga's own, rest on the lovely face above him, with a look Olga Ventnor has seen in the eyes of many men before to-day, and which certainly, in the present case, stirs her pulses no more than if Frank were her pet Spitz dog. It is a face that can be very mutinous and imperious, as he knows to his cost, a face that can be as exasperating as it is alluring, and *that* is saying much. Something akin to irritated impatience and pain stirs within him as he looks.

> "As you sit where lusters strike you,
> Sure to please,
> Do we love you most, or like you,
> Belle Marquise ?"

he quotes, under his breath.

"I told you not to talk !" says Olga, austerely ; "but a talker you are or nothing, my poor Frank. There! I think that will do. How Hilda will thank me in her secret soul for this treasure !"

A saucy smile dimples the perfect mouth, the sapphire eyes glance down laughingly at the figure on the grass. But Frank, still gazing, is absorbed in his poem.

12

> " You had every grace in heaven,
>   In your most angelic face,
> With the nameless finer leaven,
>   Lent of blood and courtly race ;
> And was added too, in duty,
> Ninon's wit, and Bouffler's beauty,
> And La Valliere's ' *Yeux Caloutes*'
>   Followed these.
> And you liked it when they said it
>   On their knees,
> And you kept it, and you read it,
>   Belle Marquise ! "

"The words must have been written for you, I think—you fit the portrait—fair, heartless, icy—admirably well. I wonder if you *have* a heart, like other people, most beautiful Olga, or if, as in the case of the Marquise, that inconvenient essential was left out ? "

"I think I have got your exact expression, or, rather, lack of it," goes on Miss Ventnor, very busy with her work, and evidently quite deaf. "This sketch is worthy of being immortalized in oils and forwarded to the autumn Exhibition. What were you saying a moment ago ? Something uncivil, I think, from the sound. But you generally *are* uncivil, and unpleasantly personal in your remarks, I grieve to observe, when you do me the honor to address me. Nothing in the world, my dear Frank, is in worse form than vituperation, and it pains me to observe that you are falling sadly into the habit. And poetical vituperation is worst of all. You will excuse my mentioning this. The cousinly—I may almost say the maternal —interest I take in you must plead the pardon of rebuke."

Livingston laughs again, and takes up the sketch-book, but the sting of her indifference rankles. It is

so real, the pang is in that. She is indifferent to all
men, she is more than indifferent to him.

In her beauty, her pride, her grace, and her power,
she is like some young queen, looking with blue,
scornful eyes upon her adorers and slaves.

As he turns the leaves of the sketch-book he suddenly stops, a look of surprise, of pleasure, of recognition flashes from his eyes. A touch of eager color comes
into his face ; he takes out a little time-yellowed,
faded, pencil-drawing from between the leaves.

"You remember it?" Olga says, calmly. "You
did that. What centuries ago it seems, and I have
kept it all this time. I wonder why? It has no intrinsic value, and certainly it could not have been for
sake of the artist. No, Frank, you need not put on
that pathetic look—I assure you it was not for the
sake of the artist. What a dowdy little thing I look,
and what a wistful expression you have given me.
Did I really look like that, at ten years old?"

For faded, yellowed, dim, it is the pencil-sketch
made by Frank fully eleven years ago.

"'Princess Olga, with the love of the most loyal of
her lieges,'" he reads at the bottom, " even then, eleven
years ago, I was in love with you, Princess Olga."

"You were in love with Lora Sleaford," returns
Miss Ventnor, composedly, " with her flame-red cheeks
and tar-black hair. You always were a person of
atrocious taste, I regret to remember. You were a
shocking boy in those days. You used to stay out until
the small hours, playing cards, singing songs, and
making love at Sleaford's."

"And you used to lie awake and watch for me—I

remember *that*. The Princess Olga of those days must have been rather fond of me, I think."

"Very likely. I used to be a dreadful little idiot, if I recall myself rightly. That picture is associated in my mind with my getting lost in the woods, and that wild creature Joanna going to tear out my hair, and all the misery and illness that followed. I wanted you to take me to play croquet with Leo Abbott that afternoon, I remember distinctly. I also remember distinctly you would not."

His eyes are upon her—trouble, longing, imploring in their pleading. - But she is not inclined to spare him.

"You would not," she repeats, a somewhat hard inflection in her voice. "You were Lora Sleaford's lover in those days. You wanted to go to her, no doubt. You broke your promise to me. You left me, whistling a tune, that sketch of myself to comfort me, and a childish ache and loneliness that I do not forget to this day. You are right, Cousin Frank, I must have been fond of you then. I wonder what absence of yours could give me a heart-ache now?"

A triumphant smile lights her face, an exultant sense that it is in no man's power to touch, or move, or hurt her.

"None, I am quite sure, though it were the absence from which there is no return," he answers, coldly.

"I wandered away," she goes on, retrospectively, "and lost myself in the woods, and you—how little you cared ! Ah ! well—all that is a decade of years ago, and Lora Sleaford is the butcher's lady over there, with a waist two yards round, and no end of little butchers growing up about her. I saw her yesterday,

Frank, in the midst of her jewels, and thought of your first love, and the banjo business, and laughed to myself. No peony, no pickled cabbage was ever so glaringly purple as her cheeks. What a mistake first love is, to be sure !"

"Or last love, or any love, in your eyes."

"Or any love—we are so fatally in the power of those we love. They can so wring our hearts ; their going is such misery, their loss such despair. You see, heartless as I am, I can imagine all that."

"Having seen a great deal of it, having caused wholesale slaughter wherever you went. Only you took care your knowledge should be from observation—never from experience."

"Never from experience. You sound sarcastic, Frank, but it is very true, nevertheless. As to caus· ing it—your great gallantry compels you to say so, no doubt. Poor little yellow pencil sketch ! Put it back. It is the only souvenir of my childhood, and of—you —I possess. Let me cherish it still."

He does as he is told—people do obey her as a general thing—she is more than a trifle imperious even in trifles, this queenly Olga, and Livingston is not inclined to rebel. He is conscious of irritating pique always, when with her ; her words wound and vex him.

She is a merciless mistress—it is questionable if any lover of hers has ever been a happy man, even in the first fleeting hour of his fool's paradise—most certain is he to be supremely miserable a little farther on.

He turns the leaves of the book mechanically, but he hardly sees the sketches, full of vigorous life as they are. Olga is almost as skilled an artist as himself.

"Look there!" she says, laying her finger on a page, "does that resemble any one you know?"

It is a young man in the dress of a monk, standing in a striking attitude, his handsome head thrown back, one hand shading his eyes. His cowl has fallen on his shoulders, his left hand rests on the head of a huge dog.

Both stand listening intently. It is in water-colors —a steel gray sky is above; around, nothing but snow —a white, frozen world.

Livingston looks, and is conscious, in some queer way, that the face of the monk is like his own.

"It is a monk and a dog of the Hospice of the Great St. Bernard," says Olga. "I saw him one evening from my bedroom window, listening and looking like that. Do you not see the likeness, Frank? He is your image, height, features, complexion, only he was more distinguished than you, and had much more courtly manners. He looked as if he might have been a young Austrian prince, come there to renounce the world, and live for God and his fellow-men. I was very much impressed—I *know* he must have been of noble blood—he had the manners and bow of a court chamberlain. And sitting there, that cold, bleak, gray evening, I sketched my handsome young monk and his dog. How grave he looks—as if the old life of courts and kings were a dream—the shadow of a dream with a touch of loneliness in the profound peace. And I thought of *you*, Frank, and imagined you in cowl and robe, and with that look in your eyes——" she breaks off with a laugh, this malicious coquette, as Livingston looks up, certainly with a very different expression from that in the peaceful, pictured face.

" 'I envy them, these monks of old.
  Their books they read, their beads they told,
  To human weakness dead and cold,
    And all life's vanity.'

There is something grand in the idea, is there not? to
renounce all that life holds of brightest and sweetest,
at that age, and for that reason? Turn another leaf."
  "I am tired of sketches," he says, impatiently, but
turns as he says it. "This is Geoffrey Lamar!" he
exclaims.
  " Drawn from memory—yes," she answers. "Frank,
where *is* Geoffrey Lamar?"
  " Heaven knows ! slaving at his profession, poor fellow, I suppose, to support his mother and sister."
  "I never understood that matter rightly," Olga says,
"except that Geoffrey made some great sacrifice for
honor's sake, and renounced for himself and Leo all
Mr. Abbott's wealth. What was it about?"
  " Heaven knows again. I suppose Geoffrey does;
he is the sort of fellow to know his own mind pretty
thoroughly. I fancy the money was illy come by,
some one had a better claim than even Leo, and so
Geoffrey gave it up. Noble, as you say, but a trifle
Quixotic, for the missing heir, whoever he may be, it
seems cannot be found. But if the heir is never found
it will make no difference to Lamar. He will work
like a galley-slave until the day of his death, for his
mother and sister, but he will never permit them to
touch a penny of dishonorably-gotten gain. There
are not many like that."
  Olga says nothing, but a sort of glow comes into
her face—a look that is never there except when she
listens to some deed heroic.

"He is of the stuff that made paladins of old," goes on Livingston, "with uplifted notions on every subject under the sun—a sort of Sir Galahad, you know, to ride to the aid of damsels in distress. Witness his adoption of Sleaford's Joanna. By-the-bye, I wonder whatever has become of Wild Joanna. I must step in and inquire of Mistress Lora one of these days. Not that she is likely to know."

"When did you see Geoff—the Abbotts, last?" Olga inquires.

"I saw Geoff in New York, but 'we met by chance the usual way.' He does not live there, but somewhere out of the world, where he is working himself to skin and bone, judging by his look. They have sunk the Abbott, and call themselves Lamar now—the old pride, you know. I do not see much sense in it myself. They might at least use the property until the missing heir turns up. I would have liked to go and see Leo, but Geoffrey's manner was cold and discouraging. And one cannot force one's self whether or no, you know."

"I do not know. *My* experience—of you—is particularly the reverse, but I suppose cousins are always an exception. As you are here, Frank, you may as well make yourself useful, and carry my sketch-book home. I am going."

She rises—a lofty, slender, white figure—picks up her cashmere and gold wrap, puts on her pretty hat, and turns to go.

"Come, Frank!" she says, and glances back, with one of those brilliantly sweet smiles that are as fatal to men as the siren song of the fabled Lurley. What is Frank that he should resist? He is but mortal, and the spell of the enchantress is upon him. Is he in love with her? really in love? He asks himself that question sometimes, but never when by her side. Then the glamour of the white witchery is upon him, and he lives but to do her bidding. Coldness, coquetry, are forgotten now; he picks up the big flat book, throws on his hat, and is by her side. And he thinks of a fitting couplet—though remembering recent rebuke he does not quote it:

" You throw off your friends, like a huntsman his pack,
For you know when you will you can whistle them back."

All the way to Ventnor Villa Olga is very silent and thoughtful. The sun is setting as they reach it, and she lingers a moment to look at its rose and gold beauty. But she is not thinking much of the sunset—not at all of the young cavalier by her side.

"Like a paladin of old," she muses, dreamily. 'Yes, it is true. He is noble, great, good, self-sacrificing. I wish—I wish I could see—Leo Abbott—again."

CHAPTER II.

AFTER THE CONCERT.

HE lamps are lit in the pretty drawing-room of the villa. Dinner is over, and the one guest, the Reverend Ignatius Lamb, sits near Mrs. Ventnor's sofa, talking earnestly. The ex-rector of St. Walburga's is the incumbent of a beautiful little church in the village now, not so rich or rare a gem certainly as St. Walburga's in the days of

12*

Mrs. Abbott—still, an extremely pretty structure. Gothic as to style, mediæval as to painted saints on golden backgrounds, aristocratic as to congregation, and all that there is of the most ritualistic, as to doctrine.

Mrs. Ventnor, pallid, languid, graceful, reclining on her couch, listens with weary interest. She has a pew at St. Chad's, and is especially anxious about the success of Mr. Lamb's latest project—that of founding a convent and an orphan asylum, on a grant of land recently presented to the church by Colonel Ventnor. The order is quite a new one, the Sisters of the Suffering—Mr. Lamb himself the founder, and to establish the Mother House in Brightbrook, with an asylum and a day-school, is a project very near to the reverend gentleman's heart.

"I saw the Reverend Mother last week," he is saying to Mrs. Ventnor, " and it was she who proposed this concert. For obvious reasons, it is more convenient at present than either a picnic or fair. Mother Bonaventure knows this singer—this Miss Jenny Wild —knew her before she entered religion—you understand, and speaks of her in the very highest terms. Her moral character—Miss Wild's, of course—is perfectly unexceptionable. And she is more than willing to assist us by giving a concert and donating the proceeds. She is said to excel in charities indeed, and is especially interested in orphan children. In addition to her concert she promises two hundred dollars. All this, with the noble donation of your excellent husband, my dear madam, will enable us to start work at once, without incurring pecuniary liabilities. Everything is arranged, and the concert takes place on Monday evening. Miss

Wild is at present in New York, but will reach
Brightbrook on that day. May I hope, my dear Mrs.
Ventnor, that you will endeavor to be present?"

"I go nowhere of late," Mrs. Ventnor responds,
languidly, "as you are aware. My wretched health,
you know—but assuredly, if possible, I will be present
at the concert."

"And Miss Olga—we may, I presume, count upon
her without fail."

The door opens as he speaks, and the Reverend
Ignatius pauses, and is conscious of a shock—not an
unpleasant one. He holds distinct views upon the
celibacy of the clergy, and has always advocated them,
but at this moment he feels that under certain influences a man and an Anglican priest may be untrue
to the convictions of his life, and yet be excusable.

She comes in, tall, slender, white-robed, her lovely
hair falling like a bath of sunshine over her shoulders,
her gold and snow drapery trailing about her, a faint
flush on her cheeks, a starry light in the blue, blue
eyes. Behind her comes her faithful shadow, Frank,
and the Reverend Ignatius' frowns slightly, and
realizes that handsome distant cousins are a most dangerous and objectionable class of men.

"My dear, how late you are," mamma murmurs, as
Olga stoops and kisses her, "we have dined without
you. Dr. Gillson, you know, is most peremptory on
the point of my always dining at the same hour."

"Pray make no excuses, mamma—it does not matter in the least," Olga says, gayly. "Frank and I will
dine *tete-a-tete*. We have been quarreling all the afternoon, and can recommence over our soup. Anything

new in Brightbrook, Mr. Lamb? What of the new convent?"

"Olga thinks of renouncing this wicked world, and going in for Mother Abbess. The role would suit her, I think. She has rather the look at this moment of a vestal virgin—a Norma—a Priestess of the Sun. That sort of people never cared for anybody but themselves, and were made of ice-water more or less, I believe."

"My dear Frank, how often have I told you sarcasm is not your strong point? You mean to be cynical, but in reality I am almost sure I should like it. The habit of the Sisters of the Suffering is in admirable taste—a trained black robe, a white coif, and long black vail are always picturesque and becoming. What of our fair, Mr. Lamb—or is it to be a picnic?"

Mr. Lamb explains. It is to be neither. It is to be a concert—a ballad concert, with Miss Jenny Wild as prima-donna, and Monday next is the appointed night.

"Miss Jenny Wild? Jenny Wild? I do not know that name. Who is she? Do you know her, Frank?"

"Never heard her—heard of her though. Sings in character—ballads chiefly, and is very popular. Good contralto they say, but seldom comes to New York. It is not to be supposed you would know her, Miss Ventnor—scampering over the face of the earth as you have been for the past five years. Come to dinner. I do not know how it may be with you, but I am consumedly hungry."

They go. Frank may be in love with the exquisite face across the table, but that fact does not impair his appetite to any serious extent. If it exists, it is perhaps a love of the eyes, not of the heart, for he is distinctly conscious of being much more comfortable away from his adored one than with her.

Her presence, her triumphant beauty, have upon him the effect of a fever. He seeks to woo and win her, and he feels that if he succeeds he will be in a state of unrest and discomfort all the rest of his life. She exacts too much, her ideal is too high ; he can never reach it ; it is always uncomfortable to dwell on the heights. Still, the family expect it of him, and to show the white feather in love or in war is not the nature of a Livingston. In an off-hand sort of way he has been making love to his pretty cousin ever since he can remember, but to distinct proposal he has never yet come. In his pocket, to-night, a letter lies from his mother, urging, entreating, commanding him to speak before he leaves Brightbrook. Business calls him away on Tuesday next, and the Rubicon must be crossed between then and now. He is not a nervous young man as a rule ; but, truth to tell, the thought makes his heart beat a little quickly. Perhaps it is not to his discredit that he is a trifle afraid of this regal Olga. He is not the first man who has feared this chill, white goddess. This is Thursday evening. He has still one, two, three, four days and nights to screw his courage to the sticking-place, and put his fate to the touch, to " win or lose it all."

" I will speak to-morrow," he thinks, looking at her across the cut flowers and crystal. " Hang it all ! why should I be afraid ?

" 'Praise as you may, when the tale is done,
She is but a maid to be wooed and won.' "

But to-morrow comes and he does not speak. He

does not feel sentimental, as it chances, and no fellow
can propose in cold blood. And Saturday, and Sunday, and Monday come, and still golden silence reigns,
and his fate hangs in the balance. And Monday evening is the evening of the concert, and there is no longer
chance or time.

The whole Ventnor family go. Olga, in India muslin, with touches of crimson here and there in her pale,
crisp draperies and laces, is, as ever, bewildering. A
fairly fashionable assembly fills the hall, and Miss
Ventnor finds an acquaintance who seems to know all
about the musical star of the night.

"A very charming songstress, I assure you," the
lady says. "She travels with her guardian and his
wife—Germans, I believe—and has a very sweet and
powerful contralto, with an odd sort of pathos in it
that most people are captivated by who hear her sing.
I have seen her give nearly a whole evening's enter-
tainment herself, singing song after song, in character.
with a rapidity and power quite amazing. It is very
good of her to proffer her services in this way ; but
then she *is* good ; it is quite like her. She is the most
generous and large-hearted creature in the world—and
beyond reproach, I assure you. In all quarters Miss
Wild is most highly spoken of."

"Yes?" Olga says, indifferently. She is not much
interested, naturally, in Miss Wild or her character.
Her glass sweeps the hall, and she is busy acknowledg-
ing bows. It is something of a bore to be here at all,
after seasons of Patti and Nilsson abroad. Still, it is
for Mr. Lamb, and she is Olga Ventnor—and *noblesse
oblige.*

The curtain rises ; the stage is handsomely decorated. A slim, dark young man, with great Italian eyes and accent, appears, and sings, "Let Me Like a Soldier Fall," in a very fine baritone voice. Then there is a piano solo—Liszt's "Rhapsodie" No. 2, performed in a masterly manner by Herr Ericson, and then Miss Jenny Wild is before them, and "Love My Love" is ringing through the concert-room, in a voice that makes even Olga Ventnor, difficult as she is, look up in pleased surprise. And looking once, she looks again. The singer, a tall, finely-formed young woman, dressed simply enough, in dark silk, is a person to command from most people a second glance. It is hardly a handsome face, but it is a striking one; the features are good, the eyes dark and brilliant, and with an intensity of expression not often seen. There is vivid dramatic power in her rendering of the song—the voice has that sweet, touching, minor tone Olga has heard of. But something beyond all this strikes and holds Miss Ventnor. "As in a glass darkly" she seems to recognize that face, that voice. She knits her brows, and tries to recall. In vain—Miss Jenny Wild refuses to be placed. She concludes her song, and disappears in the midst of a tumult of applause.

"She is really a very fine singer," Olga says to the lady by her side, "but it is the oddest thing—I seem to have seen and heard her somewhere before."

"You have attended some of her concerts, perhaps?" the lady suggests.

"No, it cannot be that—this is the first concert I have attended since my return to America. Frank!" imperiously, "are you asleep? What are you thinking of, sitting there, with that dazed look?"

"Of Miss Jenny Wild. Somewhere—in some other

planet, perhaps—I must have met that young lady before. Ah! she is good-natured ; she responds to the
encore. Here she is again."

Miss Wild reappears, bowing graciously to the
hearty call she has received. Her fine dark eyes
calmly survey the house, and lift and rest for the first
time on the Ventnor party. They fall on Frank
Livingston, and meet his puzzled glance full.

A slight flush rises to her face, a slight smile dawns
about the lips, then her graceful figure is drawn up,
and she is singing " Within a Mile of Edinboro' Town."
The old, ever-welcome favorite is listened to with delight, and a great basket of flowers is presented to the
singer. Olga hands Frank her bouquet.

" Throw it," she says ; " she deserves it. She sang
that delightfully. Miss Jenny Wild is worth coming to
hear. But, oh! *where* have I seen and heard her before?"

Frank throws the cluster of white roses with un-
erring aim—it lights at the feet of the songstress.
She stoops and picks it up, and again that slight
glance, and flush, and smile rest on Livingston, as she
bows and quits the stage.

The Italian sings again. Herr Ericson performs a
ringing Rondo, and Miss Wild sings the grand aria,
" Nabuco " from Verdi, quite magnificently, and again
is rapturously encored. Once more she responds with
another Scotch song, " Sleeping Maggie," and once more
her eyes look and linger with evident amusement on
the profoundly puzzled face of Frank Livingston.
Then the concert is over, and they are out- in the sweet
darkness of the June night.

" *Who* is Miss Jenny Wild?" cries Olga, impatiently ; " I hate to be puzzled, and she puzzles me.

Frank, I command you! find out all about her, and
tell me why her face and voice are so ridiculously
familiar. And she has, evidently, seen *you* before—
she did you the honor to look at you more than once
in the most marked manner."

" I go to-morrow," is Frank's answer, "and whether
I shall ever return to discover Miss Jenny Wild's an-
tecedents, or for any other reason, depends entirely on
you, Olga, and what you will say to me to-night!"

The hour has come—the two are alone, lingering
for a moment before saying good-night and going in.
They stand on the piazza ; the June stars shine above
them ; the silence of midnight is around them.

She glances at him in surprise ; she is humming
" Within a Mile of Edinboro' Town."

"' For I cannot—wunnot—wunnot—wunnot buckle
to !'" she sings, and then breaks off to laugh.

" What a tragical face ! What a desperate tone !
What a dramatic speech ! You go to-morrow, and
whether you will ever return depends on what I will
say to-night ! Really, Frank, the concert, and the
impassioned singing of Miss Wild have been too much
for you. Must you really go to-morrow ? I am sorry.
Hurry back."

" *Are* you sorry, Olga ? Shall you miss me ? Do
you care for me, I wonder, the very least in the world ?
Oh, you know what I mean ! Do not laugh at me, for
God's sake !" with almost angry impatience. " You
have laughed at me long enough ! I love you, Olga !—
I want you to be my wife !"

The words, thought of so long, come abruptly
enough—roughly, indeed. He sees in her face the
familiar, mocking look he knows so well—a look

nothing seems to have power to soften or change. But at the irritated passion of his voice and face it dies out, and she looks at him with smiling, gentle, half amused eyes.

"I like you so much, Frank, that I am sorry you have said this. You do not mean it, do you? We have been playing at flirtation all our lives, and, by mistake, you have fancied the play earnest to-night. You are not in love with me—you do not want me to be your wife. You would be miserable if I said yes, and you know it. But fear not. I am not going to say yes."

"Say it and try! I will risk the misery. All my life will be devoted to you, every thought of my heart, if you will marry me, Olga."

"Marry you!" she repeats; "marry *you*, Frank!" There is that in her tone makes Livingston redden angrily and throw back his head. She laughs a little in spite of herself. "I never thought of such a thing in my life," she says, with cruel coolness.

"Do you mean to tell me," the young man demands, in no very tender tone, "that you did not know it was a compact made and agreed to years and years ago?"

"Never!" she answers, with energy, "never! In such compact I had no share—of such compact I never heard. Oh, yes!" contemptuously, in reply to his indignant glance; "I have heard hints, innuendoes, seen smiles and wise glances; but do you think I heeded them? They are the impertinences relatives seem to think they have a right to. There is but one person on earth who has a right to speak to me of such a thing—my dear father—and he has been silent.

And I do not care for you, Frank—in that way. I am very fond of you—there never was a time when I was not, I think," she says, and holds out her hand with the sweet, alluring smile that makes men her slaves, "there never will come a time when I shall not be. But not like that. There is not a friend I have in the world I would not sooner lose than you; so shake hands and forget and forgive all this. Let us say good-night and good-by, and when you return—say in three or four weeks—you will have forgotten the fancy of to-night. Do not look cross, Frank, it does not become you—and come in."

She slips her hand through his arm, and, half laughing at his moody face, draws him into the house. The gas burns low in the drawing-room, the piano stands open; she strikes the keys as she stands, smiling over her shoulder, and sings:

> " The fairest rose blooms but a day—Good-by!
> The fairest spring must end with May,
> And you and I can only say:
> Good-by, good-by, good-by!"

CHAPTER III.

AFTER LONG YEARS.

HE morning that follows this night of the concert is bleak and raw for June. A drab sky frowns on a sunless world; the wind is as much like November as the month of roses, and the weather-wise predict rain. But in this threatening state of the weather Miss Jenny Wild hires a pony carriage, and starts all by herself for a drive.

Not for an aimless drive—she seems to know very well where she wants to go. She is very plainly dressed, in black, a straight dark figure sitting upright in the little carriage, a black straw hat, with a blue vail twisted round it, on her head. She pulls this vail over her face as she drives through the village, and, glancing hardly to the right or left, takes the woodland road, and pulls up at the Red Farm, erstwhile Sleaford's.

Here she sits and gazes for a long, long time, with darkly-thoughtful face and brooding eyes, at the dreary and deserted house. There her most miserable childhood was spent ; working in that kitchen her most miserable girlhood wore on ; in that attic room how many supremely wretched nights of cold, and pain, and isolation, and heart-break the child Joanna struggled through ! In that adjoining chamber her merciless task-master had met his fate, and passed to his death. In that parlor, with its shattered panes, how many a jolly revel had been held, in which *her* part was only additional drudgery. And yet she had liked them, too; there were light and music, and laughter and dancing, and youth, and at one of them she had first seen Frank Livingston's gay, handsome face—the same face, older, manlier, she had looked upon again last night. Out of yonder broken gate she had watched him come one never-to-be-forgotten morning, with his fair little cousin in his arms. Last night he had sat by that fair young cousin's side, and listened to her singing. Always these two are associated in her mind, and always with a sense of dull, morbid pain. In that gloomy kitchen she first saw Geoffrey Lamar, the true, noble-hearted friend who had done all in his power to lift her out of her misery

and out of herself. Here wild Joanna suffered and
slaved, was beaten and girded at; from here she fled,
out into the world, with George Blake! And to-day
she might have been George Blake's wife, if chance—
or Providence—had not thrown in her way Frank
Livingston, and so in a moment changed her whole
life.

She turns from the eerie spot at last, and goes on
to Black's Dam. Here, too, time and decay have lain
their ruinous finger. The old mill, her shelter and
solace so often, has fallen to utter decay, the pond is
almost dry—silent desolation reigns. She turns from
it with a shudder, and drives away. Great drops of
rain are beginning to patter, but she cares almost as
little for a wetting now as in the old days. She drives
to Abbott Wood—the old gate-keeper lives still in the
vine-wreathed Gothic lodge, but he can give her no
news of his missing mistress.

A lawyer from the city does everything that is to
be done in these latter days. Of Mrs. Abbott or Mr.
Geoffrey no one seems to know anything. The rain
falls heavily as she drives through the lovely, leafy
avenues, up to the grand, silent, somber house. The
blinds are down, the shutters closed; it looks as if it
were mourning for those it has lost. She does not go
in, though she is invited to do so by Mrs. Hill. She
feels she cannot look at those fair, empty apartments,
filled by the haunting faces of half a dozen years ago.
Her own is among them—the restless, unhappy, aimless Joanna of seventeen. She is neither aimless nor
restless now. She has found her niche and work in
life, and they suit her well. But happy? Well, she
is hardly that, and yet a very different, a much wiser,

gentler, nobler Joanna, than the dark, discontented
protégée of Geoffrey Lamar. Softened and good she
has grown, through years of kindness and affection
given to her lavishly and loyally by the Herr Professor
and Madame Ericson. All that is best in her has
its day at last. Of friends she has many ; of lovers
she has had her share ; of admirers more than she
cares to remember. And love has redeemed her, and
"Miss Jenny Wild" is all that they say of her, and
more, giving of her abundance to all who ask and
need.

That afternoon Professor Ericson and his family,
as he calls them, leave Brightbrook. By the morning
train Mr. Frank Livingston has gone up to New York,
and while Miss Wild is recalling the days of her youth,
he is spinning along, a cigar between his lips, the
morning paper in his hand, far from the scene of his
despair. Truth to tell, he looks anything but despairing this morning, in a most becoming English suit of
the very roughest gray tweed, fresh, vigorous, good-
looking, alert. Broken-hearted at his rejection he has
a right to be, and may be ; but a broken heart is becoming to some people, and Livingston is apparently
one of them. In his secret soul there is rather a sensation of relief, that as the train bowls along it bears
him in its throbbing bosom a free man ! He has done
what destiny and his Maker, and the united houses of
Ventnor and Livingston expected of him, and she has
said No, and there is no appeal. And when Mr. Livingston dies, and worms eat him, whatever the imme-
diate cause may be, he is comfortably convinced it
will not be love. So, in a fairly cheerful mood, he
surveys his fellow-passengers, unfolds his Brightbrook

paper, and reads what the musical critic of that sheet has to say about last night's concert. Miss Wild is lauded, and Livingston is disposed to laud also. She sang remarkably well, and looked very imposing. That grand aria from "Nabuco" is still ringing in his ears, and it occurs to him once more to wonder why her face should be so oddly familiar. Not a pretty face, he decides, but a good one, a striking one, and once seen not easily forgotten. And then he turns to another column and subject, and forgets all about it.

He spends three or four days in New York, among old friends and old haunts. His principal object in coming to town is to tell his mother the result of his proposal, and so make an end of that business at once and forever ; but his mother has gone on a visit. He proposes to follow her, for he knows it is a subject on which she is more than anxious ; but it is news that will keep, and he does not hurry himself. On the evening of the third day he sees by the bills that Miss Jenny Wild is to give one of her character concerts, and makes up his mind to go.

"Perhaps I shall be able to place her this time," he thinks, "and so get rid of her altogether. I believe I was dreaming of her half the night last night."

So, a little after the commencement of the concert, Mr. Livingston saunters in, and finds a large and fashionable gathering. Many of the faces present are familiar ; one lady in a private box bows, and smiles, and beckons, and in a few moments he is shaking hands with Mrs. Van Rensselaer and her daughters.

"So glad to meet you once more, my dear boy," that great and gracious lady exclaims, " and looking so extremely sun-burned and well. We heard you had

returned with the Ventnors, and were staying with
them at that charming villa. And how is dear Mrs.
Ventnor, and the lovely Olga, after their prolonged
European tour ?"

" Mrs. Ventnor is much as usual, and Olga is rather
lovelier than usual," says Frank.

"And when are we to congratulate you, Mr. Livingston ?" says the elder Miss Van Rensselaer, a dashing and daring brunette, but not quite so young as she
used to be. " Ah ! we hear more than you think, we
stay-at-homes. We expected Olga would have cap-
tured a duke at least, so many rich American girls are
making brilliant matches this year. And yet there
she is, *la belle des belles*, back again and—as we understand—unattached ! But you can open the mysteries,
no doubt."

" I only know Olga refused half the peerage !" says
Livingston, with calm mendacity. " As for your very
flattering hints, Miss Van Rensselaer, you do me too
much honor in inferring *I* have anything to do with
it. I might as well love some bright particular star,
and so on, as my beautiful Cousin Olga. Such
daughters of the gods are not for impecunious artists
like myself. Ah ! here is Miss Wild, and as Marguerite, singing the famous ' Jewel Song.' How well
she is looking, and in what capital voice she is to-
night."

" You have seen her before ?" Miss Brenda Van
Rensselaer inquires.

" Once before, at a concert last Monday night. Her
voice has the ringing of mountain bells, and what
pathos and dramatic force she has. She would make a

fine actress. It strikes me Miss Wild grows on one. I like her better now than I did even then."

"Oh! she is lovely," cries Miss Brenda, gushingly. "We are the greatest friends. She is received by the very best people. She is perfectly charming in private life, and, unlike most artists, always so willing to sing. She comes to us to-night after the concert; mamma has a reception. I think her drawing-room songs are even more beautiful than her stage singing."

"Come and make her acquaintance," says Mrs. Van Rensselaer, graciously.

"Thanks—I will," Livingston responds.

He is exceedingly taken by Miss Wild, he loves music almost more than he does art, and her voice, her look are so sympathetic that they draw him irresistibly. Besides, he wants to discover what is that familiar look about her that so perplexes him now.

" Who is Miss Wild?" he asks, as, in the midst of hearty applause, she quits the stage.

"Ah! who, indeed?" returns the elder Miss Van Rensselaer. "Find somebody to answer that if you can! No one knows; she arose first a little pale star out West, and went on shining and enlarging until she is the star of first magnitude. You see her now. Hark to the clapping—she will return in a moment— they always encore her songs. Flattering, but rather a bore, I should think. Here she is; what will she give us now, I wonder?"

An hour later he stands in the Van Rensselaer drawing-rooms, and awaits his introduction to the cantatrice. He cannot tell why he is so vividly interested in her, unless it is caused by that puzzling familiarity. But interested and impatient he is, and as he

13

has never been to meet any artist of the kind before.

"Mr. Livingston, Miss Wild," says, simply, his hostess, and he looks down into two dark, jewel-like eyes, into a smiling face. He is conscious of bowing and murmuring his pleasure—another moment and some one else has claimed her, and she turns—is gone.

He looks after her with knitted brows, and ever deepening perplexities. That tall figure, that gentle, earnest face, those great gem-like eyes—they are in some mysterious way as well-known to him as his own face in the glass. He tries to approach her more than once as the evening wears on, but she is always surrounded. The charm of her manner evidently carries all before it, as well as the charm of her voice.

Presently, when he is about to give up in despair, he hears her singing, and makes his way to the piano. The words she sings he has never heard before—the air is tender and very sweet.

> "My darling! my darling! my darling!
>   Do you know how I want you to-night?
> The wind passes, moaning and snarling,
>   Like some evil ghost on its flight.
> On the wet street your lamp's gleam shines redly;
>   You are sitting alone—did you start
> As I spoke? Did you guess at this deadly
>   Chill pain in my heart?

> "Out here where the dull rain is falling,
>   Just once—just a moment—I wait;
> Did you hear the sad voice that was calling
>   Your name, as I paused by the gate?
> It was just a mere breath, ah, I know, dear,
>   Not even Love's ears could have heard;
> But, oh, I was hungering so, dear,
>   For one little word.

" Ah, me! for a word that could move you,
  Like a whisper of magical art!
  I love you! I love you! I love you!
  There is no other word in my heart——"

She looks up ; her eyes meet his. Has she been
conscious of his presence there all along ? Her hands
strike the wrong chords ; there is a jar and discord ;
a flush rises over her face ; she laughs, and suddenly
breaks off.

" Oh, go on !" half a dozen voices cry ; " that is
lovely."

" I sing it from memory," Miss Wild says. " It is
a little poem I lit upon the other day in a magazine,
and it seemed to fit some music I had. I will sing you
something better instead."

She sings " Kathleen Mavourneen," and looks no
more at Frank Livingston. He stands wondering, and
of his wonder finding no end. He turns over absently
some sheets of music bearing her name, and as he
does so, from one of them a written page falls. It is
the song she has broken off. Instantly he commits
petty larceny, and puts it in his pocket.

" It will serve as an excuse to call upon her and
restore her property," thinks this " artful dodger."
" Find out who she is I must, or I shall perish misera-
bly of curiosity."   .

" Kathleen Mavourneen " is finished, and she makes
a motion to rise ; but her listeners seem insatiable.

" Only one more—one little, *little* one, dear Miss
Wild," a young lady says.

She pauses, glances at Livingston's absorbed face,
smiles, and begins, " My Ain Ingleside." And then,
in one second, like a flash, a shock, the truth bursts

upon him. He has heard that song before ! In the
drawing-room of Abbott Wood he has heard the same
voice sing it ! He stands petrified, spell-bound, breathless, his eyes on her face. Sleaford's Joanna ! Yes,
yes, yes ! the reddish, unkempt hair shining, dark,
becomingly   dressed,   the   sweet   voice   perfected,
womanly, and sweet, but still—Sleaford's Joanna !

How it comes about he does not know, but five
minutes later he is standing with her alone, both her
hands clasped close in his.

" It is !" he exclaims ; " I cannot be mistaken. It
is Joanna !"

" Sleaford's Joanna," she answers, and tears slowly
fill her eyes, though her lips are smiling. " I saw you
knew me, puzzled as you looked, and thought the old
song would put an end to your evident misery. Yes,
Mr. Livingston, after all these years, it is Joanna."

" And I am the first to find you," he says, triumph-
antly, " that is a good omen. Tell me where you live.
I *must* come to see you, and talk over the old days.
You shall not make a stranger of so old a friend,
Joanna."

" So old a friend !" she draws away her hands and
laughs. " Were you and I ever friends ? Ah, yes,
come and see me. It does me good to look at a Brightbrook face. ˙ And I am glad—yes, glad, that yours is
the first."

" And that is Sleaford's Joanna," Livingston thinks,
going home through the city streets, feeling dazed and
in a dream ; " fair, stately, famous ! What will Olga
say when I tell her this ?"

CHAPTER IV.

"CARRIED BY STORM."

HEN Mr. Frank Livingston carries his blighted affections away with him from Brightbrook and his fair, cold cousin Olga, it is, as has been said, with the intention of seeing his mother and making an end of that, and then starting off for a summer sketching tour, through Canada and British Columbia.

That was his intention. The last week of June is here, and so is Mr. Livingston. Canada and British Columbia—places misty, afar-off, unseen and undesired. Three weeks have come and gone, warm, dusty weeks, and every day of these twenty-one days has seen him by the side of Miss Jenny Wild, and for more hours a day than he cares to count.

Miss Wild is still singing—not every night, but one or two evenings a week. She is a favorite with the musical public, and her concerts are always well attended. On the nights she sings, a slender and exceedingly handsome young man may be observed in one of the front seats, drinking in with entranced looks every note of that sweet, bell-like voice. Miss Wild on the stage, in trailing silks and stage adjuncts, is a very imposing and graceful person.

She has a face that lights up well, dark, pale, and clear ; great star-like eyes, and the most beautiful smile and teeth—the young gentleman in the front seat thinks—in all the world. She is hardly handsome—at times she is positively plain ; but yet there

are others, when, flushed and sparkling with excitement and applause, her dark eyes shining, she is
brilliantly attractive. She possesses, in an eminent
degree, that magnetic unknown grace, quite apart from
beauty, and called fascination. Her smile enchants;
her eyes hold you ; her voice haunts you ; her tricks
and graces of manner captivate before you know it.
Where the charm exactly lies no one can tell, not her
most bewitched admirer, but it is there, subtile and
irresistible. The tones of her voice, the words she
says and sings, the light of her eyes and her smile
linger in the memory of men after lovelier women are
forgotten. Perhaps it is a little in her abounding
vitality, her joyous life, her lavish largeness of heart,
that has room and to spare for all who come. Friends,
admirers, lovers, if you will, she has many, and foremost among them Frank Livingston. For Frank
Livingston to be in love, or what he calls such, is no
new experience. He has loved many women, and been
cared for, more or less, a good deal, in turn. Handsome, *insouciant*, inconstant, he is yet a gallant and
gracious young fellow, for whose faults fair flirts are
quite as much to blame as his own intrinsic infidelity.
Three weeks ago a young lady refused him—at present
he is the ardent admirer of another. In any case he
would have taken his rejection with philosophy, and
consoled himself promptly—possibly with some good-
looking young squaw, if he had gone to British Columbia. He has not gone to that chilly land, and Miss
Jenny Wild, the songstress, has found favor in my lord's
sight. She bewitches him—her force of character, her
great popularity, the number of his rivals, the evident
preference she shows him, turn his head. He ignores

past and future, he lives in the present—in the sunlight of those dark, entrancing eyes. He spends every afternoon by her side, in the park, in the streets, in her parlor. He sketches her in half a hundred attitudes—he is painting her portrait—he is perfectly happy!

For Miss Wild—well, Livingston cannot quite make her out. Her eyes and smile welcome him always; she takes his bouquets, she sings him the songs he likes. Her doors are open to him when closed to all the rest of the world. And something in all this puzzles him. If it were any one else, it would be most encouraging preference; but this is Joanna, and Joanna is different. He does not understand her. He is by no means sure of what her answer would be, if he were inclined to speak to-morrow. She likes him—yes, of that there can be no doubt; but if he were to say, "Joanna, will you be my wife?" he has very strong doubts of what her answer would be. But he really has no intention of asking any such thing. The present is delightful; it is charming to be with her—that suffices. To-day is good—why lift the vail that hides to-morrow? To be *epris* is one thing, to ask the lady to marry one is another.

———

"And so to-night is your last appearance for the summer?" he says, "and you all go to your Newport cottage to-morrow? Well, New York is no longer habitable, of course; but what an elysium I have found it for the past month! I, too, shall go to Newport, Joanna!"

"And that sketching and hunting tour in British

Columbia ? And that visit to your anxious mamma ?
What of them ?" she asks, laughing.

They sit alone in the cool, green-shaded parlor,
Joanna doing lace work, Frank on an ottoman more or
less at her feet, with the Browning he has been reading aloud tellingly, on his knee.

"I *must* see my mother," he answers, frowning
impatiently, "but it will be a flying visit. As for
British Columbia—well, British Columbia will always
be there, and other summers will come. But the
chance of going to Newport—in this way—may not
occur again."

"I think it had better not occur now. Start on that
visit to Mrs. Livingston to-morrow, and take train from
there to Montreal. It will be best, believe me. You
have had a surfeit of Newport and surf bathing, I
should think, before now."

"Neither Newport nor surf bathing will be novel-
ties, certainly. But I do not go for them, you know
that. Do you forbid me to follow, Joanna ?"

"Why should I ?" she says, and her dark eyes rest
on him a moment. "I like you to be with me. No,
do not say anything complimentary, please—I was not
angling for that ; I mean what I say. It brings back
the old times and the faces I seem to have lost out of
my life. That past is a dark memory enough, and
yet it holds good things—Mrs. Abbott, Geoffrey, and
dear little Leo. I can never regret its pain when I
think of them."

"And does it hold no one else ?" he asks, jealously.

"Ah, you were no friend of mine in those days.
Do not deny it—I have an excellent memory for the
few who cared for me in that desolate time. And you

were not among them. Why should you have been?
I was only an ugly and uncouth creature, rude in manner, and look, and speech. I was not of your world
then. I am not now. No, the gap is not bridged over
yet. Do you think I do not know it?—do you think
I do not know it never can be? I am a singer, I am
popular, I make money, if that is all—fashionable
people like Mrs. Van Rensselaer ask me to their parties because I sing and amuse their guests. But I am
nameless, homeless, a vagabond, and a wanderer. And
to know *who* I am is the one unsatisfied desire, the one
ceaseless longing of my heart. Surely I must have a
name—surely in some veins the same blood must flow.
There were the Sleafords—I do not know to this day
whether they were related to me or not."

"'A little more than kin, and less than kind,'"
Livingston quotes. "What does it matter, Joanna?
You have hosts of friends who love you for yourself.
You have made a name the world honors. Why
regret what you may be better without knowing?"

Her work has dropped, her hands clasp her knees
as she leans forward, in the old fashion he remembers;
her great eyes look dreamy, and wistful, and far
off.

"I would give half my life to know. I will never
rest until I know. The Sleafords I have lost sight
of; even Lora had left, and gone West before I had
reached Brightbrook. For the boys—it is doubtful if
they could tell me anything, even if I found them.
The secret of my life Giles Sleaford alone held, and
he carried it with him into the grave. I would give
all I possess to know. You cannot understand this—
you who have always had name, and home, and re-

13*

lations, and love—this ceaseless heart-hunger for some
one to whom we *belong*. Ah, well! it is folly to sigh
over the inevitable. But all the same, it leaves me
to-day what I was six years ago, and you—you had
much better be wise, and go to Canada, and shoot
moose! The past weeks have been pleasant—yes—
but they are over. Say good-by to-morrow, and do
not come to Newport."

"I shall never be wise if that is wisdom," he says,
coolly. "I am always happiest when with you. Let
me be happy in my own way. I shall make that
filial visit, of course—that cannot be postponed—
but I shall return and spend ·my summer at Newport."

She smiles and says no more. She resumes her
work, and he his Browning. If Livingston cannot
understand her, neither can she understand herself.
All her life he has been in her eyes something different from other men. In her ignorant youth he
was the "Prince Charming" of her fairy tales. In
her dreary girlhood a slight, a word from him could
stab her as no other had power to stab. She does not
understand why this should be—she only knows it is
so. There is no reason why she should care for him.
There are a hundred good and sound ones why she
should not. The fact remains—she *does* care for
him; she will care for him possibly to her life's end!

That night is Miss Wild's last appearance for the
season, and that night the house is thronged with her
admirers and friends. That night she is brilliant as
she has never been brilliant before, as she never will
be again, for it is the very last time she will ever face
an audience! But though she does not know it, some

thrilled, excited feeling sends a streaming light into her eyes, a deep flush into her too-pale cheeks, a ringing sweetness and power into her voice.

She sings as she has never sung before. She bears her audience away—she is recalled again and again, flowers are flung to her, the theater rings with excited applause. Foremost—wholly carried away, is Frank Livingston. Always excitable, the success of to-night turns his head. She is bewitching--she is a very queen of song—she is radiant in her triumph—she is irresistible! Head and heart are in a tumult—this is love, and he will win her—this bewildering woman, who turns the brains of all men!

It is all over—it has been an ovation—and they are in her rooms—Herr Ericson and madame his wife, the Italian baritone, and Frank. In her trailing silks and laces, with sapphire ornaments, she looks absolutely handsome—she looks like a goddess in Livingston's dazzled eyes. They are alone in one of the softly lit rooms—her piano stands open, but it is he who strikes the silvery chords, looking up with eyes that flash in her smiling face. It is he who sings, in an excited, exultant voice, the little song he purloined, the song he first heard her sing at Mrs. Van Rensselaer's party :

"Do you think I am ever without you?
　　Ever lose for an instant your face,
　Or the spell that breathes alway about you,
　　Of your subtile, ineffable grace? ·
　Why, even to-night, put away, dear,
　　From the light of your eyes though I stand,
　I feel as I linger and pray, dear,
　　The touch of your hand.

"Ah, me! for a word that could move you
　Like a whisper of magical art!

> I love you! I love you! I love you!
> There is no other word in my heart.
> Will your eyes, that are loving, still love me?
> Will your heart, once so tender, forgive?
> Ah! darling, stoop down from above me
> And tell me to live."

"I love you! I love you! I love you!" he cries, and rising, takes both her hands in his feverish clasp. "Joanna, I love you! I always have from the first, I think, but to-night you have carried my heart by storm!"

She does not speak. His flushed face, glowing eyes, and ringing voice, hardly lowered as he speaks the passionate words, tell her of the wild excitement within.

"My darling, stoop down from above me and tell me to live!" he repeats; "do you hear, Joanna? —I love you! I tell you, you have carried my heart as you do your audience, by storm!"

She stands silent. But the hands he clasps are not withdrawn; the sweet, dark, tender eyes do not droop —they are fixed on his face.

"Silence is consent!" he gayly cries. He draws a ring off his little finger, and slips it on one of hers. "I bind you with this," he says, "for to-night, to-morrow I will bring you a better."

He tries to clasp her, but she draws suddenly back.

"Oh, do not!" she exclaims, almost in a voice of pain.

They are the first words she has spoken, and there is a tone akin to terror in them. But she smiles a moment after, and looks down at the ring.

"You are all my own," he says ; "I love you and I claim you. Wear that until to-morrow. My darling, you sang and looked like an angel to-night."

"Supper ish waiting," says the stolid German voice of stout Madame Ericson ; "you had better come."

They go, and Livingston quenches his fever and excitement in iced champagne.

Somewhere in the small hours the little party breaks up, and he goes home through the summer moonlight full of triumph and exultation, still humming softly to himself the haunting words of the song.

But long after he is asleep, long after she is forgotten, even in his dreams, Joanna sits in her room, and watches the slender yellow July morn lift itself over the black, silent streets, full of troubled pain and unrest.

"Carried by storm," she repeats to herself ; "carried his heart by storm ! Ah ! Frank Livingston, *is* it your heart, your fancy, your excitable imagination— what ? But whatever it is, my love—my love, I love you ! "

CHAPTER V.

"LITTLE LEO."

"NIGHT brings counsel," says the adage, and "colors seen by candle-light do not look the same by day," says the poet. Both are exceedingly true. Livingston rises next morning, and his first thought, as he recalls all that passed last night, is one of simple, utter, intense consternation. Carried away by the excitement of the moment, by the charm of her eyes, her voice, the appearance of the crowd, he has asked Sleaford's Joanna to be his wife. The memory absolutely stuns him. All the fever of his throbbing pulses is allayed now, and he knows he no more is in love with her than he was with his cousin, Olga. Once again, as often before, his heated, hot-headed recklessness has played him false, his fickle fancy led him astray. He has asked the last woman in the world he should have asked to be his wife, and she has not said no. She has said nothing, he remembers that now ; but in these cases saying nothing is equivalent to saying yes.

Well, his fate is fixed—he must be true to her he has asked ; she must never know of this revulsion of feeling—Sleaford's Joanna must be his wife. It is thus she forces herself on his imagination—no longer as Jenny Wild, the singer, fair and stately, but wild, ragged, devil-may-care—she rises persistently before him. He does all he can to banish the memory—in vain. The image of the little barefoot tatterdemalion, the drudge of Sleaford's, is the only image rebellious recollection will bring up. And last night he told her he loved her.

It is with a very gloomy face, a very impaired appetite, Mr. Livingston sits down to his breakfast. He is not much of a hero, this fickle Frank—less of a hero than usual, even at this crisis of his life. But un-happily—or the reverse—the world is not made up of heroes, and Livingston goes with the majority. What will his mother say, his fretful, ambitious, fastidious mother ? What will the Ventnors say ? What will

Olga?—Olga, who has always especially disliked and distrusted Joanna—Olga, who has pride of birth enough for a royal princess. He can see the wonder, the incredulity, the scorn of the blue, chill eyes.

But it is too late for all such thoughts, what is done cannot be undone, he has chosen and must abide by his choice. He must keep faith with her, and she deserves a much better man. She shall never suspect that he regrets. He will inform his mother—the sooner the better; he will accept her wrath and her reproaches, he will marry Joanna out of hand, and hurry her away with him to Italy. That will look like flight, and flight will look like cowardice, but he has not much trust in his own moral courage. In Italy they can live as artists live—he certainly has nothing very brilliant to offer his bride—he will cast off the idleness of a life-time, and go to work with a will. Of course, Joanna must go on the stage no more; poor he may be, but not so poor as to compel his wife to work for her living.

" In Rome I can keep her on black bread and melon rinds!" he says, with a rather grim laugh, " until fame and fortune find me out. She is the sort of woman, I think, to whom love will sweeten even black bread and melons. Though why she should care for me Heaven knows! She is worth a million such weak-minded, vacillating fools as I am!"

He takes his hat, and tries to clear the cloud from his brow, and to look like his natural self, as he hurries through the sunlit, hot, hot, streets, to Joanna's cool, green-shaded, up-town bower. He is not very successful perhaps, or her eyes are not easily baffled, for in one long, grave, steadfast glance she reads all his

trouble in his tell-tale face, then turns slowly away.
The rooms are littered with trunks, bags, boxes, and
all the paraphernalia of a flitting.

"You find me in the midst of my exodus," she
says, dropping his hand, and going on with her work.
"I always oversee my packing myself. So many
things are sure to be left behind. Find a seat if you
can, although it is hardly worth while to ask you. In
ten minutes we start."

She is putting on her hat, and twisting a gray tissue
vail around it, before the glass, as she speaks. Except
that first earnest, searching look, she has not turned to
him once, although there is no slightest change in her
pleasant friendly manner.

"Joanna!" he begins, impetuously, a touch of
remorse stinging him, "you must still wear the ring I
gave you last night. I protest, I forgot until this moment all about the other."

He does not think of all that his words imply. It
is early hours for a lover to forget. She says nothing
—her white slender hands are uplifted, arranging the
hat. He glances at them, and sees no ring."

"What !" he says, "you have taken it off already ?"

"Your ring ?" she says, quietly. "Oh, yes, it was
too large. Take it back, wear it again—pray do ; it
is of no use to me. I may lose it, carrying it about,
and indeed I cannot wear it. It is greatly too large
for anything but my thumb."

She laughs, and holds it out to him. He can do
nothing but take it.

"Very well, as you say, it must be too large ; I will
send you a more suitable one before the week is out.

I, too, am off this morning, Joanna, to hunt up my missing *mother*, and tell her all !"

She turns a little pale, but her eyes are fixed on the glove she is buttoning.

" Pray do not," she says, earnestly. " Oh, pray do not—just yet. Give me time, give yourself time. You are not sure of yourself—wait, wait ! There is no hurry. Truly, truly Frank, I would much rather you did not. Promise me you will not speak to your mother."

" Carriage is waiting, Jenny, my dear," says Professor Ericson, popping in his bald head, " and not a second to lose. Good-morning, Mr. Livingston. Time and trains, you know, wait not for any man."

" Promise," she exclaims, looking at him with those dark, intense, serious eyes.

But he only smiles and clasps her gloved hands.

" I will write to you," he says, "and send you that ring. You will wear it, will you not ? I promise you it shall be pretty, and not too large. And do not let your countless admirers nor the dissipations of Newport make you forget during my enforced absence. I shall not be a day longer than I can help, and I shall have much to say to you of my—of our future plans, when next we meet."

Nothing more is said. He places her in the carriage beside Madame Ericson, and leans forward to talk until it starts. It has not been a very lover-like meeting or parting, and he notices that Joanna is very pale as she leans out with a smile to wave her hand in adieu. Then they were out of sight, and he is thoughtfully stalking along to the depot to take the train to his penitential destination.

It is a long, hot, dusty, disagreeable ride. Livingston sits in the smoking-car, and plays euchre, and
gets through unlimited cigars and newspapers, and the
grimy hours as best he may.

Twilight is falling, misty and blue, as he reaches
his journey's end, and, glad to stretch his legs a bit,
he starts off briskly to walk to a hotel. The streets
are crowded; the lamps are lit, and, twinkle through
the summery gloaming. Suddenly there is a com-
motion, a shouting, a scattering and screaming of the
crowd. A pair of horses have taken fright at something, and started at a furious pace along the streets.
There is a rushing and shrieking of women—the
runaways dash across the sidewalk, upsetting everything and everybody, and lashing out at all obstacles.
Stop them! stop them! shout a score of hoarse voices.
They flash past Livingston like a black whirlwind,
and he leaps aside barely in time. A young girl beside
him is less fortunate. The carriage-pole strikes her,
and she is flung heavily to the ground, directly at his
feet. The excited crowd dash by, heedless of the
prostrate figure, and Livingston, stooping down, lifts
her in his arms, and finds her insensible, and bleeding
freely from a cut in the head.

This is a situation! He glances about in consternation, and sees near the glowing globes of a
druggist's. To hurry thither, to summon assistance,
to place her in a chair, and support her there while
the man of drugs examines her wounds, is but the work
of a moment.

"A very nasty little cut," the druggist says, "and
unpleasantly close to the temple. Still, she is not
killed, and this wound will not amount to much if

she has received no other hurt. Knocked down by
the carriage-pole, you say? Poor young lady! Hold
up her head, sir, if you please; I will stop the
bleeding, and bind up the cut with a strip of
plaster."

Livingston obeys. He looks for the first time
closely at the drooping face before him, and finds
his interest and sympathy considerably heightened
by the fact that it is an exceedingly pretty face, despite
blood-stains and pallor. She is a very young creature,
not more than sixteen to look at, with a dusk, sweet
face, and quantities of wavy dark hair. The long
lashes rest on ivory-pale cheeks. With gentle touch
the druggist puts aside the loosened braids of hair, to
bind up the wound. Two lines he has read somewhere
occur to Frank's memory:

> "Love, if thy tresses be so dark,
> How dark those hidden eyes must be!"

"A pretty little soul," he thinks. "I wonder who
she is, and what we are to do with her next?"

Even as he thinks it, there is a flutter of the drooping lids, a quiver through all the slight frame, and
then slowly two dark, deep eyes unclose and look up
in bewilderment into the strange faces bending over
her—the faces of men.

"Oh! what is it?" she says, shrinkingly. "Where
am I? What has happened? My head——" She puts
up her hand in a frightened sort of way, and her lips
begin to quiver like a child's. "Oh! *what* is it?" she
says again.

"You were knocked down by a runaway horse—do
you not remember?" Livingston says, gently. " Your

head is hurt a little, but not much, I hope. Do you
feel hurt anywhere else ?"

She looks at him—dark, solemn, childish eyes they
are—and her lips quiver still.

"I—I don't know. Oh ! let me go home, please !
I must go home !" She essays to rise, then falls back,
with a little sob of pain. " My foot hurts me," she
says, sobbing outright; " but, oh, please, I want to go
home !"

She is indeed like a child. Livingston takes her
hand in both his, and tries to soothe her as he might
a child.

·" You shall go home ; do not be distressed, do not
be afraid. I am sure you are not much hurt. I will
take you home. Stay here, while I go and get a carriage. I will not be a moment."

She looks up at him again, and to his utter amaze
says this :

"I know you. You are Frank Livingston !"

"Good Heaven !" the young man exclaims, stunned
by this unexpected speech, "and who are you ?"

Instead of answering, she droops back in her chair,
so white, so death-like, that the druggist springs over
his counter for a restorative.

" Never mind asking her questions now," he says.
" Do you not see she is fainting ? Go for the carriage,
and get her home as quick as you can. She ought to
be put to bed, and attended to at once. She has had
a severe shock."

Livingston obeys. In a moment he is out of the
store—almost in another he is back with a cab.

" She is better again," the shopman says. " Take
her home at once. It is at 37 Pine street, she says—a

mile off or more. Tell the man to drive very slowly, and as easy as he can. Her ankle is hurt, I think. You will have to carry her to the carriage."

This is neither difficult nor unpleasant. He lifts the light, youthful figure in his arms, and carries her with infinite gentleness and care, and deposits her on the back seat. Then he gets in opposite her, gives the cabman the address, and they are driven slowly through the lamp-lit city streets. He looks at her in intense curiosity, as she sits before him, her head drooping against the back, her eyes closed, her face drawn into an expression of silent pain. He can ask her nothing now. She looks almost ready to faint away for a third time.

" Poor little soul !" he thinks, exceedingly sorry for her—" poor little pretty child. I wonder who she is, and how she comes to know me ?"

But conjecture is useless ; he cannot place her. Long before they reach 37 Pine street, what he has feared comes to pass. She droops forward, and faints dead away from sheer exhaustion and pain.

Livingston will never forget that drive ; it is always twilight, lit with yellow stars of light, and the slender figure lying inert and senseless in his arms.

They reach their destination at last—a cottage set in a pretty garden. A lady comes hurriedly out of the door as they draw up. There is still light enough to see her face plainly—a pale, handsome face—and Frank Livingston utters a cry.

" Good Heaven !" he exclaims, for the second time, " Mrs. Abbott, is it really you ?"

His cry is echoed, and it is her only reply, for she catches sight of the drooping figure in the carriage.

" My Leo ! my Leo !" she cries out, "oh, what is this ? What has happened ? Oh, great Heaven, is she dead ?"

" My dear Mrs. Abbott, no, only hurt a little, and unconscious just at present from the shock. Do not alarm yourself—indeed there is no need. Let me carry her in and send for a doctor at once. I am sure she is not seriously hurt. I will tell you all about it in a moment."

He carries her into the parlor, and lays her on a sofa. In a moment Mrs. Abbott has recovered the self-repressed calm habitual to her. She give a few hurried directions to the driver, and then bends over her pale little daughter.

" I have sent for my son," she says. " I chance to know where he is. Frank Livingston, is this really you ?" She holds out one slim, transparent hand, and looks wonderingly in his face. " Tell me all about it, and how you come to be with my little Leo like this."

" And it is Leo—little Leo ?" he says, gazing down at the still white face, " dear little Leo, and I did not know her. What a stupid dolt I grow. She recognized me at once. Accident has been good to me to-day, since it has thrown me in the way of the friends I have been longing for the past five years to meet."

He tells her what has happened in rapid words, and as he ends, a latch-key opens the hall-door, and a young man hurriedly enters.

" An accident ?" he says, in alarm. " Leo hurt ? Mother, what is this ? "

It is Geoffrey Lamar. He kneels beside his still insensible sister, without a glance at the stranger, pale with alarm, and takes her wrist.

"Geoffrey, look here," his mother says, "do you not recognize your friend?"

"Frank!"

He springs to his feet and holds out both hands.

"Dear old Geoff!"

And then there is a long, strong, silent clasp, a long, glad, affectionate gaze. Then Geoffrey returns to Leo.

"What is this?" he asks again. "What has happened to Leo?"

Livingston repeats his story, and in a moment Dr. Lamar is in action. He carries his sister up to her room, followed by his mother, while Frank sits below and anxiously waits. He looks out across the darkening flower-beds to the starry sky and thinks how strangely, after all these years, he has found his friends. Half an hour passes before Geoffrey returns.

"Well?" Frank anxiously says.

"It is not particularly well, still, it might have been worse. The shock is more to be apprehended than the hurts—she is a tender little blossom, our poor Leo. She has injured her ankle, in addition to the cut in her head. How fortunate you chanced to be on the spot. Thank you, Frank, for helping my little sister."

He holds out his hand, all the love his heart holds for that little sister shining in his eyes. Livingston takes it, and gazes at him. What a distinguished-looking fellow he is, he thinks, how gallant a gentleman he looks, how thoroughbred, how like his mother in that erect and stately poise of the head, that clear, steady glance of the eye.

"You have not changed in the least, Frank," Geoffrey says. "I would have known you anywhere."

"*You* have changed, old fellow," Frank returns, "but not for the worse. And so you have been here all the time, our next-door neighbor almost, while I have been looking for you high and low. What paper walls hold us asunder ! What are you about ? Practicing your profession ? "

"As you see, and after an up-hill struggle enough, conquering fate at last, I am happy to say. And now that you have found us, we mean to keep you for a while," Dr. Lamar says, gayly. "So make up your mind to stay until further notice. Our mansion is not particularly commodious, as you may see, but we always manage to have a spare room for a friend. And of all the friends of the old time, my dear fellow, you know not one can be more heartily welcome than yourself."

There is little pressing needed. Frank does object, but those objections are easily overruled. It puts off the evil hour of maternal tears and reproaches, and that is something. So he stays, and his secret will be his secret for a few days longer, at least.

CHAPTER VI.

"JOAN BENNETT."

JOANNA sits in almost total silence during the short drive to the depot. The look in Livingston's eyes haunts her, the forced gayety of his tone has struck on her heart like a blow. She has known it will be there sometime,

·but not so soon, not the very morning after his impulsive declaration.

"Carried by storm." Ah, but not held long. More than he has yet felt himself she has read in his face—pain, regret, the resolution to make the best at all cost of the most fatal words of his life.

Professor Ericson chatters like a German magpie ; luckily, like the magpie, he waits for no answer. They reach the station barely in time to get tickets, checks, and seats, and then are off through the jubilant sunshine of the brilliant summer morning. Madame Ericson composes herself by a shady window with a German novel ; the professor goes off to the smoking car, and Joanna is left undisturbed to gaze at the flying landscape, and muse over lovers who propose in haste and repent just as hastily. As it chances—if things ever chance—her seat is near and facing the car door. As it opens to admit the conductor on his rounds, her glance alights for a second on the figure of a brakeman standing on the platform.

She leans forward, with a sudden eager interest that drives even her lover from her mind, to look again. Surely, that strong, tall figure, and all that blue-black curly hair, are familiar. He turns for a moment, sending a careless glance backward to where she sits, and Joanna sinks back in her seat with a gasp.

For years she has been seeking him vainly, and he stands before her now, when no one could be farther from her thoughts.

They are near New York before Herr Ericson returns. Joanna seizes upon him at once.

"There is a brakeman on board this train that I know," she says, eagerly. "I want to see him—I

14

must see him, and you will please hunt him up for me,
and tell him so. Perhaps you have seen him—a tall,
dark, good-looking young man. He was out there not
half an hour ago."

The professor stares a moment, then laughs.

"Mein Gott! She wants to see the handsome
young brakeman! Shall I tell him to call on Miss
Jenny Wild, the celebrated vocalist, or —— "

"Look! look! There he is," Miss Wild exclaims,
unheeding, "standing on the platform. No, do not
speak to him until Madame and I are in the carriage;
then give him my card and tell him to appoint an hour,
and I will be at home to receive him.· Say no more than
that; he will not refuse, I am sure; he will be too curious. It is the most fortunate thing in the world; he is
a person I have been wishing to see for years and years."

They rise and leave the train, find a hack, and take
their seats, always with an eye on the tall, dark young
brakeman. He *is* a handsome fellow, as he leans in an
attitude of careless strength against the car, his straw
hat pushed back off his sunburned, gypsy face, a red
handkerchief knotted loosely about his throat.

"He might stand as a model for a Roman bandit,
at this moment," Joanna thinks, with a smile; "the
dark and dashing brigand of romance. There! the
professor has accosted him, and now—see the profound
astonishment depicted on his face!" she laughs softly,
as she watches the puzzled amaze of the young man,
and that laugh clears away the last of the vapors.
After all, Frank Livingston has not hurt her very
badly, judging by that clear laugh.

"He will come," says the professor, returning, and
wiping his warm face, " but he is a greatly bewildered

young man. He denies knowing any Miss Jenny
Wild—thinks she must be mistaken in supposing she
knows him, but will be at her service, if she likes, in
an hour. I told him that would do—will it ?"

"Admirably," Joanna says, still laughing. "I saw
his incredulity in his face ; he is watching us distrustfully at this moment. An hour is short notice ; but
short or long, I shall be most exceedingly glad to see
him."

Promptly at the hour's end, the young brakeman,
in much the same costume as on the car, with the
addition of a linen coat, presents himself at the cottage
and inquires for Miss Jenny Wild. He is ushered
into a pretty parlor, and in the subdued light, sees
advancing a tall and elegant-looking young lady in
navy-blue silk, with a creamy white rose in her hair,
a smile of welcome on her lips, and one hand extended.
She stands without a word before him. The young
man stands in turn, and gazes, more puzzled perhaps
than he has ever been before in his life. She is the
first to speak.

"Well," she says, laughing outright, "will you not
shake hands ?"

"*I* don't mind," the young fellow answers, and
takes in his great brown paw the slim, cool member
she extends, "but I'll be blessed if I know you ! And
yet it does seem to me I've seen you before, too."

"I should think so—seen me, felt me, boxed my
ears many a time and oft !"

"What !"

"Ah ! you would not do it now, I dare say. You
are much too gallant, no doubt, but such is the fact,

Look very hard, Judson. Surely five years cannot
have changed me so *very* much."

"By Jupiter!" Judson Sleaford shouts, "it is—it
is—our Joanna!"

"Your Joanna—Sleaford's Joanna—Wild Joanna!
Yes—Miss Jenny Wild now, though, to all the rest of
the world. Dear old Jud! how glad I am to see you
at last!"

He holds her hands and stands gazing at her, eyes
and mouth wide with wonder.

"Joanna! Our Joanna! got up like this—a swell
—a high-toned young lady—dressed in silk and roses!
Well, by George! And here I've been looking for
you high and low for the past five years! Upon my
soul, Jo, I can hardly believe my eyes? *Is* it you?
Why, you used to be ugly, and now I swear you
are——"

"Ugly still, Jud—fine feathers make fine birds,
that is all. But sit down, I am dying for a long, long
chat with you. Dear old fellow, how nice, and brown,
and well you are looking!"

She draws forward a puffy chair of satin and
springs, and Judson Sleaford sinks down on it. But
his black eyes are still riveted on Joanna's face; he
cannot believe them. He is trying to recall the bare-
footed, red-haired, fiercely-scowling child he remembers
so well, and place her side by side with this smiling,
charming, "high-toned" lady, so good to look at, and
make one of the two. And he cannot. No man
could. Every trace of *that* Joanna is gone!

"I can't believe it," he cries out. "It is all a
fraud! It isn't Joanna at all. You can't be. Why,
she had red hair, and you——"

"Have red hair still—not so rosy though as in those days. Don't stare so, Jud. Your eyes will drop on the carpet! It is I, myself—I, Joanna—no other. I wish it were."

"Why?" bluntly—"why should you wish it? I think you are one of the luckiest girls that ever was born."

"Do you?" she says, a tinge of bitterness in her tone. "Because I wear silk dresses and live in a Newport cottage? Well, it is better certainly than life at the Red Farm, but as for being the luckiest girl ever born——"

"What do you call it then?" he demands—"having the fortune of a princess left you in this way? By Jove! I call it the greatest stroke of luck that ever was heard of, out of the Arabian Nights."

Joanna stares in turn.

"The fortune of a princess? What do you mean? I have had no fortune left me. I sing for my living, and make a very good one, but as for fortune——Well, pay for my dresses, and so on, and have some pocket-money left, if you call that the fortune of a princess."

It has seemed that by no possibility can Judson Sleaford stare harder than he has been doing, but at these words he absolutely gasps.

"Do—do you mean to say," he demands, as soon as he can speak, "that you don't know?"

"Don't know what?"

"Good Lord above! Do you mean to tell me Geoffrey Lamar never hunted you up after all?"

"Geoffrey Lamar? I have not seen or heard of Geoffrey Lamar since I left Brightbrook nearly six years ago."

Judson Sleaford falls back in his chair, and looks helplessly at her.

"And all this—this cottage and furniture, and that dress, and—and everything—do you mean to say you work for and earn all that?" ~

"I work for and earn all that. I have never had a penny I did not work for and earn. I do not know what you are talking about. I wish you would cease staring and explain," cries Joanna, almost losing patience.

Jud takes out his red handkerchief and wipes his heated face. His amazement at finding Wild Joanna in this stately young lady, walking in silk attire, is not for a moment to be equaled by the amazement he feels at finding her ignorant of who she is. Mingled with the amaze is delight that it has been reserved for him to tell her.

"Then, by thunder, this is the luckiest day's work, Joanna, you have done in a long time! Just let me catch my breath, will you, and don't hurry me. I'll tell you everything directly, everything you've been wanting to know all your life. First of all let me ask you some questions. You know rich John Abbott shot himself?"

"Yes, I know that. Poor Mrs. Abbott."

"Ah! poor *Mr.* Abbott, I should say. You don't happen to know *why* he did it?"

"Certainly not. I only saw it in the papers, and the reason assigned was temporary aberration of intellect."

"Yes, jest so. Temporary fiddlestick! He knew what he was about—he was going to be found out, and was afraid of the law and his high and mighty missis. So he put a bullet through his brain, and got out of it that way. Then—do you know what Mrs. Abbott and young Lamar did then?"

"Shut up Abbott Wood and left the place. Yes, but even that I only discovered a few weeks ago. One can hardly wonder—so sensitive as Mrs. Abbott was, and after so shocking a tragedy. I am not surprised she has never returned. But where are they, Judson?"

"You would like to see them?" he asks, looking at her curiously. "You are as fond of them as ever?"

"Can you ask? They were my friends when I had not a friend in the world. They did all they could to lift me out of the misery and degradation they found me in. As fond of them as ever! I tell you, Judson Sleaford, I would lay down my life for Mrs. Abbott."

"Ah!" Jud says, in a peculiar tone, "and for Geoffrey Lamar?"

"And for Geoffrey Lamar. What I am to-day I owe to them. All I have, or ever may have, I owe to them. Why do you look like that, and speak like that? What do you know of them? Tell me where they are, if you know that."

"I don't know that. And you need not be in a rush to find them as far as they are concerned. I dare say, if the truth was known, you're about the last person in this world they want to see. Why, I heard Geoffrey Lamar as good as swear to find you, if you were above ground, and restore you to your rights, and *this* is the way he keeps his word!"

"Heard him swear! Swear to whom?"

"To dad—poor old chap—the night he died."

"And restore me to my rights? What *are* you talking of, Jud?" she asks, in a maze of wonder.

"I'm talking of what I heard with my own ears, though nobody knows to this day I heard it. I'm talking of what I heard dad tell young Lamar on his death-bed, and young Lamar swore to tell you. He hasn't done it, it seems. Dad sent for him to do justice to you at last, and tell him what hold he had over his step-father, who you were, and let him right you, seeing he was your friend."

"Who you were!" She hears those words and starts to her feet. She stands before him, her hands clasped, her eyes wild and wide, her lips breathless and apart.

"Who I am! Judson—at last!"

"Ah! don't be in a hurry, Joanna. I don't know whether you will like it or not when you know—so fond as you are of Mrs. Abbott, too. I tell you it knocked Lamar over like a bullet. If ever you saw a corpse take a walk—I don't suppose you did—he looked like that when he left the house. But he believed what he was told, and dad gave him the paper that proved your father and mother's marriage, and your baptism, out in San Francisco. He needn't deny it, for I saw it all, if you ever have to go to law about it—and I would, by Jupiter! Fortunes like that don't go begging every day, and you're the rightful heiress of every stick, and stone, and penny. Fight it out, Joanna, and I'll stand to you through thick and thin."

"But who—who—*who* am I?" Joanna cries out. "Tell me that—never mind the rest. *Who* am I?"

"Oh, I forgot," Jud says, coolly and slowly. "Your

name is Joan Bennett, and you're the eldest daughter, and sole heiress, of the late John Abbott, Esq., millionaire!"

CHAPTER VII.

THE STORY.

"OU see, it was the night dad died," says Jud Sleaford. "You know about that, don't you? It all began about you. You had run away with Blake while dad was away attending a prize-fight. When he came home, and heard of it—it was the very dickens of a day, I remember, in the way of wind and rain—he just mounted, and rode straight as a die for Abbott Wood. I reckon he thought Mr. Abbott had made off with you, or had some hand in it. He was stone white with rage. What would have happened there and then, if Abbott had been at home, the Lord only knows. He was not, and dad came back, in one of his black rages. But it seems he had left word for Abbott to follow; and Abbott *did* follow that very same night."

Jud is rapidly telling his story, and a very vivid narrator he is. The first overwhelming shock of surprise is over, and Joanna sits listening, pale, breathless, absorbed.

"We were all off to a dance, I remember," goes on Judson, "only the girl was at home. Early in the morning, as we were driving back, we were met by old Hunt—you know, next place to ours—with the word that there had been a row at our house, and that dad was done for. We hurried on, and there we found

14*

him, poor old fellow, 'weltering in his gore,' as the
stories put it, and almost at the last gasp. Almost,
but not quite. Dad was so uncommon strong, that he
gave death a tough tussle for it before he would go.
We got him to bed, sent for the doctor, and from first
to last I was his nurse. The girls were afraid of him,
he was as savage sick as well, poor old dad, and Dan—
but you know what Dan was—he wouldn't be paid to
enter the room.

" Well—I took care of dad. I gave him his medi-
cines and his drinks, and that, and did the best I knew
for him. By and by he got back his voice, and the
first thing he says was : 'Send for the young swell—
young Lamar.'

" ' Abbott's step-son ?' I says, for, of course, we all
knew from the girl that Abbott had been there, and
that it was in a fracas with him he had got his death-
blow. And dad's eyes shot out sparks of fire after their
old fashion.

" ' Can't you hear, you fool ?' he says, in a fierce
whisper. ' Abbott's step-son, young Lamar. Go for
him, bring him here at once. I have something he
ought to know to tell him. He must come.'

" Of course, I went. It was another pelting storm,
and when I got to the house I saw the missis. I gave
her the message. Young Lamar was in New York, but
she telegraphed for him at once, and that same afternoon, just before dark, he came, and I took him up-
stairs to dad's room.

" Now dad, although he was dying as fast as he
could, kept up a wonderful deal of strength to the very
last. His voice sounded much as ever, a little weaker,
but to hear him you would never know he was so near

his end. And he had worked himself up into a fever, waiting for Lamar. He could not die, he said, until he had seen him. I brought the young fellow in, and offered to fetch a light, but dad wouldn't have none. He ordered me out of the room, and I went, but only as far as the closet where we hang clothes. You remember how thin the partitions were, and the holes in the lath and plastering? I was curious to know what he had to say so particular. I was sure it was some revenge he was going to take on John Abbott. I sat there and listened, Joanna, and found out all about it and *you* at last."

There is a brief, breathless pause. Jud draws a long breath. Joanna hardly seems to breathe or stir.

"Oh, go on!" she says, in a whisper, and young Sleaford resumes.

"I'll tell it in my own way—not in dad's—he cursed a good deal, you know, and abused Abbott. You won't care for that. It seems that long before, when Abbott was quite a young man, and just beginning to get on in California, dad came there, a widower, with all of us, from Liverpool, and a sister of his with him, who took care of us. This sister, it appears, was a good-looking young woman, and John Bennett— that was Abbott's name then, and his right name— took a fancy to her, and her to him, and he made her his wife. His wife, mind you, all right, and tight, and legal. Well—he lived with her for a while, and was good enough to her and that, and gave dad a helping-hand as well, and then all of a sudden he started off somewhere up country to the mines, on a spec, intending to come back all fair and square when his business was settled, and not meaning desertion, or

anything like that. But that's what it proved to be—
he did not come back—dad never set eyes on him
again till he set eyes on him as the rich John Abbott,
of Brightbrook, and his wife never saw him in this
world more. Whether they have met in the next is
more than I know ; she was alive and well on the
night dad told the story.

"Well, Bennett—or Abbott, whichever you like—
had struck a vein of luck up there in the hill country,
among the mines, and wasn't coming back. It was a
wild region, no women there, and he didn't want to
fetch his wife. So he wrote ; all honest and square,
you see, at first, and sent money. Then the wife had
a baby—*you*—and got a fever of some sort after, and
went straight stark out of her mind. At first her
husband was anxious about her, got nurses and so on,
but after a time, as that seemed to do no good, he
sent word to dad to put her in an insane asylum, and
he would pay the damage. The young one—you again
—was to be put out to nurse, and be took proper care
of. It—you again—was christened Joan, after its
mother, Joan Bennett. Bennett didn't come himself,
you understand—was too busy making money, but he
sent the needful to dad, and dad obeyed so far as to
put his sister in the asylum, and pocket the money sent
for you. Things went on like that for a couple of
years, then all at once Bennett disappears, and from
that day not a trace of him was to be found. After
that dad went to the bad. While Bennett sent money
it was well enough, but dad always hated work, and
shirked it, so poverty came, and he dodged about with
us 'uns from pillar to post, until at last, after some
nine years of it, he settled us in a wild part of Penn-

sylvania to shift for ourselves, and started off himself
on the tramp. There's a fate in these things, maybe.
He tramped along until he came to Brightbrook, and
there, of course, one of the first people pointed out to
him was the rich man of the place, Mr. John Abbott.
Of course dad knew his man at a look. There he was,
as large as life, as rich as Rothschild, with a new wife,
a new daughter, a new name, and a step-son. The
other wife, the lawful wife, was alive and well, out in
San Francisco, as dad knew, and here he was, a blooming bigamist, with proudest, piousest lady in the land,
for number two.

"Well, dad was tickled, you may believe. All
this time he had kept you, not because he wanted you,
or cared about you, but because he didn't know what
to do with you. You were a trump-card in his hand
now.

"He took a night, and thought it all over, before
he showed himself. Abbott was in his power, he
knew, but he did not dislike Abbott, and he made up
his mind not to be too hard on him, to get a good living out of him, and let him off at that. He didn't
bear no malice, he didn't want to show Abbott up,
there was nothing to be gained by that, there was
everything to be gained by holding his tongue. Dad
didn't want to be a gentleman, and rob Abbott outright, he only wanted to be flush in his own way. As
to deserting his crazy wife, and taking up with this
handsome lady, dad didn't blame him for that either,
it was only what he would have done himself. As to
you, he made up his mind to say you were dead. He
didn't quite know why, but he thought that if Abbott
guessed who you were he might try to spirit you

away. Then, when he had thought it well out, and
settled his plans, he waylaid Abbott, in company with
Colonel Ventnor, and I heard him laugh as he told
Lamar that night—ay, dying as he was, he laughed,
when he thought how struck of a heap John Abbott
was when he first saw his face. After that I needn't
tell you what followed. He got the Red Farm give
to him, sent for us 'uns, and settled us all there. You
know the life we led, jolly for us, but deuced hard for
you, I must say. Dad owned he fairly hated you after
that, why he didn't know, but he did. All the hate he
might have bestowed on your father, he gave to you;
so you were ill-treated morning, noon, and night.
And I'm ashamed to say by me as well as the rest. I
ask your pardon now, Joanna."

The young fellow says it with real feeling; he is
honestly sorry, and she sees it. She gives him her
hand, and he starts to find how cold it is.

"You need not," she says. "You alone never
were cruel to me, Judson! But, oh, my childhood!
my youth! What a childhood, what a youth has
been mine!"

"Ah!" Judd says, with a hard breath of sympathy.
"Well then, the next was the coming of Geoffrey
Lamar, and the sudden interest he took in you. Perhaps. John Abbott suspected—nobody knows—he refused to let you come to Abbott Wood. You remember the evening Lamar came and told you so? Dad
took the matter in hand, through pure contrariness
and cussedness, as he owned; he went to the big
house, and he *made* Abbott let you come. His wife
should look after you, and nobody else; his daughter
should be your companion; his high-toned step-son

your friend. And he had his way. And now,
whether Mrs. Abbott suspected or not, I don't know—
that's what I've puzzled over many a time since. Did
she suspect, and did she do all that kindness to you to
quiet her conscience, knowing she was wronging you
all the time? I can't make it out. Them fine ladies
will do a great deal sooner than lose their money and
position. Was she one of them, or not? As to
Lamar, I do believe it was all news to him. I tell you
he looked like a corpse. And no wonder. There it
was! his mother was not that man's wife—a fellow
like that, that at his best was like the dirt under her
feet; his little sister was a—illegitimate ; and they
were prouder than Lucifer! You can guess how
Geoffrey Lamar felt as he sat and listened to the story
of his mother's disgrace, told by the lips of a dying
man."

Joanna has covered her face with her hands. Oh!
she can guess it—the shame, the horror, the appalling
force of that most horrible blow! Oh, Geoffrey!
truest friend! noblest heart that ever beat! and *this*
was his reward for saving her !

"When you ran away with Blake," goes on Jud,
"dad suspected foul play on the part of Abbott,
thought he had a hand in the business, and went there
at once. That night they had it out. Dad had the
certificates of your mother's marriage and your baptism,
and swore to expose Abbott. There was a struggle.
Abbott strove to master dad, and get them. Dad
pulled out a knife, and would have stabbed Abbott
without doubt, but that he slipped forward, fell on
his own weapon, and stabbed himself. Then Abbott
fled. At first dad did not realize how badly he was

hurt, and had strength enough left to replace the
papers in their hiding-place before he called for
help.   But the girl was frightened and wouldn't
come.   He tried to crawl from the room, but fainted,
it seems, from loss of blood.   There he lay, wounded
and bleeding, until morning—if he had been cared for
in time he could have lived, not a doubt about it.
And that was the story he had to tell Geoffrey Lamar.
He gave him the papers, told him where to find your
mother, and so sent him away.   I saw young Lamar
as he left the house—I never want to see a face look
like that again.

"That night dad died, but first of all he cleared
John Abbott of any share in his death.   I suppose he
thought he had had revenge enough.   And so he
had.

"Well, we buried poor old dad.   I never said a
word to anybody—it was no good, I had no proofs;
Lamar had them, and you were gone.   Abbott carried
things with a high hand with Dan, turned us out as
fast as we could bundle.   And I don't wonder.   For
my part, I was ready to go.   I was tired of life on
the farm.   Lora married, Liz came to town, Dan went
to sea, and I drifted up to the city.   Then, one morning, about six weeks after, I picked up a paper, and
the first thing I saw was the suicide of the rich man
of Brightbrook—nobody knew why.   But I knew.
I wrote to Lora, and heard how Mrs. Abbott and her
son and daughter had left the place, and that Abbott
Wood was shut up.   It has been shut up ever since.
It stands there to-day, and you are its mistress, and
heiress by right of every penny John Abbott—or
Bennett—has left."

Her hands drop, she is deadly pale, her eyes burn in the fixed pallor of her face.

"As for Lamar, it is strange," Jud continues, slowly, "and yet, perhaps it is *not* strange either. He promised dad, on his word of honor, he would hunt you up, and see you restored to your rights, and he has not done it. You see, to do it, all the world would have to know of his disgrace, and his mother's and Leo's, and they all are so infernally proud. Still, Lamar seemed the sort of fellow to do right at any price, and not stop to count the cost. He hasn't this time, it seems. It must have been a tremendous blow to Mrs. Abbott. I wonder where they are? In Europe somewhere, I suppose, flourishing on your money. It ain't fair, by Jove, and I'd hunt them up if I was you, and have my rights. Your mother's living, or was then—you can find and bring her forward, and I'll swear to all I've told you. Possession is nine points of the law, they say, and they have that and the money, still——"

"I must find them!" Joanna cries; "but oh! not for that—not for that! I must find my mother— my mother! *mine!* that I—I, Sleaford's Joanna, should have a mother! Oh, Judson, help me—I must find my mother at once, at once, at once!"

"And the fortune?" says Judson, looking at her curiously.

"The fortune! Ah, dear Heaven, what is fortune, a thousand fortunes, to that? To find my mother! my poor, lonely, imprisoned mother! And I must find Mrs. Abbott and Geoffrey Lamar. What they must have suffered! Ah, *what* they must have suffered!"

"And what they have kept—don't forget that. They

. have the fortune all this time. And they never looked for you."

"They have—they must ; I will not believe it. Oh ! if they were not good, not noble, not unselfish, then there is no goodness, no nobility, no unselfishness on earth. I will not believe it. Mrs. Abbott never knew. I would stake my life on that. Geoffrey has looked for me—I believe it as I believe in heaven. To doubt them would be for me ruin. I could no more have faith in honesty or truth on earth. Oh ! I shall find them ; I shall know no rest until I have found and comforted them, as much as I can comfort—until in ever so little I have returned to them what they so freely, so generously gave to me. The bread they cast upon the waters shall return to them ; the waif they tried to rescue shall prove her gratitude and love. And Leo is my sister—dear, dear, dearest little Leo ! Oh, my God ! what a grateful heart I ought to have this day—what a happy girl I ought to be ! And I am. I will find them—I will comfort them. I will find my mother—I will devote my life to her. Help me, Jud —help me in this, and thank you, thank you a hundred times for what you have told me to-day !"

Her face is transfigured ; it is, young Sleaford thinks in wonder and awe, like the face of an angel— lit with love, wet with tears, more than beautiful, with the beauty of a noble, a true, a grand, unselfish soul.

"I will do all I can," he says, rising. "I didn't think you would take it like this. I will hunt the world over if you say so. Joanna, you're a trump, and no mistake ! "

"Come this evening," she says ; "give me until then to think."

She sinks down, and once more covers her face. And so Judson leaves her, with bated breath, and hushed footfall, and solemn—feeling a sensation upon him as though he were going out of church.

But in the garish sunshine, in the bustling, busy, outer world, his old self returns as he sets his hat rakishly on his mop of blue-black hair.

" I'm blessed if I ever see any one so changed," he thinks in wonder ; "she's no more like *that* Joanna than—than I'm like an archbishop. We did our best to spoil her, and a little more might a' done it, only there's some sort *can't* be out and out spoiled, do what you will, and she's one. She's a stunner—she's a brick —she's fit to be an angel, and with the angels stand. But for all that, Lamar and his mother will wish her at the dickens the day she hunts 'em up. It's nature— I would myself, in their place."

<hr>

CHAPTER VIII.

HOW JOANNA CAME BACK.

" EOFF," Leo says, with some hesitation, " what is the matter with Frank ?"

" Matter with Frank ?" repeats Geoffrey, looking up from the evening paper, abstractedly, " there is nothing the matter with Frank. He looks in very good health."

"I don't mean his health," returns little Leo, pouting, " I mean—I mean his looks. A person may have something the matter with him, and still his liver and lungs be all right."

"Oh, you mean the secret sorrow sort of thing, do you?" with an amused look. "Well—yes—come to think of it, Livingston does look a trifle hipped—as if he had gotten a facer, somehow, in the set-to with life. But it is only what he must expect, as well as the rest of us," says Dr. Lamar, philosophically, going back to his paper. "As we ride onward in life, care mounts the crupper with most of us."

"It seems odd it should with him," Leo says, half to herself, and with a touch of regret. "Whenever I wished to recall the happiest, brightest face of old times, his was the one that always started up. It never used to wear a cloud. And now——"

"I see typhoid is spreading," remarks Dr. Lamar, glancing up from his sheet, "and two or three cases of malignant typhus have appeared. This looks badly and the sanitary state of this city is a disgrace to——"

But Leo does not wait for the conclusion of this uninteresting speech. She has caught a glimpse of some one coming up the road, and starts to her feet; she knows that tall, graceful figure, that negligent walk.

Brother and sister have been for some time out here in the scented summer dusk. Mamma is reading one of her pious little books in her room, and their guest went to the city in the afternoon. It is their guest who approaches, with a certain air of weariness and boredom, now. In his hand he carries a large bouquet, whose fragrance heralds his approach.

"Ah, Livingston," Geoffrey says, genially, "back? Good evening. Were you successful? Did you find your mother?"

"No," Frank says, moodily, "I did not. There is

a fatality in it, I think. It has been a regular game of
hide and seek. She left yesterday for Saratoga.
Where is Leo?"

The sound of the piano in the dusk of the parlor
answers. Leo is well enough to limp about all day,
and sing in the twilight. Hers is a voice like herself,
low, and soothing, and sweet, suited to nothing more
pretentious than little home songs and tender love dit-
ties. It is one of these she sings now, "Take Back the
Heart thou Gavest."

It is too dark to read. Dr. Lamar lays down his
paper, and essays conversation on the cheerful subjects
of typhoid and typhus. But Frank's replies are mono-
syllabic; he is listening to that gentle little plaint with
a savage sort of soreness at his heart. Even here his infidelity faces him, in the innocent voice of the singer,
in the mournful words of the song.

Geoffrey sees he is not in the mood for talk, and
resigns himself to listen also. Little Leo's singing is
always pleasant to the fraternal ear. Certainly, Livingston is very much changed, he thinks, he used to be
rather a rattle-pate; melancholy and Frank never used
to be on speaking terms. Can it be connected with
Olga? the young doctor wonders. He sighs as he
wonders; she rises before him, a vision of pure, pale
loveliness, a daughter of the gods, divinely tall and
most divinely fair—no other he sees equals her. Happy
Frank, if he is to win her. But is he worthy? He is
the sort of a fellow to fancy himself in love many
times, but Olga Ventnor has a deep nature, a strong,
steadfast heart; the man she gives herself to should
be brave, and loyal, and true.

A good fellow enough, Frank—a fellow to make a

different sort of girl happy, but never Olga Ventnor.

The song ends ; silence falls ; Frank rises and approaches the piano.

"A melancholy ditty," he says, half-smiling.
"Will you have some white roses, Leo? They used
to be your favorite flowers—used they not? You see
I remember old times and tastes. And as a reward of
merit, sing for me again—something not quite so
heart-broken this time."

A flush rises to Leo's dusk, mignonne face. She
does not thank him for his floral offering other than
by that fleeting blush, but she buries her pretty little
nose in their sweetness, and gives them a surreptitious
kiss, a little for themselves, a great deal for their
giver.

"I will sing whatever you like," she says, in that
shy, sweet way of hers. "I sing all Claribel's songs,
and like them best—they are so simple, you know, and
so, just suited to me."

"So sweet, you know, and so suited to you," amends
Livingston, rallying, and dropping into this sort of
thing from sheer force of habit.

"Shall we have lights?" Leo asks.

The half-light is charming ; his presence sets every
little youthful nerve thrilling as he leans, tall and dark,
against the piano.

"Not unless you wish it. I like this hour ' 'twixt
the gloaming and the mirk,' as the Scotch say. Can
you not sing from memory?

"Oh, yes," Leo answers, and sings. It is another
of Claribel's ; not sad this time, but with a gay, lilting
refrain :

"And I will marry my ain love,
For true of heart am I."

"True of heart !" Livingston thinks ; "true of
heart !" Is it in him to be that to any one ? he wonders. It is a noble quality, truth of heart ; but noble
qualities seem to have shaken hands and parted from
him of late.

It is precisely five days since he first came to the
Lamar cottage, days that have flown so pleasantly that
their flight has been unfelt. All his life is about to be
changed ; on the brink of that supreme change he
may surely linger for a moment, Sybarite that he is,
looking neither backward nor forward. But the brief
respite is at an end ; this is the close of the last day.

"Sing 'Robin Adair,' " he says, in the pause that
follows ; "you used to sing it long ago ; and I will return to Geoff and smoke while I listen. It will be my
parting remembrance of you—this twilit room, · and
the words of the old Scotch song."

"Your parting !" she exclaims. The little brown
hands on the keys falter and fall, in the dusk ; the
small face whitens. "What do you mean ?"

"That I tear myself away from this enchanted
spot, this 'Island of Tranquil Delights,' to-morrow
morning by the 9.50 train ; and 'Robin Adair' shall
speed the parting guest. Ah, little Leo, it is five long
summer days since I came, and the good days of this
life are not long-lived. My pleasant visit is ended ;
to-morrow I go back to grim reality, to grim duty, to
grim New York. I will carry this picture with me,
and paint it some day—this half-lit interior, this open
piano, and—you. Ah, little Leo ! little Leo ! believe
me, I am sorry to go."

And then he stops suddenly, and goes off to Geoffrey and his cigar ; and little Leo is left to realize the swift, startling truth that her heart will go with him to New York or wherever he chooses to take it, and that she will follow her heart, oh, so gladly ! so lovingly ! if that blissful day ever comes when he will ask her. But just at present she is a maiden unasked, and her duty is to be " plucky," and sing " Robin Adair," while he smokes over there in the garden chair.

And she does it bravely, too, to the end. If the sweet voice is low, it is always low ; if it falters, it is a pathetic little ballad ; if it closes with something like a sob, the last chord of the accompaniment drowns that.

The summer darkness is friendly and hides much. But she sings no more. She comes close to her brother and, sitting on a low stool, nestles her head against his knee. He lays his hand lightly on that dark, drooping head.

"Tired, little Leo ?" he says, gently. "Does the ankle hurt ?"

"A little," she answers, in a stifled voice.

Opposite, Livingston sits smoking, silent, dark, in deepest shadow. Overhead there is a primrose, star-lit sky, around them sleeping flowers and fragrant shrubs, summer stillness, a faint breeze, and the noise and lights of the great city afar off.

As they sit there, a silent trio, Mrs. Abbott—Lamar she calls herself now—descends and joins them. She looks very frail and white, but the rare beauty and stately grace remain.

" In the dark ?" she says, smiling. " Why do you not light the parlor, Leo, and go in ?"

"It is pleasanter here, mother," says her son, bring-
ing forward a chair. "Have you a wrap? Yes, I see.
Well, sit down ; it is a lovely night—let us enjoy
it."

" 'Let us crown ourselves with roses before they
fade,'" quotes Livingston out of the dusk. "My roses
fade with this evening. To-morrow I go, and I shall
bear with me the memory of one of the pleasantest
visits of my life."

There are exclamations from Mrs. Lamar and
Geoffrey. Leo says not a word.

"So soon ?" Mrs. Lamar says. "Oh ! I am sorry."

She is sorry. It has seemed wonderfully good to
see a face out of the old life—the old life that has had
its pleasures and its friendships, as well as its bitter
pain.

"Thank you for saying that," Frank returns ;
"thank you still more for the tone of sincerity in
which it is said. Mrs. Lamar, I wish you would do
me a favor ; I wish you would let Olga Ventnor come
and see Leo."

There is a movement in the quiet figure leaning
against Geoffrey's knee, but she does not speak.

"Olga !" the lady says, startled. "Oh ! indeed I
do not know. All that is at an end——"

"You have chosen that it shall be," says Frank ;
"there is no other reason why. And it is a little unjust to Leo, I think. She has no friend of her own
age, and—pardon me—it must be a little lonely for
her sometimes."

"No, no—oh, no !" from Leo ; "no, no, indeed,
mamma. Do not think that."

"And Olga is dying to see her," pursues Living-
15

ston, unheeding ; "and Olga is a charming girl, I
assure you. Quite all she promised to be, and more.
How often have I heard her long to see you all again !
Come, Mrs. Abbott—come, Lamar, be generous to old
friends—say she may come."

"I see no reason why she may not," Geoffrey
answers, slowly ; "but it is a matter of feeling with
my mother, and one for her decision alone. Would
Miss Ventnor care to come ?"   ·

"Do you ask that, Lamar ? If I tell her, she most
assuredly will not come to see *you.* Does your remembrance of Olga lead you to think she is one of the
'out of sight, out of mind' friends ? You hardly do
her justice."

"You are her loyal knight, at least," Dr. Lamar
says, and laughs a little constrainedly, "and plead her
cause well. Will congratulations be premature, or are
they an old story by this time ? We are such ancient
friends and cronies all, you know, that it is not imper-
tinent to ask."

There is a tremor in the figure leaning against his
knee, then a strained, painful hush, in which she can
count her own heart-beats. A brief pause follows ;
Livingston removes his cigar to knock off the ash with
care, and speaks :

"If you mean an engagement between me and my
cousin Olga, there is certainly no need of congratula-
tion. We are not engaged, and we never will be.
But we are excellent friends and cousins all the same."

"But I thought—we all thought," says Mrs. Abbott, surprised, "that it was an understood thing
you and Olga were to marry. We thought the families——"

"So did I," says Livingston, with a half laugh, "and on that hint I spake. We were all mistaken, it seems. Olga thought differently, and has reserved herself for a better man."

"Ah ! and that better man——"

"Is mythical at present—has not yet put in an appearance. But no doubt he will, and Olga will wait serenely, although it should be a score of years hence. She will certainly never make a mistake matrimonially. What principally concerns *me* is, that I was not the man."

There is a pause. Frank resumes his cigar, Leo's heart its wonted beating, but with a sudden contraction of pain that she cannot define. He has asked then, and been refused.

"Refused !" thinks little Leo, looking shyly over at him in the dark : " how very strange !"

"She has had many offers, no doubt?" says Mrs. Abbott, at last. "Olga must be very lovely."

"She has the loveliest face ever seen out of a picture or a dream," Frank says, but he says it without one faintest touch of enthusiasm. "Men raved about her abroad. She has been painted again and again—her beauty is almost without a flaw. But you will see her for yourself. Only say the word—she will be but too glad to come."

"Could we be churlish enough to refuse? Yes, bring her, Frank, dear, fair, little Princess Olga ! It is good of her to remember us all so long."

" Five years is not an eternity, Mrs. Abbott. And I doubt if fifty would enable those who ever knew to forget *you*."

Mrs. Abbott smiles.

"My dear Frank, you are as charming as ever. You always had a faculty for saying nice things. I am afraid you are a flirt—I think, indeed, I have heard it whispered that you always were. Leo, do you not hear? Have you nothing to say? Olga will come."

"I am glad, mamma."

"Only that, and you are generally so enthusiastic! You are strangely quiet to-night. Are you in pain? Your ankle——"

"Oh, it is all right, mamma," poor little Leo cries out.

In pain—yes—but the pain is not in anything so unromantic as an ankle. If he is not engaged to Olga, what then is the matter? Is it that her refusal has hurt him so deeply, in spite of his forced lightness of manner?

"There is another friend of the past," Dr. Lamar says slowly, after a silence, "whom I suppose you have never met in all your wanderings up and down the world. I mean Joanna!"

The name falls so unexpectedly, that all start at its sound. Livingston in the darkness turns quite white.

"Why do you suppose so?" he answers, and his voice is not quite steady. "I *have* met Joanna!"

There is a universal exclamation.

Dr. Lamar starts to his feet, his mother clasps her hands, Leo sits erect, and looks eagerly.

"You have met her!" Geoffrey cries, excitedly. "You know where she is! Mother, you hear this? At last!"

"I have met her—I know where she is," Livingston answers, surprised at the amount of excitement they showed; "is there anything extraordinary in that?"

"There is this—that I have˙searched, and caused search to be made everywhere all these years in vain. I had almost made up my mind she was dead—so impossible has she been to discover. And all this time you have known where she was——"

"Not all this time, if you mean these six past years—only within the past two months," says Frank, feeling oddly cold and conscious, and wondering what they would say if they knew.

"And where is she? In New York?"

"At Newport, I think, just now. How exercised you are over the matter, Lamar. I always knew, of course——"

"My dear fellow, you know nothing, absolutely nothing, of the truth. It is the most important concern of my life to find Joanna. She is safe and well, and married to Blake?"

"Safe and well, but not married to Blake, or anybody else."

"What! She ran away with him, you know——"

"I know," Frank says, wincing; "but she ran away from him, as you must recall, after."

"It was true, then? Odd girl—strange, wild Joanna! And what became of her—what did she do? No harm befell her, I trust?"

"None whatever, but much good. She found friends, honest and real friends, and she has worked her way to comparative fame and fortune. She is *wild* Joanna no longer. She is a refined and thoroughly well-bred young lady, with gracious manners, and all womanly sweetness, and goodness, and grace."

He speaks warmly, his handsome face flushes in
the dark.

"Thank Heaven !" he hears Mrs. Abbott murmur,
and Geoffrey, too, seems deeply moved.

"I am more thankful than I can say," he says,
after a little. "I always knew the elements of a noble
character were there, crushed, warped, as they had
been. Thank Heaven, indeed ! But tell us about her,
Frank. You can form no idea of how deeply we are
all interested in the well-being and history of Joanna."

So Frank tell it. Out there, in the sweet summer
dark, he tells the story of provocation, and reprisal,
and flight, and pain, and struggle, and hardly-won
victory. Joanna has told it to him—simply, unconscious of its real pathos—and he repeats it tenderly,
dwelling on all her goodness, her free generosity, her
brave great-heartedness, her bounty to all weak,
oppressed, and suffering things.

"She gives like a princess, freely, with both hands,
to all who need," he says. "I know that the dearest
desire of her heart is to see you all again. She speaks
very little of herself, but that much I know."

"Will you bring her to us ?" Mrs. Abbott says,
with repressed eagerness, great tears in her eyes.
"Oh, my poor Joanna ! my poor, wronged, ill-treated
child ! Bring her to us, Frank, at once, at once !
Geoffrey, you cannot go for her, I know—if you
could——"

"Quite impossible, mother, quite unnecessary also.
Livingston will tell her and she will come. I will write
to-night and say—well, something of what there is to
be said—and she will come. The rest she can learn
here. Frank, you have done us to-night a service for

which I thank you with all my heart. You do not understand now, but you will later. Get in lights, Leo. I will write my letter at once, before I am called away."

So they leave the sweet-smelling garden, and the starry sky, and go in. Lights are brought. Geoffrey sits down to write, Mrs. Abbott goes to the piano and plays dreamy sonatas, Leo gets some needlework, Frank sits near, with the paper Geoffrey has thrown down, and says little. Presently it is eleven, and the letter is finished—a very long one, and it is bedtime, and they all stand up to say good-night and good-by.

"But you will soon return with Olga?" Mrs. Abbott says.

"Olga will soon be here," he answers, with a smile, but Leo notices he says nothing about accompanying her. Then it is her turn, and those two hard words, "good-by," are spoken, and his visit has come to an end.

* * * * * *

"A gentleman for you, Miss Jenny." Her maid hands her a card. Joanna looks at it, and her face flushes. Frank returned.

She is alone in her room. A week has passed since Jud Sleaford told her his story, and no action has been taken yet. She hardly knows why she waits, but it is for Livingston's return, and now the week is up, and he is here. She goes swiftly to where he waits, and he comes forward, both hands outstretched.

"You did not expect me so soon?" he says, the first salutation over. "No, I know. But the oddest thing has happened. Whom do you think I have met?"

She has no idea, she says, and smiles at the bright eagerness of his face.

"Leo Abbott—Geoff—their mother—and I have been stopping with them ever since."

"Frank !"

"I thought you would be astounded. You cannot be more delighted than they were, when they found out I knew you, and where you were. They have been looking for you, it appears, all this time. You know they have given up everything—the Abbott property, I mean—and Geoffrey supports them by his profession. They are living in comparative poverty and obscurity, but are one and all as delightful people as ever. Here is an epistle for you, from Geoff, long enough to make one jealous, and, Joanna, they count upon your going to them at once."

She takes the large letter, and looks at the clear, bold, familiar writing.

"I thank God," she says, softly, "I have got the desire of my heart. And I thank you, Frank, for being the bearer of good news. And you have been there ever since ?"

"My mother had gone," he says, hastily. "She had left for Saratoga before I left New York. I mean to go after her there at once. It reminds one of 'Japhet in Search of a Father,' and seems almost as fruitless a search," he laughs.

"Do not," she interposes, and lays her hand on his arm, "as a favor to me—at least not yet. Wait. Tell me about them. Is Leo pretty ? "

"Very pretty."

She glances at him a moment.

"And Mrs. Abbott ? " she says, then.

"As beautiful as ever, but less proud, less cold. You know what I mean. As for Geoff—dear old fellow, he is looking splendidly. Shall you go at once, Joanna? They will literally be in a fever, I think, until you are with them."

"I will go to-morrow."

"And I may accompany you, of course? Then I must inform Olga, who wishes to visit them too. They will owe me a vote of thanks, I fancy, for restoring them to their friends."

"Go for your cousin at once, for I intend to go alone. Yes; I will have it so. I prefer it. Do you think I cannot travel alone?" laughing, and lifting her brave, bright face. "Have you yet to learn I am strong-minded, and amply sufficient unto myself? And, Frank, do not tell your cousin any more than your mother. Tell no one until I give you leave."

"But, Joanna——" he is beginning, impetuously, when Professor Ericson enters, and cuts him short. Joanna informs him of to-morrow's journey, and that Mr. Livingston will dine with him, and so his opportunity is gone.

He dines and spends the evening, but he does not see Joanna for a moment alone. And next day she departs, holding to her resolution to go unescorted. He sees her off, and takes the train for Brightbrook and his cousin Olga. Will they meet, he wonders, these two, at the Lamar cottage, and if so, how? Will Olga be simply, chillingly civil? And how is it that Lamar and his mother take the finding of Joanna so greatly to heart?

In the late afternoon of that day a cab sets Joanna down in front of the Lamar cottage. They have not

15*

expected her so soon, and Mrs. Abbott alone is in the house. As she sits the door opens, a tall young lady enters hurriedly, and falls on her knees beside her, and clasps her in her arms.

"Mrs. Abbott," the familiar voice cries, "it is I. Oh! my friend, kindest, truest, dearest, best, look at me—bid me welcome—say you forgive me—say you are glad to see me. It is I—Joanna—come back."

CHAPTER IX.

HOW JOANNA PAID HER DEBT.

HEY sit in the half-lit parlor, the lights turned low under shades, and Joanna listens once more to the story Jud Sleaford has told. Her hand is clasped in Mrs. Abbott's, Leo nestles beside her after her usual clinging, childish fashion, and Geoffrey is the narrator. No sound disturbs him, there are tears in his mother's dark eyes, otherwise she is calm. In the startled eyes of little Leo there are wonder and fear, but she says nothing, although what she hears now she hears for the first time. For Joanna, she sits quite still, quite calm, and listens to the end. Even then there is not much said—there is not much that it is easy to say. Leo buries her face in Joanna's lap, and is sobbing softly.

"Oh, how could papa—how could he—how could he?"

It is not in that tender little heart to blame any one too hardly. She is afraid to look at her mother, at Joanna, her sister, both so deeply wronged. Her sister, how strange that thought. A thrill of gladness goes through her as she clasps her closer in her arms. She has grown so famous, she bears herself so nobly— it almost compensates. And she will be a great heiress —Joanna—it is her birthright, all that splendor and luxury—beautiful, lost Abbott Wood.

Ah, her heart aches for Abbott Wood often and often, her fair, stately home, down by the sea. All is Joanna's now. Not one spark of envy or jealous grudging is in her—all good fortune that can befall her Joanna deserves, has bravely earned. *They* were the usurpers, and held from her for years what should have been hers. Her own sister ! How good, how comforting is that thought. She has never felt the need of a sister, mamma and Geoffrey have always sufficed, but it is a rare and sweet delight to find one at this late day. And this is why everything had to be given up, why mamma took her former name, why papa shot himself.

" Poor papa ! he used to be so fond of his little Leo."

She sobs on, her face hidden, the sobs stifled in Joanna's lap. No one has a tear for the dead sinner but tender-hearted little Leo.

All this time they have been talking, brokenly, dis-connectedly, but Leo has not been listening. She has only been hearkening to her own thoughts. Now Joanna gently lifts the bowed dark head.

" Crying, little Leo ? Why, I wonder ? Surely not because poor Joanna is your sister ? Ah, my dar-ling, it is the one bright, bright spot in all this dark-ness, and sorrow, and sin."

" Oh, my dear ! my dear !" Leo says, flinging her

arms about her, "do you not know I feel that? I
thank the good God for giving me so great a gift. I
love you, Joanna—no sister was ever more dear, but
I cannot help thinking of—of *him*. He was fond of
me, you know."

She droops her face again, crying with all her heart.

"Fond of you, my little one?" Joanna says, her
own eyes moist. "I wonder who would not be fond
of you? And we all love you the better for those
tears. But you"—Joanna lays her hand on Mrs.
Abbott's, and looks up with wondering eyes into her
calm face—"how you bear it. I wonder as I look at
you. And you used to be so——"

"So proud, so imperious, so exacting, so haughty.
Ah, say it, Joanna! Do I not know it well? I needed
the lesson I have received—the only blow, I believe,
that could have humbled me. All other things—sick-
ness, poverty, death itself—I could have borne and
kept my pride; this I could not. Pride had to fall.
I bore it badly enough at first—in agony, in rebellion,
in despair. I *would not* believe such shame, such disgrace, could touch me. I lay for weeks at death's door.
I was wicked enough to wish to die. But all that is a
memory of the past now; I am happy—yes, quite
happy, Joanna, with a deeper, and a truer, and more
lasting happiness. Do you remember the ninth Beati-
tude of St. Francis de Sales—'Blessed are the hearts
that bend, for they shall never break.' I have no fear
of a broken heart, now."

Joanna stoops and touches, with loving lips, the
worn, white, thin hand.

"And now," Geoffrey says, briskly, coming back
to the practical, "there is nothing for you to do but

to step into the property, and take the reins of government out of the hands of Blaksley & Bird. They have managed the estate very well in all these years, and your income must have accumulated like a rolling golden river. What a rich young person you are, Joanna—quite a modern Mademoiselle Fifty Millions! And yet how quietly you sit there and take it all."

Dr. Lamar says this in rather an injured tone. Joanna laughs.

"What would you have?" she says; "that I should throw up my hat and hurrah? We don't do that when we come into a fortune—the luck is something too solid and substantial. Besides, it comes to me so—well, not pleasantly. It is not a comfortable reflection, that the best, the dearest friends ever forlorn waif found in her need, are thrust out to make room for—I had almost said, the viper they had nourished. It takes all heart out of your millions, Geoffrey."

"Oh! if you look at it in that light," says Geoffrey, coolly; "being a woman, of course you will take the romantic and unpractical side of it first. But having taken it, look at the other—at the birthright usurped for years. And as our going out was inevitable, you must know what a delight it will be to us all to see you step in and reign at Abbott Wood instead of a stranger. You have grown such a regal-looking young woman, Joanna, that you will grace the position and the house. I know of no one," says Dr. Lamar, making a courtly bow, which includes the two ladies, "so fitted, in mind and person, to succeed its late illustrious chatelaine!"

They laugh, and all restraint and embarrassment fly. Time has so softened the past, so blunted the pain, that they can bear to talk of it all with hardly a pang.

"We have kept it a secret hitherto, even from Leo," says Geoffrey, " because, until you were found, nothing could be gained by telling. Now, everything had better be told, and the sooner you are installed at Abbott Wood the better. What are your plans, Joanna? Whatever they are, for the future remember you are to command me. I consider myself quite as much your brother as Leo is your sister."

She stretches out her hand.

"More than brother always, Geoffrey—best and stanchest of friends. And so I may command you in all things? You promise this?"

"Undoubtedly—in all things."

"Very well—the first command I issue is, that you will not say one word of this to any one. To the lawyers, if you like, but make them the only exceptions. Not one word, remember, to any living soul."

" But, my dear Joanna——— "

"But, my dear Geoffrey, you have pledged yourself blindly to obey, and must abide that rash promise. I will it so."

"And Joanna is queen regnant now, it must be 'as the queen wills !'" cries Leo, gayly.

" Well—if I must, I must, but I see no sense in it. And your plans? for that is not one. But perhaps it is too early for you to have formed any."

"No—my plans, such as they are, are formed, and are few, and simple enough. In the first place, I leave the stage."

"Of course !" promptly—"*that* goes without saying."

"In the second," smiling, "I stay here a week or two, with you all, if you will have me."

"If we will have her—oh!" says Leo, opening wide her velvety eyes.

"Then I start for San Francisco, escorted by my dear old professor, who would escort me to the world's end, at an hour's notice, and take my mother, my poor mother, out of her prison of years."

"Good child," says Mrs. Abbott. "You will find her well, too. Geoffrey had a letter from the doctor, only a fortnight ago, saying so, and saying she still keeps calling for you. Ah! Joanna, that fatal fortune will do some good after all—it will rescue her."

"In Joanna's hands it will do much good," says Geoffrey, with decision. "Well, and after that?"

"After that—after that the deluge! I hardly know. Thus far I have planned, and no farther. I do not quite realize it all yet. My plans and wants will increase, I suppose, as I do. But oh! through it all, this fairy fortune—this strange, tragical story, there is one thing I *do* realize to my heart's core—how glad I am to be with you all again. What would it all avail but for your goodness in the past. Geoffrey, my first friend, I cannot thank you—indeed, I will not try—but you know, you *know* what I feel! And Leo is my sister—my very, very own sister. It is better than a score of fortunes. And you!" she puts her arms suddenly about Mrs. Abbott, "my dearest! my dearest, my more than mother, how good you were to me, in those long gone days. Your lessons of love, of patience, of gentleness, seemed to be thrown away then, but I hope—oh! I hope, they have come back, and borne fruit. Nothing good is ever lost, it all returns sooner or later. I have found my own mother, but I can never love her better than I love you."

It is a scene, and these women weep together, and when, an hour later, good-nights are said, it is a very happy little household that retires to sleep.

But Joanna does not sleep—at least for hours. She is excited, she wants to be alone, to think. She has the room lately vacated by Livingston. Some relics of him yet remain—a glove on the table, a flower given him by Leo, dead and dry on the window-sill. It is of him she is thinking—he is rarely absent long from her thoughts. He is coming to-morrow with his cousin Olga. He must not know, not yet, not yet. In these dim plans of hers for the future, his figure does not appear ; she tries to place him there, but she cannot. A week with Leo, and already the abrupt mention of his name sends a flush into the dark, mignonne face. Is it so, then ? And he ? She is the sweetest little blossom possible, a tender, gentle, adoring little heart, the sort to sit at her husband's feet, and worship, and see no faults. No, in the picture of her future, Joanna cannot fancy him, try as she may.

Next day he comes, and with him Olga Ventnor.

Dr. Lamar is very busy in those days, and disease and death are very busy, too, in the city.

He and they do battle by day and by night; he has very little time to give them at home. Fever is spreading and will not be stamped out ; the weather is hot, damp, murky, oppressive—real fever weather, and in the pestilential purlieus many lie ill unto death these July days. He is indefatigable in his profession, he seems to live in his carriage, he begins to look fagged and worn, strong and robust as he is, splendid in his

flawless vitality.   His mother grows anxious, and begs
him to spare himself, but in vain.

Coming home on this sultry evening, tired, de-
pressed, hungry, out of sorts, his mind filled with grim
sick-rooms, and the grim faces of poverty and disease,
he sees a vision !   Standing in the parlor, alone, the
last light full upon her, dressed in some gauzy, silky
robe, that floats like a cloud softly over the carpet,
her golden braids twisted coronet-fashion around her
head, a diamond star flashing at her throat, he sees—
Olga.

It comes upon him like a shock, a shock of rapture.
He has not been thinking of her at all, and she is before him, a dream of light, of loveliness.   He stands
quite still, quite pale, unable for a moment to advance
or speak, looking at her.   It is she who comes forward, blushing slightly, smiling and holding out her
hand.

"Are you going to swoon at my feet, Dr. Lamar ?
Do not, I beg—I would not know in the least how to
bring you to.   Yes, it is I in the flesh—Olga—shake
hands and see.   How unflatteringly amazed you look,
to be sure !   And yet," with the prettiest of pouts,
"you must have known I was coming."

"I had forgotten," says Dr. Lamar.

The words are not flattering, but he still holds her
hand, and gazes at her as though he could never gaze
enough.

"Complimentary, upon my word !   But it is just
like you all—out of sight, out of mind.   Leo and your
mother had not forgotten, sir !   Men have no memories.
Will you not come in ?   The house is thine own—or do
you mean to stand staring indefinitely.   You remind

me of the country swain, who sighed and looked, sighed and looked, sighed and looked, and looked again. If you sigh and look into the dining-room it will be more to the purpose. Your dinner is waiting there, and your mother has been left lamenting over your prolonged absence, and the fowl that is spoiling while it waits."

She runs on gayly—she sees all the surprise, the admiration in his face, and she likes it. She is a hero-worshiper, this fair, white Olga, and Geoffrey Lamar is her latest hero. She does not understand very clearly, but for honor's sake he has given up a fortune, and gone out single-handed to fight with fate. He is a hero in that to this romantic young lady; he is working himself to death among the poor and suffering, heedless of rest, or food, or comfort, he is a hero in that also. And it is a grand thing to be like that. She adores strength, bravery, unselfish deeds. And— what a distinguished-looking man he has become, but then he always had that *air noble* even as a boy, which she admires so much, and sees so seldom.

Dr. Lamar is off duty that evening, really off duty, and enjoys his home circle with a zest, a delight that is not untinged with pain. To sit and look at that lovely face is a pleasure so intense that he is almost afraid of it. Frank is there, near Leo ; Mrs. Ventnor, too, is present, talking earnestly to Mrs. Abbott.

They have much to say and hear, of the past five years, and once mutual friends. She and her daughter, with Frank, are stopping at the hotel near by—the bandbox cottage accommodates but one guest at a time. That one, Joanna, is at the piano, playing softly—so softly that she disturbs the talk of no one. Livingston tries to be devoted, and turns the music, but she sends him away.

"I play from memory," she says, "or I improvise. It is my way of thinking aloud ; and I like to be alone when I think. Go and talk—go and amuse little Leo," smilingly ; "she hates to be alone."

So he goes, and thus paired off, the evening passes delightfully. It is an evening Geoffrey, for one, never forgets. Olga is by his side ; Joanna is playing softly, softly, and a little sadly. Is *she* happy? Her face tells nothing. The others are—he is, supremely so. Outside there is the summer darkness, the stars, the whispering wind. Yes, it is a picture he will recall to his dying day.

Miss Ventnor has met Miss Wild, the vocalist, with some surprise, and extreme curiosity. And so she is Joanna?—really ? How stupid of her and Frank not to have recognized her at once. But she has so changed—so improved. Miss Wild will pardon her, she trusts, for saying as much. After all, she is privileged, being such a very old—acquaintance. May she congratulate her ?—her voice is enchanting, she envies her whenever she hears it. How charming that they should all meet again like this. And so on—more than civil—gracious, indeed—quite the manner of some fair young grand duchess, so uplifted that she can afford to stoop and be sweet.

Joanna smiles at it all, not embarassed, not overwhelmed, and responds very quietly. Olga does not dream—none of them do—the double secret she holds, her manner to Livingston is so simply that of a friend. Still, he feels uncomfortable, and urges her to let him tell. "Wait, wait," is all she will say. It is her answer to Geoffrey, too, when he reiterates his wish to make known her real position to the Ventnors. " Oh, wait," she says ; " time enough for all that." And they obey her. She has a strong will, this gentle Joanna, and it makes itself felt. She knows her own mind, and adheres to it. She forms her own plans, and abides by them. She has great faith in time, and waiting, and patience, to set the most crooked things straight. A little, indeed, is revealed—she has discovered her mother, out in San Francisco, and Joanna is going there to join her next week. It is her intention to return with her and make another brief visit to the Lamars.

After that—Livingston glances at her with a somewhat anxious face, but she smiles back at him with a brightness all her own. She has the brightest smile, the frankest laugh, in the world—in her presence there is a sense of comfort, of peace, of rest. That subtile fascination of manner has its effect on them all, and her singing charms care from every heart. Mrs. Ventnor is bewitched—Olga says so laughingly ; she is ready to listen for hours, rapt, if Joanna will only sing.

"I repeat it," Miss Ventnor says, " you have bewitched mamma, Miss Wild. She is under the spell of a musical enchantress. What sorcery is in that voice of yours that you steal our hearts through our ears ? "

This is very gracious. Olga goes with the majority, and does real homage to her old foe. The clear, noble face, the quiet, well-bred manner, the siren charm of voice, win golden opinions from her, fastidious as she is.

"I never saw any one so changed as that—that

Joanna," she says, half laughingly, half petulantly, to
Frank; "she is a witch, I think. Even *I* cannot resist. There is a sort of charm about her—I cannot define it, but perhaps you can see—that compels one's
liking in spite of one's self."

"And why in spite of one's self, Mlle. Olga? Why
should one try to resist?"

"Ah! why? We were always antagonistic, you
know. And so you *can* see it? Now, really you are
sharper-sighted than I took you to be. I thought *you*
saw nothing but little Leo's *riante* face!"

"What?" Livingston cries, conscience-stricken;
"do you know what you are saying? Leo! What is
Leo to me?"

"I do not know what Leo may be to you at this
present moment," says Olga, coolly, "but if things go
on, she will be Mrs. Livingston to you before long.
Deja! we go fast, my friend. *Your* heart goes out
through your eyes, it seems. And only two months
ago he proposed to me! What a crushing blow to my
vanity! As for little Leo——"

But the door opens, and little Leo comes in with
Joanna, and the cousins part—Livingston covered with
confusion as with a garment, and Olga's sapphire eyes
laughing with malice.

The days go by; Joanna's week has nearly merged
into two. They hold her by force, it seems; Mrs.
Abbott's pleading eyes, Leo's pleading lips, Geoffrey's
pleasure in her prolonged stay. The Ventnors are
still here; Livingston is every day, and all day every
day, almost, at the cottage.

Dr. Lamar works as hard as ever, spares himself as
little as ever, and begins to really look haggard and

ill. His mother and Joanna watch him with anxious eyes, and what they fear comes to pass. Olga's hero goes down on his battle-field, but facing and fighting the foe until he falls, prostrate and conquered.

And then there are tears, and panic, and terror in the bright little household, and a sudden scattering of the happy circle. And in this hour, Joanna comes forward to pay her debt, to pay it, if need be, even with her life. She is calm and self-possessed, where all is dismay. She takes Livingston aside, and speaks to him as one having authority.

"Last night I spoke to Geoffrey," she quietly says: "he felt this coming on, and knew he could rely upon me. He wished to be taken to the hospital, but that I would not hear of. He wished me to go, but that was still more impossible. Then we decided what to do, and you must obey. You must leave at once, and take Miss Ventnor, and her mother, and Leo with you, to Brightbrook, if you are wise; this city is not safe. I remain with Mrs. Abbott. A professional nurse is coming, and his friend, Dr. Morgan, will attend. To obey is the only way in which you can help us, and with the help of Heaven, Geoffrey will be restored to us soon."

"But, oh, Joanna," the young man cries out, "it may be death to you!"

She smiles; it is a smile that goes to his heart.

"If Heaven pleases, but I think not. I am so strong, so well, I have never been ill in my life, and I am not in the least afraid. I do not think that for me there is the slightest danger. But for your cousin and Leo, there may be much. Take them away, Frank, and do not come here any more."

"I will take them away," he answers, "but as for not coming here any more——"

He does not finish the sentence; he turns to go. Then suddenly he comes back, and clasps her closely in his arms, and kisses her again and again.

"God bless you, my own darling—my brave, noble, great-hearted Joanna, and make me worthy of you in the time that is to come."

Olga Ventnor, and her mother, and Leo are taken away. Not willingly, rebelling, and under loud protests and tears on Leo's part, white, mute grief on Olga's. Her heart burns as she thinks of Joanna there in the post of danger, by his side, and she here, selfishly safe and free.

But she says little. What is there for her to say? and maiden pride is very strong in Olga Ventnor. They see that she is pale, that as the days go on she grows thin as a shadow, that she wanders about like a restless spirit, that she listens breathlessly to the report Livingston brings daily, and many times a day. For they have not gone, that would have been too cruel, and Frank hovers constantly about the cottage, intercepts the doctor, waylays the nurse, and tries to catch glimpses of Joanna. There are not many glimpses of Joanna to be had; she literally lives in the sickroom, she shares the nightly vigils, she snatches brief naps in her clothes, while she insists upon his mother taking her proper rest. No Sister of Mercy, no adoring wife, could have watched, nursed, cared for him more devotedly than does she. And the days pass—the long, sunny, summer days. Everything

that medical skill can do, that tireless nursing can do,
are done. And they triumph. There comes a day
and a night of agonized suspense, and waiting, and
heart-break—a night in which Olga Ventnor knows in
her agony that if Geoffrey Lamar dies, all that life
holds of joy for her will die too—a night in which
Leo weeps, and Livingston roams restlessly, and
Joanna watches, and waits, and prays. And as day
dawns, and the first lances of sunshine pierce the
darkened sick-room, she comes out, white as a spirit,
wasted, wan, but oh! so thankful—Oh! so glad—Oh!
so unspeakably blessed. Frank Livingston starts up
and comes forward, pale too, and worn, and thin.
He does not speak—his eyes speak for him.

"Do not come near," Joanna says, remembering,
even in that supreme hour, prudence. "Go home
and tell them all to bless God for us. Geoffrey will
live."

He goes and tells his glad news. Mrs. Ventnor
and Leo cry with joy, and are full of outspoken
thanksgiving, but Olga is silent. And presently she
rises, feeling giddy and faint, and goes to her room,
and falls on her knees by the bed, and there remains,
bowed, speechless, motionless, a long, long time. And
whether it is for Geoffrey she is praying, or—Joanna
—she can never tell.

CHAPTER X.

"THE TIME OF ROSES."

" NEVER thought to see it again, the dear old place. Nowhere in the world can ever seem so much like home to me as Brightbrook. It is good, good, good to be back !"

So says little Leo, drawing a long, contented breath. She stands leaning against a brown tree trunk, her hat in her hand, the sunshine sifting down upon her like a rain of gold, flecking her pink cambric dress, her braided dark hair, her sweet, soft-cut face, the great black velvety eyes.

Those dark eyes gaze with a wistful light in the direction of Abbott Wood, whither she has not yet been. Sitting in a rustic chair, near, Frank Livingston looks at her, thinking, artist-like, what an unconscious picture she makes of herself, and with something deeper, perhaps, than mere artist admiration in his eyes.

They are all here, the Lamar family, and have been for two days. To Leo it is as though they had never quitted it. The villa, the village, the faces of Frank and Olga, everything seems as if she had only left yesterday. The gap of years is bridged over ; she is rich and prosperous Leo Abbott once more. Only her old home she has not seen ; she longs to go, but dreads to ask.

In an invalid chair, close by, sits her brother, very much of an invalid still, pallid and thin to a most in-

10

teresting degree, and petted by all the womankind
until Livingston declares in disgust the after coddling
must be ten times harder for Lamar to bear up against
than the fever bout.   Olga is an exception.   Olga,
now that she has gotten him safely here, feels a limit-
less content, but she does not " coddle." She watches
the returning appetite, the growing strength, the
gradual return to life and health, with a gladness, a
thankfulness words are weak to tell, but she pets not
at all.   She treats him a trifle more tenderly, perhaps,
than the Geoffrey Lamar, vigorous of strength and
life, of some weeks back ; but feel as she may, Olga
Ventnor is not one to wear her heart on her sleeve for
any man, sick or well.   She is a fair, a gracious, a
lovely young hostess, full of all gentle care for the
comfort of her guests ; but Geoffrey is her mother's
especial province, and to her mother she quietly leaves
him.

It is rather against his will, truth to tell, that Dr.
Lamar is here at all ; but very little voice was given
him in the matter—his faint objections were overruled by a vast majority, and he was en route hither
almost before he knew it.

Colonel Ventnor had come for his wife and daughter, alarmed for their safety, and, finding the patient
convalescent, had waited a few days, and abducted
him, willy nilly.   The cottage had been shut up, and
the family are safely here, recuperating in the fresh,
sea-scented breezes of Brightbrook, and Olga and Leo
at least, in their hidden hearts, supremely happy.

For Frank and Geoffrey—well, their roses are certainly not thornless.   For Geoffrey, he finds himself
yielding irresistibly to the spell of other days, and it

threatens to be a fatal spell. In those other days it was different—he might have hoped then—now hope would only be another name for presumption. He has loved Olga ever since he can remember, it seems to him, and even when he thought her assigned to Livingston, had hoped, feeling confident of being able to hold his own with that careless wooer. But all that has been changed ; in those days he was the heir presumptive of a very rich man ; in these days he is a penniless doctor, able to earn his daily bread, and little more. And for all the best years of his life it seems likely to be so. For himself, he has quite made up his mind to it, has not been unhappy, but now—now, after this inopportune visit, after long days spent in her society, it will be different. He can hardly love her better, and yet he dreads to stay. He will spoil his life for nothing ; a hopeless passion will mar all that is best in him, a love she must never know of will consume his life, eat out his heart with useless longings and regrets.

Meantime Joanna speeds on by day and by night, on her long journey to her mother. Her prediction has proven true—she does not take the fever. And the doctor tells them all that to her indefatigable nursing more than anything else do they owe Geoffrey's life.

"Thank her if you can, young man," Dr. Morgan says ; " she never spared herself by night or day. But for her you would be a dead man this morning."

But Geoffrey does not even try to thank her—there are things for which mere words, be they never so eloquent, are a poor return. Others overwhelm her with tears and gratitude—his mother, his sister, Mrs. Vent-

nor. Olga says little, but it is at her Joanna looks.
She is very pale in these first days, with a tense sort of
look in her blue eyes ; but she holds herself well in
hand, and even Joanna turns away disappointed, from
that still, proudly calm face. Only when they say
good-by does a glimpse of Olga's heart appear. She
is the last to say it, and they are alone. She has held
out her hand at first with a smile, and the conventional
good wishes for a pleasant journey. Suddenly she
flings her arms around Joanna's neck and holds her almost wildly to her.

"You have saved his life," she whispers, kissing
her again and again. "I will love you while I live
for that."

And then she is gone.

Joanna looks after her, a glad, relieved, triumphant
smile on her face.

"It is so, then," she says, softly, "in spite of all—
in spite of pride. I am so glad—so very, very glad."

And now they are all here, and the five last miserable years seem to drift away, and the old time—"the
time of roses"—comes back. Leo visits Abbott Wood
to her heart's content—no one objects—and wanders
sadly under the trees, and down by the blue summer
sea, through the glowing rooms, speaking of her mother's refined taste, her father's boundless wealth.

Poor papa ! Leo's tender little heart is sad for
him yet. Here is the chapel, beautiful St. Walburga's,
with its radiant saints on golden backgrounds, the
crimson and purple and golden glass casting rays of
rainbow light on the colored marbles of the floor, the
carven pulpit with its angel faces, from which Mr.
Lamb's meek countenance used to beam down on them

all. Up yonder is the organ where mamma used to sit and play Mozart and Haydn on Sunday afternoons. How silent, how sad, how changed, it all is now. Here is her own white and blue chamber, with its lovely picture of Christ blessing little children, its guardian angels on brackets, her books, and toilet things, all as they used to be.

Here is Geoffrey's room, bare enough and without carpet, for his tastes were preternaturally austere in those days, with lots of space, and little else, except an iron bedstead, and tables, and chairs. And books, of course—everywhere books. And a horrid skeleton in a closet, on wires, and a dismal skull grinning at her under glass.

Leo gets out again as quickly as may be, with a shudder at Geoff's dreadful tastes. Her first visit leaves her very sad and thoughtful; she loves every tree in the old place, every room in the stately house, and it is never to be home to her any more! It is Joanna's, and, of course, she is glad of that. No good too good can come to Joanna; but for all that, it makes her heart ache. She may come to it as a visitor, but dear, dear Abbott Wood will never be home any more.

No one else goes, not her mother, not her brother; they drive in every other direction, never in that. Leo goes often, and frequent going blunts the first sharp feeling of loss and pain. Another sense of loss and pain, keener yet, follows this. What has she done to Frank? He is her friend no more; he avoids her, indeed; he is never her escort if he can help it. Sometimes he cannot help it. Olga, in her imperious fashion, orders him to go and take care of Leo, and

not let the child come to harm moving about alone.
Leo tries to assert herself, and summon pride to her
aid ; but Leo in the role of a haughty maiden is a
failure. The sensitive lips quiver, like the lips of a
grieved child ; the velvet black eyes grow dewy and
deep, with tears hardly held back. What has she done
to make Frank dislike her? He used not be like this ;
he used to be nice, and attentive, and polite. But it
is so no more. He goes with her when he must, and
talks to her after a constrained fashion, and looks at
her furtively, and seems guilty, when caught in the
act. Why should he look guilty, and glance hastily
away? There is no harm in looking at her—Leo has
a secret consciousness that she is not bad to look at.
She cannot be entirely miserable over the loss of her
old home, while she every day grows more and more
miserable over the loss of her friend.

And the days go on, and the weeks pass, and the
end of September is here. They have heard from
Joanna. Mrs. Abbott has had a brief letter, very
brief. She has reached her journey's end in safety ;
she has found her mother, has taken her from the asylum, and, after a week or two of rest, will return.
She sends her love to all. There is no more. It is
singularly short, and business-like, and to the point.
She writes to no one else. Livingston hardly knows
whether he is sorry or relieved. He has asked her to
write, but she has made no promise. In a fortnight
she will be back, and then —— They will bear the
announcement of his engagement better now than they
would have done a month ago. After all, it is as well
he waited. All sing pæans in Joanna's praise now.
He grows a trifle weary, sometimes, listening. It is all

true, no doubt ; she is a noble woman ; he will never
be half worthy of her, at his best, but—— He looks
across at Leo, sitting, listlessly enough, in a garden-
chair, her hands lying idly on her lap, her mignonne
face pale and spiritless ; the soft, black eyes heavy-
lidded and tired-looking. The sweet, childish mouth
has a pathetic little droop ; she looks sorry, or lonely,
or something. He starts up impatiently, and goes off,
angry with himself—his fate—all the world.

And now the Lamars begin to talk of going—
Geoffrey, indeed, has been impatiently talking of it,
and thinking of it, for some time, but has been met by
such a storm of reproach for his unseemly haste, that
he has been forced to desist. But against his better
judgment always, and now he *will* go. His work
awaits him. Dr. Morgan writes sarcastically to inquire
if he has fallen into a Rip Van Winkle slumber up
there in his sylvan Sleepy Hollow. He is perfectly
well again, no plea of invalidism can be put forth to
detain him, and his resolution is taken. To-morrow
he goes. His mother and sister can remain another
week, if they choose, while he has the cottage put in
order. They do choose, overwhelmed by the hospita-
ble pressing of the Ventnors, and so it is decided.

The last evening has come. Leo is away on one of
her long rambles, and, for a wonder, Livingston is
with her. It is the hour of sunset. Colonel Ventnor,
his daughter, and Dr. Lamar linger on the lawn. The
lovely after-glow, the exquisite rose-light of a perfect
September day yet lingers in the sky ; a faintly salt
breeze comes fresh from the ocean, and stirs the sleeping flowers. On the piazza, at the other side of the
house, the elder ladies sit, and after a little the colonel

feels called upon to join them. Then Geoffrey throws himself on the dry, crisp grass, rather tired after a long day's rambling, and Olga, with a smile, seats herself on a grassy knoll close by.

"I know you are used up, if you would but own it," she is saying. "*I* am, and do not mind confessing it in the least. Ten miles is as much as I ever want to do at once. I fear it was hardly wise of you, not yet fully strong, to go as far as you did."

"You will insist on keeping me on the sick list," he answers. "I believe I am as strong as I ever was in my life. I might have gone a week ago, with perfect safety. My walk will do me no harm. And it is for the last time."

There is a pause. His voice is regretful—it is hard to go. A little frown deepens between Miss Ventnor's eyebrows.

"I hate last time," she says, petulantly, "I hate saying good-by. Every year I live, every friend I part with, I hate it more and more. They are the two hardest, hatefulest words in the language. *You* must like it, though, you appear so desperately anxious to say it, and get rid of us."

He looks up at her. She is very lovely, but she is always that. Her hat lies on her lap, her delicate face is ever so little flushed, ever so little petulant, her blue eyes have an almost irate sparkle. See is dressed in pale blue, crisp, silky, cool, a cluster of pink roses in her breast, another in her hair. She looks all azure and roses, golden hair, and flower face. He turns away his eyes, slightly dazzled.

"Do you believe that," he asks, quietly, "that I am glad to go?"

"It looks like it, I confess. You have talked of nothing else but going ever since you came. And now you will leave us to-morrow, though the heavens fall."

"It would have been wiser if I had never come," he says, still very quietly ; "it would have been wiser for me if I had gone the moment I was able. I did not mean to say this, but, Olga, cannot you see—do you not know the reason ?"

"No, I do not," she answers, still petulant, although the deepening flush on her cheek tells another story. "I only know you are very perverse, and are longing to be off among your fever patients, and to catch it if possible over again yourself."

"Would you care if I did—would you care if I did ?" he says, then quickly checks himself. "No," he says, "do not answer that question. I had no right to ask it—I recall it, and beg your pardon. I did not mean to say this much, Olga, to say anything, but but having said it in spite of myself, let me say yet more. I love you, Olga, I love you with my whole heart."

There is a startling pause. Miss Ventnor catches her breath, but makes no other sign.

"Once I might have said this with something of a good grace," Geoffrey goes on ; "that day has gone by. I loved you even then, Olga. I can recall no time when I did not. But the deluge came—the whole world changed for me ; we parted, and I never thought to see you again. I did not forget you ; I never could. You were the one fair woman in all the world for me, but I never wished to meet you more. That way madness lay. But who is stronger than his fate ? You

16*

came—we *have* met, I am here, I am at your feet, I
am saying this. My whole heart is yours—perhaps it
is written in the book of fate that I am to tell you this.
It is presumption, I know, but I know, too, you will
not look on it in that light. We have been such old
friends, Olga, that you will listen, and pity, and forgive."

Pity and forgive !   And he asks nothing but that.

"I meant to go and say nothing,"—all this time he
has hardly stirred from his recumbent position, hardly
let a touch of the excitement that thrills him creep into
his voice—it is the most passive-looking of love-making,
and yet is full of repressed passion and fire. "I meant to
depart and make no sign. But my love is stronger
than my judgment. And after all it can do no harm.
You will forget, and I will take my dreams with me,
and be the less miserable for knowing that you have
heard and understood. If I were a richer man I would
plead very differently. It is that I am so absolutely
poor that gives me courage to speak at all. Despair,
you know, is a free man—Hope is a coward. When
we have nothing to hope for, we have nothing to fear.
Say you forgive me, Olga, and are still my friend in
spite of this."

"I will say it," she answers, with a great effort,
"and if you wish—more."

He turns and looks at her, surprise in his face, little
else. Certainly there is no gleam of hope. He has
settled it so completely with himself that it is impossible she can care for him, that it is not for one falter-
ing reply to upset his theory.

"Olga !" he says.

Her head is averted, her cheek is crimson, her eyes

are downcast, her fingers pluck nervously at the tufts of grass and wild flowers.

"Olga," he says again, and this time there *is* a wild, incredulous flash of delight in his eyes. "Olga!"

"Oh," she breaks out, brokenly, "cannot *you* see! Why will you force me to speak? I will *not* speak!" with a flash from the great blue eyes.

She rises suddenly to her feet, and scatters a shower of pink petals over her lover, and over the grass.

"Olga," is all he can say, in his whirl of amazement, incredulity, of mad, new joy.

There is a struggle. Then all at once she stoops, and, lightly as the touch of thistle-down, her lips rest on his forehead.

"If you can leave me—now," she says, flushed, frightened at her own temerity, breathless, laughingly, "go!"

And, as she speaks, she turns, and swiftly as a fawn flies, is gone.

CHAPTER XI.

HOW JOANNA SAID GOOD-BY.

"THINK it is odd," says Mrs. Abbott, languidly, "and unlike Joanna. She never has whims. Why should she wish us to remain here, instead of going home, as we ought, to receive her?"

Another week has gone by—nine days, indeed—and Leo and her mother are still the guests of the Ventnors. Geoffrey has gone back to his cottage home, as per previous arrangement, to have it set in

order for them, and resume his labors. One day
longer than he had intended he has staid, and both
families have been electrified by the wonderful news.
And yet not, perhaps, so very greatly. Colonel Ventnor glances at his daughter, and slowly smiles. In all
his life he has never contradicted his darling—he is
hardly likely to begin now. And he is not ambitious
of adding wealth to wealth—she is, and will be always,
sufficiently rich. As the heir of John Abbott, he certainly never would have dreamed of objecting to young
Lamar, with the best blood of the South in his veins.
As a struggling young doctor he is not less worthy of
her. He is no fortune-hunter, of that the colonel is
well assured. And Olga loves him ; his proud and
delicate darling, whose heart hitherto no man has been
able to touch. He grasps Geoffrey's hand with frank,
soldierly warmth.

"There is no man living to whom I would sooner
give her," he says, cordially. "Fortune? Ah, well,
fortune is not everything, and fortune is to be won by
the willing. You are of that number, I am sure. If
I fancied *her* fortune had to do with it, do you think
I would listen like this ? It is because I could stake
my life on the truth of the lad I have known all his
life, that I say yes so readily. Make her happy, Geoffrey—all is said in that."

Could anything be more delightful? Geoffrey
finds the whole English language inadequate to his
wants, in the way of thanks. Mrs. Ventnor is charmed
—the son of her dearest friend is the one, above all
others, she would have chosen for her son as well.

One thing only is a drawback—the story that must
be told, the one bar sinister on the spotless Lamar

shield.   But that cannot be told now ; not until Joanna returns and gives permission.   Some hint of it
he drops, necessarily obscure, before.he goes.   No plans
are formed for the present—it is understood that Colonel and Mrs. Ventnor will not agree to any long engagement.

"If you and Olga make up your mind to wait while
you win your way," he says, decisively, "it must be
without an engagement.   I will not have her fettered
while you plod slowly upward."

It is not likely, under these circumstances, they *will*
make up their minds to wait.   Geoffrey goes, and Olga
is petted to her heart's content.   For Leo, she is in a
seventh heaven of rapture, and for a day or two positively forgets Frank.   Another sister, and that one her
darling Olga !   Surely, she is the most fortunate girl
in the world.

And now here is Joanna coming back, has come
indeed, and is with Geoffrey already.   "Wait until I
join you," is what she writes.   "I have something to
say to you, my Leo, that I prefer to say there."   It is
now late on Monday evening—to-morrow morning will
bring her.

To-morrow comes.   Frank is at the station to
meet her, looking worn and anxious, as he has grown
of late.   Latterly his misanthropy, as far as Leo is
concerned, has grown upon him ; he distinctly avoids
her.   He is trying to be true, with all his.might.   If
he could fly from danger, he would fly, but that is impossible.   So he stays on, and does the best he can,
trying to think a great deal of Joanna and her perfec-
tions.   Whether she agrees or not, he means to end
this as soon as she returns, and let the world know of

their relations to each other. He will not ask her leave, he will assert himself, he will simply tell. Then Leo will understand. They will be quietly married, and go away at once. And little Leo will forget—she is such a child—and be happy with some happier man.

The train stops, and a tall young lady, in a gray traveling suit, and pretty gray hat, alights. It is Joanna, looking well and bright, and almost handsome. She smiles and holds out her hand frankly at sight of him, but her manner is more that of a cordial friend than of the woman he is going to marry.

"How well you are looking," he says. "Your long journey seems to have given you added bloom, Joanna. You are as fresh as any rose."

"It must be a yellow rose, then," says Joanna, laughing, " and pale saffron bloom. I am sorry I cannot return the compliment. *You* are looking anything but well, Frank. You have not had a sun-stroke, I hope, this summer ?"

She speaks lightly, but her glance is keen, and there is an under-current of meaning in her tone. He flushes slightly, and flecks the wheeler lightly with his whip.

"Something rather like it, I believe. But I shall rapidly grow convalescent now that you are back. I have—we all have—missed you, Joanna."

." Thank you," she says, gently. " That is a good hearing. I like my friends to miss me. How are they all ?—well ?"

"Quite well. No doubt you have heard the wonderful news. You saw Geoffrey ?"

" Yes, I saw him," smiling, " and really it was not such wonderful news. I did not faint with surprise when I heard it. But of course I am delighted, more than delighted. She will have the noblest husband in the world, and she is worthy of him. You are sure you feel no jealous pang, Frank?" laughing.

"Not one. I shall give my fair cousin my blessing on her wedding-day, with the soundest of hearts—where she is concerned. And your mother?" he says, shifting skillfully from what he feels to be dangerous ground. "You have brought her back safe and well?"

"Safe and well, thank Heaven—almost as well in mind as in body. She might have left years ago, poor darling, if there had been any one to take her. Ah! Frank, I feel that my whole life will not suffice to re-pay her for what she has suffered. And do you know, she accepted me in a moment as her child, seemed to know me, if such a thing could be possible, and came with me so gladly. She can hardly bear me a moment out of her sight."

"You should have brought her down with you. It is unfair to leave her even for a few days now."

"A few days! My dear Frank, I return by to-night's train. Meantime she is with the Professor and Madame Ericson. I have not come to stay. I have come"—her face grows grave—"on very important business, and part of it is with you. I must see Leo first."

He is stricken dumb. Their names in this conjunc-tion! He grows quite white as he leans forward to look at her.

"Joanna, what do you mean?"

She lays her hand on his, kindly, gently, but very firmly.

"Not now, Frank—later. I must first see Leo. I want her to go with me to Abbott Wood this morning. I have a fancy for saying what I have to say in the dear, beautiful old house that she loves so well, and where she—they all—were so good to Joanna. Mrs. Hill will give us lunch there. I shall not return to Ventnor Villa ; and if, when Leo goes back, *you* will come in her stead, I will say good-by to you as well."

She is smiling, but her eyes look dark and sad. He sets his lips—even they are pale.

"Good-by ! Joanna, what are you saying ? There is to be no good-by between us any more. You are mine ; I claim you. I am going to announce our engagement. It is useless for you to object. . I *am*."

"Ah, well !" she says, wearily, " wait—wait until this afternoon, at least. I am a little tired now, and —and dispirited, I think. I do not want to talk of it. Do you know," brightening suddenly, and smiling, "I met an old friend, by purest chance, in the streets of San Francisco. It was so good to see him, although I had every reason to be ashamed. I *was* ashamed too," she laughs, and colors a little.

"Who ?" Frank asks.

"George Blake—poor George ! So improved, so brown, so manly-looking, and so prosperous. He is editor and proprietor of a daily out there, and doing well. I recognized him in a moment, but he did not know me. I stopped him, however, and made myself known—made my peace with him too, I am happy to say. What a wretch I was in those days ! I look back now and wonder if ' I be I ?' You never saw any one so glad as he was to meet me, and as for all the

good-natured things he said about my changed appearance, and so on—but you would think me frightfully
conceited if I repeated the half. What is to the point
is, that he has forgiven me, and forgotten me, so far
as his old fancy is concerned.   He is engaged to be
married, and to quite a rich young lady.   Is not all
that pleasant news?"

But Livingston is not very deeply interested in
George Blake, or his successes, editorial or matrimonial.
He is filled with disquiet by Joanna's manner ; he fears
he knows not what.   She laughs and talks lightly
enough, but underneath it all he sees a resolute purpose, and he has learned to fear her inflexible resolu-
tions.   Why should she so connect his name with
Leo's ? what does she suspect ?   He has striven hard
to be loyal and true, but those deep dark eyes are eyes
not easily deceived.   The drive is not a long one, but
silence has fallen long before they reach the house.

Joanna is met, is welcomed by the Ventnors with
flattering warmth, is embraced by Leo and her mother
with effusion, and finally has a private interview with
the latter lady.   It is not a long one, but Mrs. Abbott
is very pale and grave when it is over, and there are
traces of recent tears.

"It is like you, Joanna !" is what she says ; "I can
say nothing more than that.   You are generosity itself.
I can only echo Geoffrey's words, and leave the decision to Leo, unbiased.   She is a child in most things,
but in this she must judge for herself.   You are her
sister, and your wishes should have weight.   Tell her,
and it shall be as she says."

"I have no fear then," Joanna says, gayly.   "Leo
has common sense, if she is a child, and is free from

fine-drawn notions and wicked pride. Leo, dear, run
and put on your hat. I will drive you over to Abbott
Wood, if Miss Ventnor will trust her ponies to my ,
care. I am quite a skilled charioteer, I assure you."

"To Abbott Wood?" Leo says, opening wide the
velvet black eyes.

"Yes, dear; and we will lunch there together.
Quite like old times—will it not be? Do not be a
minute. I will say good-by to the others while you
are gone."

"Good-by?" cries Leo, with dismay; but Joanna
has left her, and is already explaining the necessity
for her return that very night. She cannot leave her
mother, who pines and frets in her absence. So she
says farewell there and then, to Mrs. Abbott as well
as the rest.

"We go south very shortly," Joanna says, "and
will pass the winter in Florida. Next spring, when
we return, of course my first visit will be here."

Frank is there as well as the rest, but to him she
does not hold out her hand.

"Come and fetch Leo back this afternoon," she
says. "I can make my adieux to you then."

She and Leo depart, and Livingston quits the
family group, and is seen no more by any member of
the household. It is a day he will not easily forget;
the suspense, the dread, the pain he feels, grave themselves on his memory, making this a day apart from
all other days in his life.

Meantime the ponies prance along and speedily do
the five miles between Ventnor Villa and Abbott
Wood. It is a perfect day—sunny, cloudless, breezy,
with the odor of the sea in the crisp air, and Abbott

Wood looking more like an ancestral park and baronial hall than ever. They sweep up the noble drive
and alight in front of the house. Great urns glow,
filled with tropical plants ; the flower-beds blaze in
their autumn glory ; the deer look at them with wild,
shy eyes ; fountains tinkle and plash—all is in perfect
order. So is the house in as exquisite keeping as when
its mistress reigned there. Leo's eyes light as they
drink in all this beauty. She laughs a little, then
sighs.

"It is so lovely," she says—"the dear, dear old
home ! Go where I will I see nothing like it !"

"You love it, then ?" Joanna quietly asks.

"Love it !" Leo repeats. Her eyes flash, her lips
part, then she stops. She must not seem too fond of
it now, she remembers, lest Joanna thinks her envious.
"Of course I am fond of it," she says. "I was born
here, and every tree, and every flower, and bird seem
like old friends. But it will always seem like home to
me, now that it is yours. If it had gone to a stranger,
I think it would almost have broken my heart."

"Dear little loving heart !" Joanna interposes with
a smile.

"But it is yours, and you are my own precious
sister," goes on Leo, gayly, "and I shall expect you
to invite me here often. You are not to forget your
poor relations, you know, Mlle. Fifty Millions !"

Joanna pauses, and looks down upon her. She
lays both hands on her shoulders and smiles down into
her eyes. Very sweet, and youthful, and fair is little
Leo, with her pretty upturned face, and large lumi-
nous Southern eyes.

"It must be the other way," she says. "You

must invite *me* here, little Leo—for Abbott Wood is yours."

"Mine!" The dark eyes open wide, and stare.

"Yes, my darling—yours and yours only. From this day you are the little *chatelaine* of Abbott Wood. Do you think I would keep your birthright—the house where you were born? the place you love so dearly, where you were so good—so good—to me? Ah, no! I never thought of that. I meant to restore it to you from the first. You are my sister, my father's daughter. It was for you he intended it, and yours it shall be. Do not look at me with such wonder-stricken eyes. Could you think so badly of me as to dream I would keep it? I would not live here if I could. There are reasons——" she stops for a moment. "No, little Leo, it is yours, all the processes of law have been duly fulfilled. It is yours by free deed of gift, and with it half the fortune our father left. What should I do with so much money? Even half is the embarrassment of riches. I can never spend my income. It was for this I stopped on my way here, to speak to Geoffrey. I knew you would do nothing without his consent. He would have no voice in the matter, he left it entirely to you. It was to tell your mother, I saw her alone this morning— she, too, leaves it altogether to you. But *I* do not —you must accept. There is no compulsion, you know, Leo, dear," says Joanna, laughing and kissing her, "only you *must!* And although you cannot live here alone, and though neither your mother nor brother will ever live here with you, I foresee Abbott Wood will not be long without a mistress. I foresee," goes on Joanna, her hands still on Leo's shoulders, her

smiling eyes still on Leo's face, "that you will soon
reign here, and not alone, and I hope—oh, my little
Leo, with all my heart I hope you may be very, very
happy !"

Her voice breaks. Leo flings her arms about her
and hides her face on her breast. She is sobbing,
whether with joy, with love, with gratitude, or with
pain, she hardly knows.

Happy ! Ah, if Joanna only knew how unhappy
she is !

"I—I don't know what to say," she sobs, wildly.
"I never thought of this. It is like robbing you,
Joanna. Oh, I don't know what to do. I ought not to
take this—it is your house—I cannot bear to take it
from you."

"Luckily you have no choice. It is yours in spite
of you ! If you refused it would only be left to the
rats and Mrs. Hill for the term of their natural lives.
But you will not refuse, and one day all my predic-
tions will come true. Oh, never look so despondent—
trust me, Joanna is among the prophets. And now,
wipe those pretty eyes, and let us consider the matter
settled, and at an end forever. No more thanks, or
tears, or scenes—they make me almost as uncomfortable as if I were a man. It is luncheon hour, and
here I protest is Frank Livingston coming up the
avenue. Leo, before he comes, I want you to tell him
all about this to-morrow—I mean my story, relation-
ship to you, and so on. Geoffrey has to tell Colonel
Ventnor, of course; I have given him permission. And
with that we will let it drop, the world will never
know. I shall take my rightful name—Bennett—and
you will keep yours until you exchange it for——"

"Mr. Livingston," says Mrs. Hill, suddenly usher-
ing him in.

Joanna looks at Leo and laughs, and Leo blushes
to the temples, as both go forward to greet him.

They take their midday refection together, and try
to talk easily, but both appetite and conversation are
failures. Everything Mrs. Hill can do to tempt them
she has done, but no one is at ease. Joanna *looks* calm,
and in spite of everything, is perhaps a trifle amused
by the marked avoidance of her two guests. She reads
it all so plainly, and if there is any pain at her own
heart, she resolutely puts it away. She has made up
her mind to the inevitable, and to look back and weep
for what is forever gone is not her way.

After luncheon they wander about the grounds for
awhile ; then Leo is summoned away by Mrs. Hill to
see some of her former pets, and Joanna and Frank
stroll back to the house. The afternoon has worn on
—the sun is declining ; Joanna looks at her watch as
they stand side by side at one of the windows commanding a wide view of the sparkling sunset sea.

"Five," she says ; "my train goes at seven. Two
good hours yet. We will have time for some tea presently—a sort of stirrup-cup to speed my departure."

"Joanna !" Livingston breaks out, "this must end.
You torture me—cannot you see that ? You are like
ice—like stone—you care nothing for me at all. How
coolly you talk of going—of leaving me for an indefi-
nite period. Do you forget you are my promised wife ?"

"I have a good memory," Joanna says, "but I assuredly do *not* remember that. I have never promised
you anything in my life."

"Have you not ?" he demands. "What is it, ther ?

Have I not asked you to marry me ? Do you not wear
my ring——"

She holds out both hands—ringless.

"As my hands, so my heart—free. Yes, you have
asked me, and I—I have said nothing, only this one
word from first to last—wait. You have waited—
well, your waiting is at an end. That is why I wished
to see you here—to say that. If you ever asked me
to marry you, ever made me any promise, ever held
yourself bound to me, I give it all back. You too are
free."

He cannot speak. He stands looking at her, so
pale, so conscience-stricken, that she lays her hand
lightly for a moment on his.

"Do not blame yourself too much," she says, kindly ; "do not blame yourself at all. Indeed, you deserve none. You have tried—do you think I have not
seen?—and failed. That has been no fault of yours.
You never loved me, Frank—no, not for one poor moment. You thought so that night you were ' *Carried
by Storm* '—do you recall your own words? They ex-
pressed it exactly ; but love me—never ! Trust a
woman to know when she is beloved. Excitement, a
moment's impulse, carried you away—when you had
time to think, you repented. You would not own it
even to yourself—all the same it was there. You did
your best, your very best, to be faithful, but there are
things that are spoiled by trying. Love is one of them.
And you know I never could accept *that*. In the common acceptation of the term I am not proud, but I am
far too proud to accept a husband after such fashion
as that. If I cannot be beloved, I will go to my grave
unmarried. And I am quite sure that so I will go.

And now, Frank, you are free—free as the wind that blows, and we are friends, good friends, once again and forever."

She holds out her hand, but he does not see it. He has turned from her, and is pacing to and fro, bitterness on his face, in his heart. Inconsistently enough, the keenest sense of loss he has ever felt is upon him in this hour.

"You never cared for me—it is easy for you to say all this," he says, bitterness in his tone as well.

She smiles slightly, and turns away, and looks far off at the golden afternoon haze over the sea. Weak and unstable he is, and she knows him to be, but he has power to bring a sharp contraction to her heart still.

"Never cared for you?" she repeats, dreamily. "Frank, come here—do not be angry ; let us talk as friends. Yes, I cared for you. When I was a little child, a little, beaten, barefoot child, I cared for you. When you used to come to Sleaford's, you were in my eyes as some beautiful and glorified young prince." She laughs as she says it, but with a tremor in the clear voice. "I fell in love with you even then. You never saw me, you know, in those days, and what wonder ? I thought Lora Sleaford the most enviable creature in the world, because you seemed to like her ; I hated your cousin because you seemed so fond of her. In after years, when we used to meet here, I believe, without knowing it, I was wildly jealous of Olga, of Leo, of every pretty girl who came near you. And when I ran away with George Blake, do you know what kept me from marrying him ? Simply because I saw you— you passed through the hotel hall, and out into the street, and I *could not*. I ran away. I cared for you then, did I not ? And since, when we met, and you knew me, I was glad—ah, glad, glad ; and when I thought you were beginning to care for me, I seemed not to have a wish left in all the world. I wonder why I tell you all this ? I ought not, I know, but it hurts · me when you say it is easy for me to give you up. It is not easy—it is only right. And when that night you asked me, I was glad—ah, gladder than you will ever know. Only for a little ; before an hour was over I feared—when to-morrow came I *knew*. And from that time I never meant to hold you to your word. I care for you so much, Frank, my friend, my brother, that I give you up. We would never be happy. You would repent, and I would see it, and it would break my heart. Indeed it would, if I were your wife, and I prefer an unbroken heart. I feel this farewell now—. so, perhaps, do you, in a different way, but it will not hurt either of us, I hope, very badly. But you believe me, Frank, that it is because I have cared for you, and do, that I give you up ?"

She holds out her hand again. This time he takes it in both his. He cannot speak ; what is there to say ? It is the saddest, gentlest, humblest moment of his life. Her face, too, is sad ; her eyes wistful, her gaze still lingers on that fading light upon the sea.

"And when we have parted," Joanna goes on, after that pause, "and you meet some one you really love, and whom you know loves you, remember you are to let no foolish scruple about all this hold you back, or mar the happiness of that other. And if," slowly, "it is any one for whom I care, the obligations will be more binding still. If you feel you owe me anything,

17

repay it in that way. I will understand and rejoice.
To-morrow there are things Leo will tell you. Why
do you start? Leo is not an alarming personage—
things you ought to know, and which I prefer you
should hear first from her. And now I am tired talking, and here come Leo and Mrs. Hill. Perhaps we
can have that tea. It is time, for I am thirsty, and
must soon be off. Can we not have tea out under the
trees, Mrs. Hill? It is so delicious here in sight of
the sea."

So they have tea, and the repast is even more silent
than the luncheon. The two young ladies do their
best, but Livingston simply cannot talk. His heart is
full, and in it there is little room for any but Joanna
just now. Then it is over. Joanna looks at her watch
again.

"Half-past six. I want to say good-by here, and
see you two off before I depart myself. Mrs. Hill,
please have them bring the buggy round to take me to
the station. Leo—Frank!"

And then the supreme moment has come, and Leo's
arms are around her, and Leo is sobbing on her breast.
She holds out both hands to Livingston, with tears in
the brave, bright eyes.

"Take her away," she says, in a stifled voice; " I
cannot bear it. Be good to her, Frank. God bless
you both!"

And then, somehow, she is alone, and they are gone,
and a last burst of yellow sunshine takes them, and
they are lost to view.

She sits down and covers her face, with a long,
hard breath. Some oft-quoted lines come into her
head, and keep echoing there, and will not be exorcised,

after the fashion of such things. "So tired, so tired, my heart and I!" She is conscious of feeling tired, old, cold, worn-out. She sits, a long time, it seems to her—ten minutes by Mrs. Hill's count—and then that portly matron returns, and says the carriage is waiting.

Joanna rises at once. She is pale, and her eyes are wet, but that is natural enough. She says good-by to Mrs. Hill, and slips largesse into her palm, and goes. And all the way to the station, and all the way back to New York, as the train thunders over the iron road, it keeps monotonously beating out the refrain, "So tired, so tired, my heart and I."

CHAPTER XII.

WEDDING BELLS.

EARLY that autumn there is a fashionable wedding in New York, and the beautiful heiress, Miss Olga Ventnor, is the bride. The bridegroom, personally, is unknown to fame; but the dear "five hundred" can see for themselves that he is a very stately and distinguished-looking gentleman, and this goes far to condone his obscurity. His name, too, tells for him, one of the fine old names of the South—"fine old family, my dear, impoverished as so many fine old families have been, by the recent war," etc. That the bride, in white satin and point lace, and orange blossoms, and diamond stars, looks lovely, you know before I tell you. That the wedding presents are numerous and splendid, the wedding breakfast a triumph of culinary art; that the speech of the bridegroom is notable among stammering bridal speeches—are not these things written in the chronicles of the books of Jenkins—have you not read it all in the daily papers, and shall I bore you with a twice-told tale? "Immediately after the breakfast the happy pair departed for Europe," etc., etc.

Thus far Olga and Geoffrey. Mrs. Abbott and Leo go back to their suburban retreat, their birds, their books, their piano, their quiet life. Abbott Wood knows no change—Mrs. Hill still reigns supreme. Joanna is right in her prediction that Leo's mother will never again dwell within its walls.

"All houses wherein men have lived and died are haunted houses."

Abbott Wood is to her a haunted house, haunted by terrible memories and a dreadful death.

For Frank Livingston, he goes to New York, sets up his easel and atelier, and goes to work with an energy and will that astonish his friends. His lazy insouciance is gone—he is a holiday artist, playing at picture-making, no more. What is given him to do, he does with all his might. It is no great things, perhaps—he is no embryo Raphael or Doré—but his best he does. And he has a fair success. He paints a picture that winter that is exhibited, and criticised, and a good deal talked about. Belter, a very rich man, and a patron of native talent, buys it at a fancy price. It is a twilight scene—some bare brown fields, a dreary expanse of arid marsh, a gray frowning sky, a chill wind. You can *feel* the chill rustling of the reeds and sedge grass, a broken rail fence, and a barefoot girl leaning upon it. Her wild hair blows in the wind, her face is wan and unchildlike; her eyes, fixed on the far-off sky line, have a mournful, appealing, dog-like look. It is called "Heart Hungry."

It is Joanna, of course, as he has often seen her, in the days when he thought of her so little. He thinks of her now, almost more than of any one else, with mingled affection, admiration, and remorse. How noble she is, how generous, how great of heart! He feels that he could never have made her happy ; her nature is too noble for his. As man and wife they would have jarred. It is better as it is. All he can do is to try by constant hard work to approach ever so little nearer her level. He paints other pictures, and they sell. He is fairly successful, and each new success spurs him on to still further endeavors.

Of Leo he sees nothing ; in those busy days he has little time for visits, and besides—well, besides there is a long future for all that.

Spring comes—May, June.

With the end of June returns the wedded pair, looking happy and handsome, and absorbed in each other, of course. Almost immediately they go to Brightbrook. The Ventnors are to follow in a couple of weeks, and Mrs. Abbott and Leo have promised to spend the holidays with them. Mrs. Abbott is dying for her son, Mrs. Ventnor for her daughter. So once more they are all to be reunited, the happiest household in the world.

It is Frank Livingston who drives Olga down to the station to meet the expected guests. The color flushes into little Leo's face at sight of him—it is a surprise—nothing has been said of his coming.

"And indeed he did not want to come," says, severely, Mrs. Dr. Lamar. She makes the most charm-

ing and radiant of young matrons. "We had almost
to tear him by force from his beloved studio. You
may see for yourself how badly he is looking—quite
old and ugly. And he used to be fairly good-looking
—now, used he not, little Leo ?"

And of course at this malicious home-thrust poor
little Leo is overwhelmed with confusion, and wishes
the carriage would open and swallow her. Frank
laughs lazily. He *is* looking rather thin, but perfectly
well in all other respects. And there is an expression
of manliness, of gravity, of determination on his handsome face, which is new and extremely becoming.

"His latest work of art," says Olga Lamar, on the
back seat, to Leo, "is—guess what ? A picture of *you*.
It is painted from memory, and the commission is mine
—as you looked in your bridemaid dress, dear—I never
saw you look so pretty as you did that day. What a
trick the child has of blushing ! He has brought it
down with him, and will finish it here. It is for my
particular sitting-room. Do you know, we are going
to live in Brightbrook, and Geoffrey will actually practice in the village. They want a doctor, and he wants
work. Of course we will go to New York in winter,
but to all intents and purposes the villa will be home.
Home ! Is it not a sweet word ? We are enlarging
and improving it, in a number of ways. And we are
going to settle down into the most humdrum Darby
and Joan life you can imagine. And speaking of Joan,
reminds me of Joanna—dear Joanna ! Geoffrey had
a letter from her last night, and oh, Leo ! she will not
come. Says she is going to England for the summer ;
her mother wishes to visit her native land once more.
Is it not too bad ? And I counted so confidently on

her spending July and August with us. But so it ever
is. I would have my life-pictures like Queen Eliza-
beth's portrait, without shadow, and it cannot be. Joanna is the gray background this time, and yes—the
fact that Abbott Wood is still without a mistress. But
yet—I live in hope !"

She runs on gayly, and laughs down in Leo's somber soft eyes. She is so radiantly happy—this fair Princess Olga, in her new life, that she seems to have received a fresh baptism of brightness and beauty.

Next morning the famous picture is displayed—a
soft-eyed, sweet-faced girl in white silk and laces, with
white flowers in her dusky hair. In the shy, wide-open,
wondering-looking eyes, there is an unconscious touch
of pathos.

"Is it not charming ?" Olga cries ; "and do you
not fall in love with yourself, little Leo, only to look
at it ? *I* do. And what have you got that pleading
look in your eyes for, and why do you seem as if you
were waiting for something or—somebody ? Perhaps
the artist knows. Did she look like that on my wedding-day, Frank ? As groomsman, you ought to know.
How do you like yourself, Leo ?"

"It is much too pretty," Leo answers, blushing, of
course ; "it is dreadfully flattered. But I like to be
flattered—in that way, I think."

"You do not really think it is flattered ?" Livingston says, a few minutes later.

He is adding some finishing touches to the likeness, and has asked her to remain. The others have
moved away—they are alone, with only the summer
wind swinging the roses outside the window, the bees
booming, and the birds chirping in the trees.

"Indeed I do—grossly. And that expression—I am sure I never looked like that," with a little pout, " so sentimental, and lackadaisical, and all that."

"Is it lackadaisical?" says the artist, laughing. "Then I think I like lackadaisical looks. But you really did wear just that pathetic expression. It was a sentimental occasion, you know—and, for the matter of that, you often have that waiting, wistful look. It becomes great, dark, Syrian eyes, I think. Do you know you, have real Oriental eyes, Leo—long, almond-shaped, velvet-black."

"I think I must look like a Chinese," remarks Leo, resignedly. "They have almond eyes, have they not?" But while she laughs she tingles to her finger-ends with delight.

" You look like what you are, the fairest, dearest darling in all the world ! Leo !"—he throws down brush and maul-stick, and takes both her hands, with a sudden impulse that flushes his blond face and fires his blue eyes—" don't you know—I love you !"

" Oh !" says Leo, with a sort of gasp, and tries to draw her hands away. She turns pale now, instead of red, it is so sudden, and—somehow he looks so overwhelming.

" Have I startled you ? Dear little Leo ! You were always easily startled, I remember. I do not know that I meant to speak this morning, but the love we hide so long all in a moment breaks its bounds and overflows. I love you ! You are not angry that I say this?"

"No," Leo says, and laughs nervously ; "only curious. To how many more have you said it, I wonder ?"

She hits the truth so nearly that he winces; then he, too, laughs a little.

"Yes, I have said it to others, but I do not think I ever meant it until to-day. I have deceived myself before, and taken passing fancies for love ; that is one reason why I have waited so long before speaking to you. It no passing fancy now—I love you! I have little to offer, but at least I have enough to put me beyond the suspicion of fortune-hunting. What I have I lay at your feet, with my heart, my life. Will you take them, Leo?"

And Leo's answer? Well, it is not in very coherent words, but it is very intelligible. One look of the soft, shy eyes, one droop of the blushing face, and then that face is hidden on Mr. Livingston's velvet painting-blouse, and broken murmurs issue from Mr. Livingston's mustached lips, of which "My darling! my love! my Leo!" are the only distinct articulations the listening robins and bluebirds can catch.

And there is another wedding in September, another fair bride is given away, another young man looks nonsensically happy, another bridal breakfast is eaten, another wedding trip is taken. And Abbott Wood, under the superintendence of Dr. Lamar exteriorly, and Mrs. Dr. Lamar interiorly, is to be put in apple-pie order for the home-coming and house-warming that are to follow, and the stately mansion is to have its mistress at last. Joanna's prediction is verified—Leo will live there, and not alone.

For Joanna—well, letters come from England with cheerful regularity, and they breathe all good wishes for the happiness of the newly-wedded pair. She is well, and her mother improves quite wonderfully in

71*

body and mind. She expresses no regrets at not being able to be present at the marriage, but she promises to come and spend Christmas with them at Brightbrook. Her plans for her own future are formed and settled ; her mother wishes to reside permanently in England, and Joanna lives but to accede to her wishes. She has bought a pretty place there, she writes, and calls it Brightbrook, and so, after all, an English Brightbrook will be her future home.

*   *   *   *   *   *

So writes Joanna. But, as it chances, Joanna is not Madame Olga's only English correspondent, and it is about this time that the following letter arrives from the Lady Hilda Stafford :

"MY DEAREST OLGA :—Your last was charming. How vividly you picture your fair Brightbrook home ! How I long to see it, and Dr. Lamar, and you ! But, delightful as *your* Brightbrook may be, it can hardly equal *ours*, I fancy, and even you do not know how to be more bewitching than Miss Bennett. We owe you a debt of gratitude for your letters of introduction to us, more particularly as she has made up her mind to settle among us 'for good.' She has purchased an ex-quisite place here, and named it Brightbrook, as you know, and the neighborhood is enchanted with its American acquisition. What a voice she has ! and what a pair of eyes ! I fell in love with her at sight, and, I fancy, I am not the only one who has done so. You met Sir Roland Hardwicke, you know, while here. You have not forgotten him, I hope ; for if the fair, stately, siren-voiced Joanna does not end by becoming Lady Hardwicke, the fault will not be his. His case was hopeless from the first, and he is a splendid fellow, and quite worthy even of so noble a heart as hers. He is every inch a soldier and a gentleman, owning a handsome face, a gallant figure, a long pedigree, and a longer rent-roll. Send your blessing and approval, for I really think both will speedily be required."

Olga is delighted—Geoffrey smiles, and approves. Both remember Sir Roland Hardwicke very distinctly, a man whose favor any woman might be proud to win. But Joanna is not one to be easily won, too readily pleased, and the pedigree and rent-roll, of which Lady Hilda speaks, will not count for much with her.

"I hope—oh, I *do* hope he may please her!" Olga cries, "dear, generous Joanna! If ever any one deserves love and happiness, it is she. And, as his wife, I am sure she will have both. Lady Hardwicke! to think of Joanna—Sleaford's Joanna," laughing, but with tears in the sapphire eyes, "wearing a title at last!"

After that the letters from Lady Hilda are waited for with feverish impatience. They come often, are long and satisfactory. Everything progresses well so far as *she* can see. She is not in Miss Bennett's confidence, of course, but Sir Roland is a frequent—a *very* frequent visitor at Brightbrook, and people talk of it already as a settled thing. Every one loves her, she is the Lady Bountiful of the parish, and Lady Hardwicke (Sir Roland's mother) has graciously offered to present her at Court next season, which shows *she* approves, etc., etc.

Early in December Mr. and Mrs. Livingston return, and parties are given, far and wide, in honor of the bride. And Frank has but one secret in the world from his little wife, and that one is the fact of his brief engagement to Joanna. Somehow he shrinks from telling that—it is the one memory sacred to himself and his friend, that even his wife may not know. He feels instinctively that it would give her pain, that Joanna would not wish it, and so he hides it in his heart, as in a grave.

Two days before Christmas Joanna comes. She finds a rare household assembled at Abbott Wood to meet and greet, and do her honor. Mrs. Abbott, Olga, and Geoffrey, Frank and Leo, of course. But there are others, whose presence is a cheering surprise —a surprise over which she laughs and cries together. The Professor and Madame Ericson are there ; there, too, is portly Mrs. Gibbs, rich and rare in black silk. There is Thad, quite a slim and "genteel" young man, a little conceited and over-dressed, but what will you at nineteen ? There are the twins, Lonzo and Lizzy. There is Mrs. Hill ; and the Reverend Ignatius Lamb ; and little Miss Rice. There, in short, is every one Joanna cares for most in the world. Her mother is not with her, the wintry voyage was too much for her, but she is so thoroughly restored she can bear cheerfully to part with her treasure for two or three months.

Olga looks at her keenly. Yes, Joanna is changed —the change that love, happy love, alone works, is in her radiant face. Looking down into Olga's beautiful, questioning eyes, the quick blush and smile tell their tale. And the sapphire eyes flash with glad joy, and Olga's arms clasp her close.

" Oh, Joanna ! dearest Joanna, is it indeed so ? as

Lady Hilda says. And you love him, and are happy," she whispers, in a fervent kiss.

"Happy ! happy ! happy !" is Joanna's reply, "and I love him with all my heart."

"Such a great, brave, generous heart. Oh, my darling ! this only was needed to complete our bliss. And when is it to be ?"

"Next June, they tell me," Joanna laughs. "In May, you know, I am to be presented at court, by—by his mother. And you and Geoffrey, and Frank and Leo are to come over for the wedding, which is to be a very grand affair indeed. Olga, I think I am the very happiest and most fortunate woman in all the universe !"

There are tears in the dark earnest eyes. Olga gives her a last rapturous kiss.

"Not one whit happier than you deserve—you could not be !" is her ultimatum, and like all imperial Olga's decisions, it stands uncontradicted.

*   *   *   *   *   *

It is New Year's Eve. Christmas, with its joy bells, its good wishes, its good cheer, its happy faces, has come and gone, and the old year is dying to-night.

"It brought me a friend, and a true, true love," sings happy Leo, as she flits about the house. Fires burn, lights flash, warmth, music, feasting are within ; darkness, wind, cold, snow are without. The long drawing-rooms are fragrant with flowers, brilliant with lamps, gay with happy faces. There are only the family to-night, no outsiders, but they form a sufficiently large assembly.

Near one of the windows Joanna stands, looking out at the fast-falling snow, listening to the wind "wuthering" among the trees. She looks a fair and stately woman in her rich black velvet dress—tall, imposing, gracious. Her velvet robe suits the grand curves of her figure—it sweeps in soft, dark folds behind her on the carpet. The fine lace at her throat is caught by one large, gleaming diamond ; a knot of forget-me-nots is beneath it, another in her hair.

"You look a queen of 'noble Nature's crowning,' Joanna," says Livingston, approaching. "I must paint you in that velvet dress, and these forget-me-nots. Do you know, you have been making a picture of yourself for the past ten minutes, and that I have been lost in artistic admiration."

"And that if it had lasted one millionth part of a second longer I should have been jealous," laughs Leo, coming up ; and then there is a momentary pause. Livingston looks conscious. Joanna smiles down at the dark-eyed fairy in creamy silk and white roses.

"And do you know, what is more to the purpose than empty compliments," says Mrs. Geoffrey Lamar, sailing forward in a cloud of rose pink, silky sheen, "that you never sing for us now, Lady Hardwicke— that is to be. You have grown very stingy about that lovely voice of yours since you have been in foreign parts. Come and chant us a New Year's anthem, or an old year's dirge, for it is almost on the witching stroke of twelve."

Joanna goes, and presently her full rich tones ring through the room, but the wind of the winter night itself is hardly sadder, wilder, than the strain she sings :

"Toll, bells, within your airy heights!
Wail, wind, o'er moor and mere !

On this, the saddest of all nights,
   The last night of the year—
The last long night, when lamps are lit,
   Like tapers round a bier ;
When quiet folk at still hearths sit,
   And God seems very near.

" The old clock strikes upon the stair,
   Time's tide is at its turn ;
And here, and there, and everywhere
   The New Year tapers burn.
Strange, dreamy anthems fill the street,
   The mists hang o'er the river,
The organ groans, the drums are beat,
   The Old Year's gone forever !"

" Oh ! Joanna, what a melancholy song !" cries
little Leo, reproachfully ; " and to-night of all nights !
You give me the heart-ache. Do sing something less
dreary."

" Hark !" says Geoffrey, raising his hand. All the
clocks in the house chime out one after another—
twelve. The bells in Brightbrook burst forth a joyous
peal—the New Year has begun. Good wishes go
round, they touch glasses in the German fashion, and
drink to each other, and " eyes look love to eyes that
speak again." And once more Joanna touches the
keys. This time it is like a jubilant burst of joy :

" Swing, bells, a hundred happy ways !
   Laugh, wind, o'er moor and mere!
On this, the gladdest of all days,
   The first day of the year!
The first sweet day, when every one
   Is cheerful at his hearth;
The first pure day, when merry sun
   Lights up a merry earth.

" Swing, bells, a hundred happy ways!
   Laugh, wind, o'er moor and mere!

On this the gladdest of all days,
  The first day of the year!
The first sweet day, when well content
  We gather round the hearth;
O God, we thank Thee, who has sent
  This New Year to our earth!"

" What a grand creature she is !" Frank Livingston thinks, standing a little apart, looking and listening ; " the noblest woman that walks the earth !"

His little bride, never content for many minutes together to be away from him, comes up, and slips her hand through his arm with the old wistful, upward look.

" Thinking of Joanna ?" she says. " Does she not sing deliciously, and does she not look lovely to-night ? Frank, I wonder, rich, accomplished, handsome as she is, that *you* never fell in love with her in the old days. I believe she never had even a passing fancy in all her life until she met this Sir Roland Hardwicke. Joanna—Lady Hardwicke ! Can you realize it ?"

But Frank does not say a word.

THE END.

1879.   1879.

NEW BOOKS

AND NEW EDITIONS,

RECENTLY ISSUED BY

G. W. CARLETON & Co., Publishers,

Madison Square, New York.

The Publishers, on receipt of price, will send any book on this Catalogue by mail, *postage free*

All books [unless otherwise specified] are handsomely bound in cloth, with gilt backs suitable for libraries.

Mary J. Holmes' Works.

Tempest and Sunshine........ ......$1 50	Darkness and Daylight.........$1 50
English Orphans................. 1 50	Hugh Worthington............. 1 50
Homestead on the Hillside..... 1 50	Cameron Pride. 1 50
'Lena Rivers 1 50	Rose Mather. 1 50
Meadow Brook 1 50	Ethelyn's Mistake............... 1 50
Dora Deane...................... 1 50	Millbank 1 50
Cousin Maude 1 50	Edna Browning................... 1 50
Marian Grey..................... 1 50	West Lawn....................... 1 50
Edith Lyle....................... 1 50	Mildred 1 50
Daisy Thornton.....(New)....... 1 50	Forrest House....(New) 1 50

Marion Harland's Works.

Alone............................$1 50	Sunnybank $1 50
Hidden Path 1 50	Husbands and Homes ... .'. 1 50
Moss Side.... .... 1 50	Ruby's Husband................. 1 50
Nemesis.......................... 1 50	Phemie's Temptation............ 1 50
Miriam........................ 1 50	The Empty Heart............. 1 50
At Last 1 50	Jessamine. 1 50
Helen Gardner.................... 1 50	From My Youth Up.............. 1 50
True as Steel....(New)...... .... 1 50	My Little Love................. 1 50

Charles Dickens—15 Vols.—"Carleton's Edition."

Pickwick, and Catalogue........$1 50	David Copperfield...............$1 50
Dombey and Son................. 1 50	Nicholas Nickleby............. .. 1 50
Bleak House.... .... 1 50	Little Dorrit... .... 1 50
Martin Chuzzlewit............. 1 50	Our Mutual Friend....:........ 1 50
Barnaby Rudge—Edwin Drood. 1 50	Curiosity Shop—Miscellaneous.. 1 50
Child's England—Miscellaneous. 1 50	Sketches by Box—Hard Times.. 1 50
Christmas Books—Two Cities... 1 50	Great Expectations—Italy....... 1 50
Oliver Twist—Uncommercial... 1 50	
Sets of Dickens' Complete Works, in 15 vols.—[elegant half calf bindings].. 50 00

Augusta J. Evans' Novels.

Beulah........ ....$1 75	St. Elmo......... ....$2 00
Macaria 1 75	Vashti.......................... 2 00
Inez............................ 1 75	Infelice ....(New)............ 2 00

"New York Weekly" Series.

Thrown on the World.........	$1 50	Nick Whiffles.................	$1 50
A Bitter Atonement....	1 50	Lady Leonora	1 50
Love Works Wonders.	1 50	The Grinder Papers...........	1 50
Evelyn's Folly...	1 50	Faithful Margaret	1 50
Lady Damer's Secret..........	1 50	Curse of Everleigh...........	1 50
Peerless Cathleen.............	1 50		

Violet Fane's Poems.

Constance's Fate; or, Denzil Place.$1 50		From Dawn to Noon...........$1 50	

M. M. Pomeroy (" Brick.")

Sense. A serious book..........	$1 50	Nonsense. (A comic book).......	$1 50
Gold Dust. Do.	1 50	Brick-dust. Do.	1 50
Our Saturday Nights..........	1 50	Home Harmonies...............	1 50

Mrs. E. P. Miller.

Mother Truth's Melodies—A new Children's picture Kindergarten...........$1 00

Ernest Renan's French Works.

The Life of Jesus....Translated.$1 75		The Life of St. Paul. Translated.$1 75	
Lives of the Apostles. Do.	1 75	The Bible in India—By Jacolliot.	2 00

G. W. Carleton.

Our Artist in Cuba, Peru, Spain, and Algiers—150 Caricatures of travel.......$1 00

Miscellaneous Publications.

Gervaise [L'Assommoir]—English translation from Emile Zola's French novel.$1 00
The Gospels in Poetry—Newly translated by Elijah H. Kimball.............. 1 50
The Two Brides—A new novel by Rev. Bernard O'Reilly, L.D............... 1 50
A Southern Woman's Story—By Mrs. Phœbe Yates Pember............... 75
Parlor Amusements—Games, Tricks, and Home Amusements, by F. Bellew.. 75
Love [L'Amour]—Translation from Michelet's famous French work............ 1 50
Woman [La Femme]— Do. Do. Do. 1 50
Verdant Green—A racy English college Story. With 200 comic illustrations.... 1 00
Ladies and Gentleman's Etiquette Book, of the Best Fashionable Society.. 1 00
Strategems and Conspiracies—Attempts to defraud Life Insurance Companies. 2 00
Beatrice Cenci—Translated from the Italian novel, with portrait, by Guido..... 1 50
Morning Glories—A charming child's book of stories, by Louisa Alcott.......... 1 00
The Culprit Fay—Joseph Rodman Drake's Poem. With 100 Illustrations..... 2 00
The Parlor Musical Album—Vocal and instrumental. Beautifully bound 1 50
Birds of a Feather Flock Together—By Edward A. Sothern, the actor...... 1 00
Trip from New York to San Francisco—Mrs. Frank Leslie. Illustrated... 2 00

Recent Novels.

Spell-Bound—By Alex. Dumas...$0 75		Widow Cherry—B. L. Farjeon..$0 25	
Heart's Delight—Mrs. Alderdice.	1 50	Solomon Isaacs— Do. Do. ..	1 50
Wired Love—By E. C. Thayer...	50	Fallen Among Thieves—Rayne..	1 50
Doctor Antonio—By Ruffini......	1 50	The Baroness—Joaquin Miller...	1 50
Once and Forever—Miss Grant.	1 00	One Fair Woman—Do. Do. ...	1 50
Under the Rose—Mrs. Wood....	1 00	San Miniato—Mrs. Hamilton...	1 00
Madame—By Frank Lee Benedict.	1 00	Another Man's Wife—Mrs. Hartt	1 50
Hammer and Anvil— Do.	1 00	He and I—By Sarah B. Stebbins..	50
Little Guzzy—By Habberton. ...	1 50	Annals of a Baby— Do. Do. ..	50
Doctor Mortimer—Fannie Bean..	1 50	Me—By Mrs. Spencer W. Coe.....	50
Lady Huckleberry's Opinions..	25	Comic Primer—By Frank Bellew..	25
Edith Murray—Joanna Mathews.	1 50	That Awful Boy.............:	50
Outwitted at Last—S. A.Gardner	1 50	That Bridget of Ours........	50
Vesta Vane—By L. King R......	1 50	Bitterwood—By M. A. Green....	1 50
Louise and I—Charles R. Dodge.	1 50	Peccavi—By Emma Wendler......	1 50
My Queen—By Sandette.........	1 50	Conquered—By a new author.....	1 50
All For Her—A tale of New York.	1 00	St. Peter's Bride—Mrs. S. Harper	1 50
All For Him—By All For Her....	1 00	Fizzlebury's Girl—De Cordova...	50
For Each Other— Do. Do. ..	1 00	Eros—A tale of love and soda water.	50
Janet—An English novel..........	1 50	Mr. Ghim's Dream.............	1 00
Innocents from Abroad.	1 50	Parlor Table Companion........	1 50
Flirtation—A West Point novel....	1 50	Trump Kards—Josh Billings.....	10
H. M. S. Pinafore—The Play . .	10	What d'ye Soy— do.	10

4   G. W. CARLETON & CO.'S PUBLICATIONS.

Miscellaneous Works.

A Harvest of Wild Oats—A Novel, by Florence Marryatt................ $1 50
Milly Darrell—A Novel, by Miss M. E. Braddon, author of "Aurora Floyd "... 1 50
Why Wife and I Quarreled—By the author of " Betsey and I are Out"...... 1 00
True Love Rewarded—A new Novel, by the author "True to the Last"...... 1 50
Threading My Way—The Autobiography of Robert Dale Owen............. 1 50
The Debatable Land—By Robert Dale Owen. 2 00
Lights and Shadows of Spiritualism—By D. D. Home...... .... 2 00
Glimpses of the Supernatural—Facts, Records, and Traditions.. .. .. 2 00
Lion Jack—A New Illustrated Menagerie Book for Boys.—P. T. Barnum....... 1 50
West India Pickles—Journal of a Tropical Yacht Cruise, by W. P. Talboys.... 1 50
G. A. Crofutt's Trans-Continental Tourist—New York to San Francisco.... 1 50
Laus Veneris and other Poems—By Algernon Charles Swinburne.......... 1 50
Parodies and Poems and My Vacation—By C. H. Webb (John Paul).... .. 1 50
Comic History of the United States—Livingston Hopkins. Illustrated...... 1 50
Mother Goose Melodies Set to Music—with comic illustrations............. 1 00
Jacques Offenbach's Experiences in America—From the Paris edition.... 1 50
How to Make Money ; and How to Keep It—By Thomas A. Davies....... 1 50
Our Children—Teaching Parents how to keep them in Health.—Dr. Gardner... 1 50
Watchman ; What of the Night ?—By Dr. John Cumming, of London...... 1 50
Fanny Fern Memorials—With a Biography, by James Parton......... ...... 2 00
Tales from the Operas—A Collection of Stories based upon the Opera Plots.... 1 50
New Nonsense Rhymes—By W. H. Beckett, with illustrations by C. G. Bush. 1 00
Progressive Petticoats—A Satirical Tale, by Robert B. Roosevelt... .... 1 50
Souvenirs of Travel—By Madame Octavia Walton Le Vert, of Mobile, Ala... 2 00
Woman, Love, and Marriage—A spicy little Work, by Fred Saunders....... 1 50
The Fall of Man—A Darwinian Satire, by author of " New Gospel of Peace"... 50
The Chronicles of Gotham—A Modern Satire, . . Do. . . Do. . :..... 25
Ballad of Lord Bateman—With illustrations by Cruikshank (paper covers).... 25
The Yachtman's Primer—For amateur Sailors. T. R. Warren (paper covers) 50
Rural Architecture—By M. Field. With plans and illustrations............. 2 00
Transformation Scenes in the United States—By Hiram Fuller............ 1 50
Kingsbury Sketches—Pine Grove Doings, by John H. Kingsbury. Illustrated 1 50

Miscellaneous Novels.

Led Astray—By Octave Feuillet...$1 50
She Loved Him Madly—Borys... 1 50
Through Thick and Thin—Mery. 1 50
So Fair yet False—Chavette 1 50
A Fatal Passion—C. Bernard..... 1 50
Seen and Unseen................. 1 50
Purple and Fine Linen—Fawcett. 1 75
Pauline's Trial—L. L. D. Courtney 1 50
A Charming Widow—Macquoid.. 1 75
The Forgiving Kiss—By M. Loth. 1 75
Kenneth, My King—S. A. Brock.. 1 75
Heart Hungry—M.J.Westmoreland 1 75
Clifford Troupe.   . Do.   1 75
Silcott Mill—Maria D. Deslonde... 1 75
John Maribel.   Do.   ... 1 75
Passing the Portal—Mrs. Victor.. 1 50
Out of the Cage—G. W. Owen.... 1. 50
Saint Leger—Richard B. Kimball.. 1 75
Was He Successful ? . . Do. 1 75
Undercurrents of Wall St. . Do. 1 75
Romance of Student Life. . Do. 1 75
To-Day. . . . . Do. 1 75
Life in San Domingo. . . Do. 1 50
Henry Powers. Banker. . . Do. 1 75
A Book about Doctors 2 00
A Book about Lawyers.......... 2 00
Manfred—By Guerrazzi.......... 1 75

A Woman in the Case—Turner...$1 50
Johnny Ludlow. From London ed. 1 50
Shiftless Folks—Fannie Smith.... 1 75
A Woman in Armor—Hartwell... 1 50
Phemie Frost—Ann S. Stephens.. 1 50
Marguerite's Journal. For girls.. 1 50
Romance of Railroad—Smith 1 50
Charette—An American novel...... 1 50
Fairfax—John Esten Cooke........ 1 50
Hilt to Hilt.   Do........... 1 50
Out of the Foam.   Do......... 1 50
Hammer and Rapier.Do.... ...,. 1 50
Warwick—By M. T. Walworth.... 1 75
Lulu.   Do............. 1 75
Hotspur.   Do............ 1 75
Stormcliff.   Do............ 1 75
Delaplaine.   Do............ 1 75
Beverly.   Do............. 1 75
Beldazzle's Bachelor Studies.... 1 00
Northern Ballads—E. L. Anderson 1 00
O. C. Kerr Papers. 4 vols. in one.. 2 00
Victor Hugo—His autobiography... 2 00
Sandwiches—By Artemus Ward... 25
Widow Spriggins—Widow Bedott. 1 75
Wood's Guide to N. Y. City..... 1 00
Loyal unto Death................ 1 75
Bessie Wilmerton—Westcott..... 1 75

www.ingramcontent.com/pod-product-compliance
Lightning Source LLC
Chambersburg PA
CBHW032338280326
41935CB00008B/374